IS
RA
EL

ISRAEL

DICKSON AGEDAH

CREATION
HOUSE

ISRAEL by Dickson Agedah
Published by Creation House
A Charisma Media Company
600 Rinehart Road
Lake Mary, Florida 32746
www.charismamedia.com

Unless otherwise noted, all Scripture quotations are from the King James Version of the Bible.

Scripture quotations marked AMP are from the Amplified Bible. Old Testament copyright © 1965, 1987 by the Zondervan Corporation. The Amplified New Testament copyright © 1954, 1958, 1987 by the Lockman Foundation. Used by permission.

Scripture quotations marked HCSB are taken from the Holman Christian Standard Bible®, Copyright © 1999, 2000, 2002, 2003, 2009 by Holman Bible Publishers. Used by permission. Holman Christian Standard Bible®, Holman CSB®, and HCSB® are federally registered trademarks of Holman Bible Publishers.

Scripture quotations marked NIV are from the Holy Bible, New International Version. Copyright © 1973, 1978, 1984, 2010, 2011, International Bible Society. Used by permission.

Scripture quotations marked NKJV are from the New King James Version of the Bible. Copyright © 1979, 1980, 1982 by Thomas Nelson, Inc., publishers. Used by permission.

Design Director: Bill Johnson
Cover design by Nathan Morgan

Visit the author on Facebook: dickson.agedah/Facebook.com

Library of Congress Cataloging-in-Publication Data: 2013946753
International Standard Book Number: 978-1-62136-679-9
E-book International Standard Book Number: 978-1-62136-680-5

First edition

14 15 16 17 — 9 8 7 6 5 4 3 2 1
Printed in Canada

DEDICATION

To Jehovah, the Creator of the universe and to
our Passover, the Lord Jesus Christ, who has so
gloriously redeemed us with His atonement blood
and to all of God's created humans who exercise faith
and joyfully await Christ's Second Advent and the
coming glory of a new heavens and a new earth.

CONTENTS

ACKNOWLEDGMENTS

THE EXPRESSION OF my profound gratitude and indebtedness goes to many great scholars and men of deep faith who have through their cerebral and spiritual books, expounded the good news of the gospel of the surely coming kingdom of God and the Messianic kingship of Jesus Christ. These are writers, living and "asleep," in whose works I have garnered knowledge which has enabled me to write this book—my first work on biblical exposition, having in the past written books on secular socioeconomic and political issues as they affect my home country, Nigeria.

I am also grateful to the following persons, Alice Forcados, Oyeodi Kitoye, and Omo-ola Adebayo for their valuable contributions to the processes that have led to the completion of this work for presentation to the publishers.

I must not forget to express my deep gratitude to my dear wife, Asele, enduring our "separation" and dutifully attending to the daily needs of our children, Preye, Pamela, Diseye, and Asa, in Atlanta, Georgia, while I take the lengthy time off from them to write this book. I am also very grateful for the editorial insights of the publishers.

TO THE READER

THIS BOOK IS written with the acknowledgment that the author's words and opinions are not sacrosanct; only God's words and pronouncements as divinely and inspirationally recorded in His manual for life—the Holy Bible are. I have also written from a close study of the authentic but not inerrant records of secular human history and God's visible and invincible commanding hands in this march of world history as unveiled in the infallible revelations and the inerrancy of the prophecies in the Scripture. As a fallible mortal, I certainly hold no claim to infallibleness and errors of judgment, interpretation, or presentation that may be found in this book are unintentional.

However, the essence of this study is to establish in the reader a rock solid faith and hope in the one and only omnipotent, omnipresent, and omniscient God—"I AM" (Exod. 3:14)—the source of eternal salvation and to the firstborn of creation, through whom all things were created and cocreator (Col. 1:15–16), Christ Jesus, who is the author and finisher of our faith (Heb. 12:2), the bread of life (John 6:35), the fountain of living waters (Jer. 17:13), the only giver of perfect peace (Isa. 26:3) and everlasting life (John 3:16) in a confused and deeply troubled Satan-dominated world. A world that is for a duration, largely controlled by powers and principalities of darkness and their human agents, promoters of spiritual wickedness in high places throughout the nations of the earth (Eph. 6:12).

The ultimate message, therefore, is hope for mankind in a world of grave uncertainties and human tragedies and liberation from the satanic dominance of Mother Earth. Hope for the poor in spirit , hope for they that mourn, hope for the meek of the earth, hope for those who thirst after righteousness, hope for the pure in heart, hope for the peacemaker, hope for the merciful, and hope for those that are being persecuted for righteousness sake (Matt. 5:3–12). This book also seeks to engender faith and hope in God-breathed promise of a new heavens and a new earth and in the universal miracle of the resurrection of the dead, the reestablishment of the lost paradise through the surely coming glory of the King of Glory, the King of kings and Lord of lords, to whom every knee will bow and every tongue will confess (Rom. 14:11); yes, faith and hope in a new world order, a theocratic kingdom and government under Christ's kingdom rule. Israel as God's ensign to nations points to this glorious end, and to the inviolability of God's Word.

Since human government has failed woefully to engender peace and with no glimmer of hope for world peace and an end to human suffering, either in the near future or even in a trillion years of continuous human government, Jehovah has decreed a redemption from selfish, wicked, corrupt, imperfect, and belligerent human leadership. He has ordained divine theocratic governance under His Spirit-begotten Son, Jesus Christ, who has been given the name that is far above other names (Phil. 2:9) as well as dominion over all powers on earth and in heaven (Matt. 28:18), as we read in the books of Daniel, Isaiah, and Revelation.

> I saw in the night visions and behold, one like the Son of man came with the clouds of heaven, and came to the Ancient of days, and they brought Him near before Him. And there was given Him dominion, and glory, and a kingdom, that all people, nations and languages should serve him; his dominion is an everlasting dominion, which shall not pass away and his kingdom that which shall not be destroyed.
>
> —DANIEL 7:13–14

> Of the increase of His government and peace there shall be no end.
>
> —ISAIAH 9:7

> The kingdoms of this world are become the kingdoms of our Lord, and of his Christ; and he shall reign for ever and ever.
>
> —REVELATION 11:15

Israel as God's ensign to nations point to this glorious end. It is to this incoming kingdom of Christ that the reader's faith and hope is drawn through the various expositions in this book. All that is presented in this study leads to the fulfillment of the good news of the kingdom, that Christ commanded His apostles to spread to the ends of the earth before the end comes (Matt. 4:23; 9:35; 28:19; 24:14; Mark 16:15; Luke 8:1; 16:16).

> *The mighty God, Jehovah, through His anointed Spirit-begotten Son, Jesus Christ, has all the power and dynamic energy through which He will attain the promised happy and glorious end to the human drama. By His divine grace, mercy,*

and perfect will for your life, may you tap into His fountain of living waters, the gift of everlasting life. May you find this book challenging, insightful, and rewarding in the kingly, healing, and salvation bearing name of our Lord and Savior, Christ Jesus. Amen.

Preface

ISRAEL: GOD'S ENSIGN TO NATIONS

And he shall set up an ensign for the nations, and shall
assemble the outcasts of Israel, and gather together the
dispersed of Judah from the four corners of the earth.
—ISAIAH 11:12, NKJV

W HY WRITE A book on Israel as God's ensign to nations?—
the nation of Israel as the sovereign Lord's clear manifestation as the omnipresent, omnipotent, and omniscient God
of human history? The history of the nation of Israel, the story of the
Jewish people is clearly one of the most intriguing, one of the most
amazing and controversial yet authentic history of our ancient, medieval, and modern world; a history that inextricably draws nations across
all continents of the world towards a common and predetermined destiny. This history is narrated in several secular historical and archaeological sources and revealed through a most reliable source, the infallible
Word of Jehovah God in written form—the Bible. Indeed, as the transla-
tors of the Zondervan New International Version study Bible point out,
the Bible "contains the divine answers to the deepest needs of humanity
as well as shedding light on mankind's path in a dark world which sets
forth the way to our eternal well-being."[1]

The way to mankind's eternal well-being is what this book seeks to
construct through a biblical revelation of the living history of Israel and
other nations of the world, in which there is constantly the active and
invincible hand of an absolute director and supreme commander in
Jehovah God. An undefeatable God, the God of infallible counsel, who
makes known the end from the beginning, and from ancient times what

is still to come: (Isa. 46:10). He is the God that all the nations of the earth, all the tribes and races have to deal with today. Nations are inevitably drawn into the battle of the ages between Jehovah God, His Christ, and the Hosts of heaven and Lucifer, the fallen angel, and his disciples. The choice of nations and people of the world is between the two forces of light and darkness, good and evil. Thus the prophet Isaiah cries out;

> How art thou fallen from heaven O Lucifer, son of the morning? how
> art thou cast down to the ground, which didst weaken the nations?
> —ISAIAH 14:12

Israel, God's ensign, and other nations of the world have been drawn into a weakened spiritual state of self-glorification by Lucifer and his powers and principalities of darkness, while individual and groups within them strive to glorify God and submit to His statutes and commandments. However, it is important to point out that the biblical context of Israel as God's ensign to all nations is distinct from the grace of the election—Israel as God's "chosen people." But the distinction is not a very sharp one. Israel as God's ensign to nations is not for the self-glorification of Israel or the Jews, but for Jehovah's own glory. Similarly, the election covenant of Israel as "God's chosen people" is not for Israel's glorification, but for the glory of God. It is for Jehovah's self-proclamation as the God of the universe, Jehovah of armies, the Lord of hosts, the Creator of heavens and earth and of mankind and nations. Through the prophet Isaiah, God tells the children of Israel,

> You are my servant, Israel, in whom I will display my splendor.
> —ISAIAH 49:3, NIV

> Thou art my servant, O Israel, in whom I will be glorified.
> —ISAIAH 49:3

Thus, the ensign and election status or privilege of Israel is intended to present clearly to the world—the universal and supreme nature of God. He is a God to whom "the nations are as a drop of a bucket and are counted as the small dust of the balance: behold, he taketh up the isles as a very little thing" (Isa. 40:15).

The New International Version translates it thus: "Surely the nations are like a drop in a bucket; they are regarded as dust on the scales; he weighs the Islands as though they are fine dust."

Before Him all nations are as nothing. They are regarded by Him as worthless and less than nothing.

God displayed His infinite capacity to deal with nations in the story of the crossing of River Jordan by the children of Israel. He told them that He would drive out nations greater than Israel, not as a result of the righteousness of the stiff-necked Israelites but because of the wickedness of those nations.

> Listen, Israel; Today you are about to cross the Jordan to go and drive out nations greater and stronger than you....When the LORD your God drives them out before you, do not say to yourself, "The LORD brought me in to take possession of this land because of my righteousness." Instead, the LORD will drive out these nations before you because of their wickedness...in order to keep the promise He swore to your fathers, Abraham, Isaac, and Jacob. Understand that the LORD your God is not giving you this good land to possess because of your righteousness, for you are a stiff-necked people.
> —DEUTERONOMY 9:1, 4–6, HCSB

Indeed, God sits enthroned above the circle of the earth and its people are like grasshoppers. He stretches out the heavens like a canopy and spreads them out like a tent to live in. He brings princes to naught and reduces the rulers of this world to nothing.

Yes, all nations are counted by God as nothing and to be counted by us, in comparison to Him, as less than nothing and vanity. When God pleases, He can as easily bring all nations into nothing (as He did with the flood of Noah's day and as He did with Sodom and Gomorrah, and other ancient nations) since He created them out of nothing. Indeed, when Jehovah God has work to do, He values not either the assistance or resistance of any human being. They are all vanity to which they will ultimately be reduced. What man, what nation has conquered death? With all his scientific and technological breakthrough and marvels, has man being able to manufacture blood? Has mankind succeeded in forestalling the devastations of the elements—earthquakes, floods, tsunamis, hurricanes, tornados, volcanic eruptions? Indeed, natural disasters show the smallness of man, his impotence in the face of awesome natural forces. But just as Christ calmed the stormy sea, the exclusive control of the elements lies squarely with Jehovah God who can direct their uses for weal or for woe.

The prophet Isaiah (60:12) warns that the nation or kingdom that will not serve God will perish and utterly wasted. Israel, God's "chosen people" stand as a good case study in this regard. For centuries they suffered desolation, captivity, and persecutions because of their disobedience, idolatry, and wickedness as well as their unbridled display of contempt to their law covenant with God. Just as Jehovah showed His mighty hands of righteous indignation and justice in the great travails and tribulations of the children of Israel, they also enjoyed momentous instances of power and goodness of God. We recall their first deliverance from Egypt, the parting of the Red Sea, (Exod. 14:21), destruction of Pharaoh and the Egyptian army (vv. 23–31), the drying up and crossing of River Jordan (Josh. 4:22), the conquest of Canaan, Jericho, Ai and other surrounding nations, and the occupation of the Promised Land. Many of the ancient nations—Assyria, Babylon, Medo-Persia, Edom (Idumea), Moab, Ammon and others—have long since been out of existence, and their handmade gods passed away with them. In our twenty-first century era, the existence of the modern State of Israel serves as an ensign to all nations of God's supreme existence as a God of history. Whether we believe or not, whether we like or not, all nations are inextricably drawn towards a common destiny under Jehovah's historic and spiritual direction of Mother Earth and the entire universe to His ultimate grand purpose—a new heavens and a new earth; a new world order under the kingdom rule of Jesus Christ on behalf of His Father, Jehovah God.

GOD CREATED NATIONS AND ALLOTTED HIMSELF A NATION

In creating the nations of the world and allocating land spaces to each, God also allotted Himself a nation so as to be actively involved in the march of history of His created humans and show through His chosen nation or people that He is in firm control. Jehovah speaks to the entire earth on this issue in the Book of Deuteronomy 32:1, 8–9 when Moses sang from divine inspiration. The Holman Christian Standard Bible translates thus:

> Pay attention, heavens, and I will speak; listen, earth, to the word of my mouth.... When the Most High gave the nations their inheritance and divided the human race, He set the boundaries of the people according to the number of the people of Israel. But the LORD's portion is His people, Jacob, His own inheritance.

The patriarch Jacob (*Ya'akov*), the house of Israel, the Jewish people became by grace the allotted heritage of God (*Adonai*), while He made other nations and assigned boundaries to them. Israel became His ensign, His banner, so that other nations could *see* and discern His supreme and majestic presence through Israel. God expected other nations to come into the same service. God's word through the prophet states, "Open the gates, That the righteous nation which keeps the truth may enter in" (Isa. 26:2, NKJV).

Through the ensign and election status of Israel, a greater ensign is given to the people and nations of the world in Jesus Christ. The first prophecy in the Bible in the Book of Genesis, even at the dawn of God's creation (and before Israel came into being), draws our attention to a time when Christ will subdue Satan for the salvation of humanity.

> And I will put enmity between you and the woman, and between your offspring and hers; he will crush your head, and you will strike his heel.
>
> —GENESIS 3:15, NIV

About the coming Christ, the Book of Genesis also reveals,

> The scepter will not depart from Judah, nor the ruler's staff from between his feet, until he to whom it belongs shall come and the obedience of the nations shall be his.
>
> —GENESIS 49:10, NIV

This is Jesus Christ, the Lion of the tribe of Judah. About 732 years before the earthly birth of Christ, the prophet Isaiah foretold his coming.

> There shall be a root of Jesse, which shall stand for an ensign of the people; to it shall the Gentiles seek: and his rest shall be glorious.
>
> —ISAIAH 11:10

This root of Jesse is Jesus Christ revealed in the Revelation 5:5 as "the Lion of the tribe of Judah, the Root of David," and in Revelation 22:16 as the "root and offspring of David, and the bright morning star."

Thus, through Israel as an ensign or banner of Jehovah's supreme existence to nations and His active involvement in the march of human history, we are bestowed with the firstborn of creation, His Spirit-begotten Son, Jesus Christ, as an ensign of Jehovah's salvation history for mankind, and Christ as the salvific medium for universal redemption; a redemption that will come with God's reclamation and restoration of the earth to a paradisiacal state under Christ's kingdom rule.

> And the seventh angel sounded; and there were great voices in heaven, saying, The kingdom of this world are become the kingdoms of our Lord, and of his Christ; and he shall reign for ever and ever.
>
> —REVELATION 11:15

Revelation 21:1–4 reads:

> And I saw a new heaven and a new earth: for the first heaven and the first earth were passed away; and there was no more sea. And I John saw the holy city, new Jerusalem, coming down from God out of heaven, prepared as a bride adorned for her husband. And I heard a great voice out of heaven saying, Behold, the tabernacle of God is with men, and he will dwell with them, and they shall be his people, and God himself shall be with them, and be their God. And God shall wipe away all tears from their eyes; and there shall be no more death, neither sorrow, nor crying, neither shall there be any more pain: for the former things are passed away.

Centuries before this revelation of Jesus Christ was given to the apostle John in a vision in the Island of Patmos, the prophet Isaiah foretold the coming government of Christ:

> For unto us a child is born, unto us a son is given: and the government shall be upon his shoulder: and his name shall be called Wonderful, Counsellor, The mighty God, The everlasting Father, The Prince of Peace. Of the increase of his government and peace there shall be no end, upon the throne of David, and upon his kingdom, to order it, and to establish it with judgment and with justice from henceforth even for ever. The zeal of the LORD of hosts will perform this.
>
> —ISAIAH 9:6–7

The prophet also paints a wonderful picture of Mother Earth under Christ's kingdom rule:

> The wolf will live with the lamb, the leopard will lie down with the goat, the calf and the lion and the yearling together; and a little child will lead them. The cow will feed with the bear, their young will lie down together, and the lion will eat straw like the ox. The

infant will play near the cobra's den, and the young child put his
hand into the viper's nest. They will neither harm nor destroy on all
my holy mountain, for the earth will be full of the knowledge of the
LORD as the waters cover the sea.

—ISAIAH 11:6-9

In the temporal and spiritual history of the Jews, we see the purity of
monotheism and the Messianic hope through which a universal salvation
will ultimately dawn for all humans. The apostle Paul pointed this out
while quoting the prophet Isaiah in Romans 15:12: "There shall be a root
of Jesse, and he that shall rise to reign over the Gentiles; in him shall the
Gentiles trust."

This is further reference to the Messianic rule under Christ and the
accession of the Gentiles (the rest of the world outside the Jews) to His
Messianic kingdom. This is a new world order where the hopeless receive
the gift of hope and salvation and in which God's lordship bursts bril-
liantly into this world; the kingdom of God that will succeed the kingdom
of the world.

And in the days of these kings shall the God of heaven set up a
kingdom, which shall never be destroyed: and the kingdom shall
not be left to other people, but it shall break in pieces and consume
all these kingdoms, and it shall stand for ever.

—DANIEL 2:44

The inspired word of Jehovah through Isaiah the prophet states,

For Zion's sake will I not hold my peace, and for Jerusalem's sake I
will not rest, until the righteousness thereof go forth as brightness,
and the salvation thereof as a lamp that burneth. And the Gentiles
shall see thy righteousness, and all kings thy glory.

—ISAIAH 62:1-2

I have set watchmen upon thy walls, O Jerusalem, which shall never
hold their peace day nor night: ye that make mention of the LORD,
keep not silence. And give him no rest, till he establish, and till he
make Jerusalem a praise in the earth.

—ISAIAH 62:6-7

The election and ensign status of Israel should therefore be understood as an inclusive, not an exclusive one, because through Israel's election of grace, we see the visible and tangible election of all nations, of all

peoples. Careful study of the Scripture shows clearly that Israel was not elected to a privilege but to a sacrifice and to a service—to serve as God's ensign to all nations, and ultimately reveal God's love for all humankind, subject to the obedience of His statutes and faith in the atonement and sacrificial blood of Jesus Christ.

The children of Israel were to serve as God's obedient children and nation, always in subjection to His laws and commandments. They were to be carriers of these laws and commandments and His divine promises to other nations. Jehovah's Mount Sinai covenant with the Israelites under the leadership of Moses buttresses the aforementioned position. In the Book of Exodus Jehovah sent a message to the "house of Jacob" (the children of Israel) through Moses.

> Now if you obey me fully and keep my covenant, then out of all nations you will be my treasured possession. Although the whole earth is mine, you will be for me a kingdom of priests and a holy nation.
> —EXODUS 19:5, NIV

So, they were to be a kingdom of *cohanim* (priests), a nation set apart, a living sacrifice. God's choice of the children or State of Israel as an ensign of His demiurgic supremacy was not unconditional. It carried with it a proviso—an absolute and whole-hearted obedience to His laws and commandments. In a world in which man acts as a free moral agent in whom God has given man a free choice between good and evil, strict adherence to His commandments became the onerous task the Israelites had to undertake in a predominantly pagan world to remain in Jehovah's favor and protection. In many instances and varied circumstances, the children of Israel failed to live up to Jehovah's expectations, not only because of their backsliding and stubborn nature and utter disregard for His infinite power and protection and His statutes and commandments, but also because of the unwholesome influences from the nations around them. Nations largely dominated by satanic forces—the powers and principalities of darkness—to which they defiantly asked God to be part of; for so they did when they requested Samuel to appoint a king to lead them as other nations and thus rejected Jehovah as their King.

> Now appoint a king to lead us, such as all the other nations have.... Then we will be like all other nations, with a king to lead us and to go out before us and fight our battles.... And the LORD told

> him [Samuel], "Listen to all that the people are saying to you; it is
> not you they have rejected, but they have rejected me as their king.
>
> —1 SAMUEL 8:5, 20, 7, NIV

Clearly, the sacred mission bestowed upon the children of Israel in Exodus 19:5—to serve as a kingdom of priests and a holy nation, and to proselytize the message to all peoples, all nations—was buried under the ceremonial concepts of peoplehood, concepts of a special and exclusive breed, which centuries of persecution and anti-Semitic prejudices made even more stubborn. As Alfred Lilienthal asserts in *What Price Israel,*

> The kingdom of God, the transfigured society came to mean clan-
> nish promise for the privileged few. Particularism triumphed and
> Judaism made a "racial hoard of God."[2]

The rejection of Christ and the new covenant of Christianity bestowed by Christ as the Spirit-begotten Son of God and the Messiah, through whom God's salvific history for mankind would be fulfilled, made impossible Israel's proselytization of the good news gospel of God's kingdom to all nations. The Jewish nation was unable to internalize the personification of Jesus (the human presence of God among men in His Son), which gave Christianity a spiritual warmth; a warmth that formalistic and legalistic Judaism has always lacked. Christianity gave God a face, made God a divine Being of immediate and intimate meaning to humans; for, after all, humans are God's image, created in God's image (Gen. 1:27). The Jewish nation failed to grasp this cosmic vision of Christhood—the "oneness" of the Father and Son.

This, however, is surprising, given the fact that the revelation of the Messiah's first and second coming was unveiled first to the children of Israel through the Jewish prophets, Micah, Isaiah, Jeremiah, and Zechariah. (See Isaiah 7:14; 9:6–7; 50:6; 53:3–4, 12; Micah 5:2; Jeremiah 31:15, Zechariah 11:12–13.)

Specifically, in prophecy to the house of David, Isaiah 17:14 states,

> Therefore, the Lord himself shall give you a sign; Behold, a virgin
> shall conceive, and bear a son, and shall call his name Immanuel.

The prophet Isaiah was bestowed with the vision of the trials, travails, and triumph of Jesus Christ.

He was despised and rejected by men....Surely he took up our infirmities and carried our sorrows....But he was pierced for our transgressions, he was crushed for our iniquities, the punishment that brought us peace was upon him, and by his wounds we are healed....He was oppressed and afflicted, yet he did not open his mouth; he was led like a lamb to the slaughter, and as a sheep before her shearers is silent, so he did not open his mouth....He was assigned a grave with the wicked, and with the rich in his death, though he had done no violence, nor was any deceit in his mouth....After the suffering of his soul, he will see the light [of life] and be satisfied....For he bore the sin of many, and made intercession for the transgressors.

—ISAIAH 53:3–5, 7, 9, 11–12, NIV

Micah states,

But you, Bethlehem, Ephrathah, though you are small among the clans of Judah, out of you will come for me one who will be ruler over Israel, whose origins are from of old, from ancient times.

—MICAH 5:2, NIV

The Old Testament Book of Genesis 3:15 and 45:10 also foretold the coming of Christ, the Messiah. The outcries of the multitude of Jews, who refused the condemnation of robber and murderer, but entreated Pontius Pilate that the Prince of life and peace should be crucified, attest to the self-exemption of the multitude of Jews to be part of Christ's Great Commission. They went as far as calling the curse of the sacrificial blood of Christ upon themselves and their offspring, for which they paid dearly over the centuries.

The multitudes of the children of Israel were unable to grasp the historic and spiritual significance of the crucified and risen Christ and to appreciate and understand the Christ event as the long intended climax of Jehovah's self-communication to the world. This "hidden Christocentricity" of a cosmic Christ remained hidden to the Jewish nation but was opened up by two of Christ's Jewish ardent disciples, John and Paul of Tarsus, who were also rejected by the Jews.

But then Jehovah did not spit out the children of Israel from His mouth. He remains faithful to His everlasting covenant with their forebears. In Isaiah 49:3 Jehovah told His prophet that through Israel, His servant, He will be glorified by all nations. In verse 6 Jehovah also promised that He will make Israel a light to the Gentiles that they may be His salvation into all parts of the universe. This promise depicts the inclusiveness of God's salvific history for all nations.

The inclusive nature of Israel's election and ensign status is attested to by the prophet Malachi who reminded the children of Israel that Jehovah God will not only be revered in Israel, but among all nations.

> For from the rising of the sun even the going down of the same, my name shall be great among the Gentiles; and in every place incense shall be offered unto my name, and a pure offering: for my name shall be great among the heathen [nations], said the LORD of hosts.
>
> —MALACHI 1:11

Isaiah reminds the children of Israel of the loving call of other nations to Jehovah's warm embrace. He points to the universal and inclusive nature of God through His divine pronouncement that Israel, Egypt, and Assyria will be a blessed people on earth, as well as Jehovah's description of Egypt as His blessed people, Assyria the work of His hands, and Israel His inheritance (Isa. 19:24–25).

The prophet Amos conveys Jehovah's question to the children of Israel in Amos 9:7 to transmit the message of a universal God. "Are not you Israelites the same to me as the Cushites [Ethiopians]?" declares the LORD. "Did I not bring Israel up from Egypt, the Philistines from Caphtor, and the Arameans from Kir?" (NIV).

The "preference" for the children of Israel can easily be understood from the natural filial love a father has for an obedient child above a disobedient one. God found obedient and righteous children in the forebears of the Israelites, the patriarchs Abraham, Jacob, and Isaac, as well as earlier ancestors like Noah. He therefore showered them with blessings passed on to their generations. It is apparent that Jehovah God does not seek worthiness but bestows it to whom He pleases. Israel was of no significance politically. It was merely a buffer zone between Assyria, Babylonia, and Egypt and was incessantly tossed around like a basketball or a football by these nations. When Israel obeyed God, they were fully protected from the predatory tendencies of the surrounding nations. But once they transgressed the covenant laws, they paid dearly for their intransigence—more than any other nation or people had perhaps done in the course of world history.

That Israel exists today as a modern "rebirth" nation-state established in 1948, in fulfillment of biblical prophecies, can only be explained as a manifestation of God's hand and divine intervention, and an indication of Israel as an ensign of His supremacy as a universal God, directing the history of nations. Israel had to carry this grace and burden of the consequences of disobedience through ancient, medieval, and modern world history at great human, material, and spiritual costs. No other nation or people had six million of her citizens annihilated in gas chambers, vans, concentration camps, and killing fields during our twentieth-century history. No other nation was enslaved for 400 years. (Only the black African continent experienced such length of slavery.) No other nation has been taken to exile for seventy years, and had wandered in the wilderness for forty years. No other people had suffered great persecutions at the scale and magnitude Israel experienced in medieval and twentieth-century Europe. No other nation or people have had to resettle, in a homeland after centuries of exile and dispersal to other nations and all continents of the world, in fulfillment of Bible prophecies. Only Israel enjoys the historical record of bestowing to the world great prophets of the Bible, Jesus the Messiah and His early apostles, as well as the two great monotheistic religions, Judaism and Christianity, spread across all continents of the world. In the history of Israel, we discern the story of the kingdom of God breaking into the world of nations at a time when national and political entities were, and are still, viewed as the creation of lesser gods and mortal men and living proofs of their transient powers.

The sixteenth and probably the greatest president of the United States of America, was bestowed with the divine revelation of God's supreme authority in the conducts of men and nations. On March 30, 1863, Abraham Lincoln issued a proclamation to the American people for a day of national humiliation, fasting, and prayer in the following words:

> Whereas, the Senate of the United States, devoutly recognizing the Supreme Authority and just Government of Almighty God, in all the affairs of men and of nations, has, by a resolution, requested the President to designate and set apart a day for National prayer and humiliation.
>
> And whereas it is the duty of nations as well as of men, to own their dependence upon the overruling power of God, to confess their sins and transgressions, in humble sorrow, yet with assured hope that genuine repentance will lead to mercy and pardon; and to recognize the sublime truth, announced in the Holy Scriptures and proven by all history, that those nations only are blessed whose God is the Lord.
>
> And, insomuch as we know that, by His divine law, nations like individuals are subjected to punishments and chastisements in this

world, may we not justly fear that the awful calamity of civil war, which now desolates the land, may be but a punishment, inflicted upon us, for our presumptuous sins, to the needful end of our national reformation as a whole People? We have been the recipients of the choicest bounties of Heaven. We have been preserved, these many years, in peace and prosperity. We have grown in numbers, wealth and power, as no other nation has ever grown. But we have forgotten God. We have forgotten the gracious hand which preserved us in peace, and multiplied and enriched and strengthened us; and we have vainly imagined, in the deceitfulness of our hearts, that all these blessings were produced by some superior wisdom and virtue of our own. Intoxicated with unbroken success, we have become too self-sufficient to feel the necessity of redeeming and preserving grace, too proud to pray to the God that made us!

It behooves us then, to humble ourselves before the offended Power, to confess our national sins, and to pray for clemency and forgiveness.

Now, therefore, in compliance with the request, and fully concurring in the views of the Senate, I do, by this my proclamation, designate and set apart Thursday, the 30th day of April, 1863, as a day of national humiliation, fasting and prayer. And I do hereby request all the People to abstain, on that day, from their ordinary secular pursuits, and to unite, at their several places of public worship and their respective homes, in keeping the day holy to the Lord, and devoted to the humble discharge of the religious duties proper to that solemn occasion.

All this being done, in sincerity and truth, let us then rest humbly in the hope authorized by the Divine teachings, that the united cry of the Nation will be heard on high, and answered with blessings, no less than the pardon of our national sins, and the restoration of our now divided and suffering Country, to its former happy condition of unity and peace.[3]

A preponderance of twenty-first-century world leaders have lost total touch with the crux of the afore-quoted Lincolnian pronouncement and divine revelation—the supreme authority and just government of almighty God in all affairs of men and of nations, and the duty of nations as well as of men to own their dependence upon the overruling power of Jehovah God. Leaders rely far more on their human intelligence and not godly wisdom to govern. They fail to appreciate the time-tested truth, learned from a close study of human history, that given another trillion years of human civilization, man will remain incapable of establishing a peaceful earth without Jehovah's divine intervention. This is because man has and will continue to dominate his fellow man to his injury (Eccles. 8:9). Indeed, one consistently recurring lesson of history is the failure of human rulership. Every civilization that has ever existed has ultimately collapsed. All good government has constantly been foiled by self-interest, shortsightedness, greed, corruption, nepotism, and especially the lust to obtain and retain power at all cost. Hence, the past and our present age is littered with wars, social unrest, and violence; rebellion, and revolutions; failed treaties, arms race, the unfair distribution of wealth, collapsed and collapsing economies; devastating natural disasters; and religious fundamentalism and terrorism.

One cannot but agree with those who contend that the only thing to be learned from history is that men learn nothing from history. The collective failure of nations and peoples to live in perfect peace with one another could also be attributed to the failure to appreciate as the prophet Jeremiah did, that a man's life is not his own and that it is not for man to direct his steps (Jer. 10:23). It is precisely because nations and governments have never learned anything from history nor are they ready to act upon any lesson they might have drawn from it that the world is in a constant state of war. It is for this reason that rulers like Iran's Ahmadinejad will deny a clear fact of history—the Jewish Holocaust—and envision a world without America and Israel.

The quest by world leaders is for international security; but like the end of the rainbow, the more they chase peace and security, the more elusive it becomes. Indeed, the quest for security and peace can be traced to the roots of past and modern day wars, yet paradoxically, our very existence today is threatened by war; and a glimpse into another century or millennium of human civilization gives no ray of hope for world peace but of increased violence. Giving our intrinsic nature—"every inclination of the thoughts of the human heart was only evil all the time" (Gen. 6:5, NIV)—and faced by a threat of our own survival as individuals, groups, or nations, we are inevitably incited to violence. In our contemporary world where ideology extends its influence into the socioeconomic system, such that personal relationships of life influence and also govern the rationale of industry and commerce, both way of life and means of livelihood inevitably become a source of concern, not only to individuals but also to competing nations.

Thus, for competing nations and the world's nuclear superpowers, the position remains that of mutual antagonism under the façade of the quest for international peace and security. We have continued to witness a scenario in which nations under the iron grip of corrupt despots and tyrants see their own actions as pure and peaceful but their adversary's as devious and aggressive. Indeed, the view that another state's policies are hostile give away to an atmosphere of rising tension producing an arms race frenzy, which in turn increases the tension and mitigates against the realization of international peace and security. What has been termed a self-fulfilling prophecy comes regularly into play; a situation in which each nation builds up its armaments to ward off the attack it predicts, but in doing so simply confirms the worst fears of its adversary. Thus, when relationship is rooted in mutual fears, it becomes difficult to establish the common ground in which to base hopes of peaceful coexistence. The current situation in the Middle East and the varied socioeconomic interests of the world's dominant military power in the region and other regions of the world is a good case study of the afore-painted scenario.

The Jewish-Palestinian impasse over the city of Jerusalem (certainly beyond man's permanent solution) and a renewed quest for the extermination of the "Zionist" State of Israel, fueled by the inordinate ambition of the world's military and economic power for military and economic dominance and the control of the vast oil reserves of the Middle East, presents a frightening yet hopeful picture of mankind's second to the last war, the war of the Great Day of God—Armageddon. (See Daniel 11:40–45; Ezekiel 38–39; Zechariah 12:1–10; Revelation 16:16.)

This is the battle that will ultimately redeem Israel and mankind, for as Rabbi Petuchowski of the United States aptly said that there will be no redeemed people of Israel and no redeemed land of Israel without a redeemed humanity. Of a truth, there are no redeemed enclaves within an unredeemed world because salvation history and human or world history are interwoven.

This is what the Scripture reveals, and this is what this book about Israel as God's ensign to nations reveals.

Let us now take a panoramic view of Israel in the march of ancient, medieval, and modern world history.

Chapter 1

ISRAEL IN WORLD HISTORY

WE ARE INFORMED from historical records that in the course of the fourth century millennium BC the first urban civilization developed and flourished in Mesopotamia and later in Egypt. The records of history also attest to the fact, that about 4,000 years before the birth of Jesus Christ, and certainly by about 3761 BC, the tradition and belief in one God had taken root amidst a pantheon of several other gods in the urban civilization of the fertile valleys of the Nile and the Euphrates where priest-dominated society had emerged. Soon the priesthood became more centralized, reflecting in the changing importance of particular gods, and in Egypt in the rise of the doctrine of divine kingship and the construction of increasingly elaborate temples and royal tombs culminating in the age of the Pyramids.

CALL OF ABRAM

The Jewish patriarch Abram (Abraham) (circa 2018–1843 BC) originally dwelt in the Mesopotamian region of Ur of the Chaldeans in Sumeria. At this time the religion of the region had reached classical form with the rise of more centralized political units in the early dynastic period. Four main gods had been developed, Anu god of heaven, Enlil god of the winds, Ninhursag goddess of birth, and Enki (*Ea*) god of water. It was in the midst of a society and people who worship these and other gods that Yahweh (Jehovah God) called on Abram (Abraham) to leave Ur of the Chaldeans (Gen. 11:31; 12:1). In Genesis 13:1–18, we read of how Abraham went from Egypt to the Negev, (the same Negev desert that the modern day Israel has turned into productive fertile area), and his separation from Lot, his brother's son. In Genesis chapter 14 is the story of the warring kingdoms of Sodom, Gomorrah, Admah, Zeboiim, and Bela (Zoar) against Chedorlaomer, king of Elam; Tidal, king of Goiim; Amramphel, king of Shinar; and Ariorch, king of Ellasar. It also tells of the defeat of Sodom and Gomorrah from where Lot and his family were taken captive and how Abraham rescued them. Historical records show that from about 2900 BC hereditary kings ruled Sumerian cities. The archaic tablets of Ur, an archaeological find, came from the early dynastic or classical Sumerian age. Some historians believe that the record of Sumerian kings began with Mebaragesi of Kish (about 2700 BC), while conflict between Sumerian cities such as Ur, Kish, and Lagash reached a climax at about 2500 BC.

In Egypt the middle kingdom reached its zenith with the twelfth dynasty (1991–1785 BC) after Amenehat I had subdued the nobility and restored prosperity. The kingdom ended about 1785, weakened by the influx of the Hyksos, a Semitic people from Syria. Between the decade 1520–1510 BC, Egypt rose again with the advent of Thautmose I who established an empire in the Near East and began the construction of the valley of the tombs of the kings of Thebes. Amenhotep III (1417–1379 BC) extended the Egyptian empire and brought peace and prosperity at home, which were threatened by the attempted religious reforms of his successor, Akhenaton, and by internecine murders. Rameses II fought the Hittites at the Battle of Kedesh (circa 1299 BC).

ISRAEL IN EGYPT

By the time of the establishment of the twelfth Egyptian dynasty of the middle kingdom in about 1991 BC, the Israelites had settled in Egypt. Joseph, Jacob's son, had been sold by his jealous brothers to the Ishmaelites for twenty pieces of silver and had been taken to Egypt. In Egypt Potiphar, an official of Pharaoh and captain of the guard, bought Joseph out of the hands of the Ishmaelites. He found favor in Potiphar's household and rose to become an overseer of his master's wealth and properties. In time Joseph suffered persecution and was jailed when Potiphar's wife falsely accused him, following her failed attempt to lure him into sexual intercourse. By divine providence Joseph was released from jail to interpret Pharaoh's dreadful dream, which he interpreted correctly. He was, as a result, elevated by Pharaoh to the position of a governor in Egypt saddled with the responsibility of storing grains and other foodstuffs in preparation for the envisioned seven years famine.

Following the coming of the foretold famine and the devastating effect on the region of Canaan and Egypt, Jacob (Israel) sent his sons to Egypt where there was abundant grain as a result of the storage of food in preparation of the seven years famine under Joseph's direction and supervision. In Egypt they met with Joseph, now the Egyptian governor Zaphnathpaaneah, who was now beyond their recognition but who recognized them. After a series of dramatic events, Joseph was reunited with his brothers and father, Jacob (Israel). He later introduced them to Pharaoh, and "gave them a possession in the land of Egypt, in the best land of Rameses as Pharaoh commanded" (Gen. 47:11). (See Genesis 37:28; 39:1, 5, 7; 41:26–45; 42:1; 47:9–11.)

SLAVERY AND MOSES

It was from this point that Jacob (Israel) lived in the Egyptian country of Goshen with his household where they became wealthy and grew and multiplied exceedingly with the full establishment of the twelve tribes of Israel (Gen. 49:10–33). With the advent of a new pharaoh, who did not know Joseph, the Israelites were gradually enslaved and ultimately ladened with bitter and hard bondage (Exod. 1:8–14). In time and at about 1593 BC, Moses, under God's mighty power, led the Israelites out of Egypt, having presented the sign of divine authority and following the judgment of the twelve plagues on Pharaoh. With Jehovah's direction Moses institutionalized the worship of a single God, Yahweh (Jehovah), to whom the twelve tribes of Israel were bound by a covenant promised them to possess the land of Canaan (Palestine).

CONQUEST OF CANAAN

The Israelites quickly conquered much of Canaan (circa 1473 BC) with the divine assistance of Jehovah. He had showed them that He is Jehovah of armies, the Lord of hosts in Egypt and through the Red Sea (Exod. 13:17; 14:31), by the waters of Marah (15:22–27), with the manna and quail (16:1–7), and in the war with Amalek (17:8–16). Moses fulfilled the vital role of mediator of the Sinai law covenant given by Jehovah God to Israel in addition to being a prophet, judge, leader, and historian (2:1–3; 22). The Law that Israel accepted consisted of the ten words or commandments and over 600 laws that amounted to a comprehensive catalog of directives and guidance for daily conduct. This law covenant or religious constitution gave form and substance to the faith of the patriarchs. As a result, the descendants of the patriarchs—Abraham, Isaac, and Jacob (Israel)— become a nation dedicated to the service and worship of God. Thus, the Jewish religion began to take definite shape and the Jews became a nation organized for the worship and service of their God. We recall that in

Exodus 19:5–6 God called them to faithful obedience of His covenant to be to Him a kingdom of priests and a holy nation.

As Israel settled in the Promised Land, having crossed the River Jordan and successfully conquering surrounding hostile pagan kingdoms (Josh. 11:1–23; 12:1–24), the barbarian invasions continued to strike the Near East obliterating the power of the Mycenaseans and limiting Egyptian and Assyrian military ambition. From about 1200 to 700 BC smaller trading societies, especially the Jews and Phoenicians, flourished. Phoenicians built colonies throughout the Mediterranean and Jews established their distinctive identity and claim to the region west of the River Jordan. Beginning with the period of the Judges, Israelite history shows continued effort by certain individuals and nomadic groups to defend the purity of the religion of Yahweh (Jehovah) against its dilution by pagan affiliation of her central rulers. This unceasing resistance to the addition of the gods to their faith reinforced the distinctive features of the Judaic tradition.

ISRAEL UNDER EARLY FOREIGN DOMINATION

Between 1100 and 1050 BC, the Philistines, a trading people, conquered the Jews who had since settled in Palestine after leaving Egypt in about 1593 BC and were at this time a loose confederation tribe ruled by Judges. In about 1020 BC, Saul became the first anointed king of the Jews with powers limited by religious traditions. Under Saul the Philistines incessantly raided the children of Israel. The biblical account records that for their evil and idolatry ways, they were sold out to the Philistines and the Amorites for eighteen years. (Judg. 10:7) They were also delivered into the hands of the Philistines for forty years (13:1) Samson came in here as Israel's great rescuer. It was he who wrought great disaster on the Philistines even unto his death in the hand of the Philistines wherein those Philistines he killed at his death were more than those he killed in his life (16:30).

KING DAVID

Not until the glorious reign of King David (circa 1077–1037 BC) (some scholars date 1011–971 BC) were the Philistines finally defeated. David moved to Hebron after the death of Saul and Jonathan where the older men of Judah anointed him as king over their tribe in 1077 BC at the age of thirty (2 Sam. 2:1–4). Saul's son Ish-bosheth was made king of the other tribes (vv. 8–10). About two years later, however, Ish-bosheth was assassinated. His assailants Rechab and Baanah brought his head to David hoping to receive a reward, but they too were put to death (4:5–12) like the pretender killer of Saul who described himself as the son of a stranger an Amalekite (1:1–15). This paved the way for the tribe who had until then supported Saul's son to join Judah, and in time a force numbering 340,822 rallied and made David, king of all Israel. David thus united Israel. (See 2 Samuel 5:1–3; 1 Chronicles 11:1–3; 12:23–40.)

David ruled for seven and a half years in Hebron before moving his capital, at Jehovah God's direction, to the captured Jebusite stronghold, Jerusalem. There he built the City of David on Zion and continued to rule another thirty-three years (2 Sam. 5:4–10; 1 Chron. 11:4; 2 Chron. 6:6). The attempt by the Philistines to overthrow David was ruthlessly met with such overpowering destruction that David called the battle-field *Baal-Perazin* meaning "owner of breakings through" (2 Sam. 5:20; 1 Chron. 14:11).

David brought the ark of the covenant to Jerusalem. He thought of building a temple—place of cedar to house the ark, to replace its tent, but was not permitted by God because of the great deal of blood he spilled in the course of the great wars he fought (1 Chron. 22:8; 28:3). However, God entered into a covenant with him promising that the kingship would everlastingly remain in his family; and in connection with this covenant, God assured him that his son Solomon, whose name is from a root meaning "peace," would build the temple. (See 2 Samuel 7:1–16, 25–29; 1 Chronicles 17:1–27; 2 Chronicles 6:7–9; Psalm 89:3–4, 35–36.) In line with God's covenant with David, He permitted and led him to expand his territorial rule from rivers of Egypt to the Euphrates, securing his borders, maintaining peace with the king of Tyre, battling and conquering on all sides—Amalekites, Ammonites, Edomites, Moabites, Philistines and Syrians. (See 2 Samuel 8:1–14; 10:6–19; 1 Kings 5:3; 1 Chronicles 13:5; 14:1–2; 18:1–20.) David became a most powerful ruler as a result of these God-given victories and was very conscious that the ultimate glory was not his but Jehovah's on whose theocratic throne he sat by divine grace and favor.

King David died at the age of seventy, but not before he had installed Solomon his son as his successor, in the face of Adonijah's attempt to install himself king. Adonijah was David's fourth son. David then counseled his and God's chosen heir to the throne, Solomon, to walk in Jehovah's ways, keep His statutes and commandments, act prudently in all things, and then would he find peace and prosperity. After a forty-year reign, David died and was buried in the City of David, having proved worthy of inclusion in Paul's honorable list of Jehovah's servants who were outstanding in faith (Acts 13:36; Heb. 11:32).

KING SOLOMON

Solomon (circa 1037–998 BC) (some scholars date it 971–931 BC) succeeded his father David. Solomon began to build the temple of Jerusalem, the house of Jehovah, on Mount Moriah (1 Kings 6:1). This was about 1034 BC. Seven and a half years after, in about the year 1027 BC, the temple was concluded. Solomon engaged extensively in trade. He built a trading fleet in the Indian Ocean. His fleet, in cooperation with Hiram's, brought in great quantities of gold from Ophir, as well as *algum* timbers and precious stones. Horses and chariots were imported from Egypt, and traders from all over the world at the time brought their goods in abundance. God blessed Solomon with wisdom, glory, and riches as long as he remained firm for true worship and obeyed the statutes and commandments; and the nation of Israel likewise enjoyed God's favor. Solomon's reign ushered in unprecedented peace. First Kings 4:25 states: "During Solomon's lifetime Judah and Israel, from Dan to Beersheba, lived in safety, each man under his own vine" (NIV).

Then Solomon transgressed God's covenant law. His government became oppressive and discontent followed the conscription of people for forced labor. He lost God's favor and wisdom to tackle the problems created by the high cost of governance due to his transgressions and thus laid the foundation for a divided kingdom.

THE DIVIDED KINGDOM

The Jewish kingdoms were divided on Solomon's death into kingdom of the Israelites in the North and Judah in the South, following religious opposition to his rule in the North. Rehoboam, who promised to chastise the children of Israel with scorpions (1 Kings 12:11), became the king of Judah with Jerusalem as the capital, while Israel made Jeroboam, son of Nebat, their king. Jeroboam led Israel away from following Jehovah and Rehoboam's intransigence, as well as the continued acrimony and disunity between them, exposed Israel and Judah to the conquest of the Assyrians and the Egyptians.

Jeroboam, king of Northern Kingdom of Israel, took refuge for a time in Egypt during the reign of Shishak (1 Kings 11:40). Shishak (known as Sheshonk I from Egyptian records) had founded a Libyan dynasty of pharaohs (the twenty-second dynasty) with its capital of Bubastis in the Eastern Delta region. In the fifth year of the reign of Solomon's son Rehoboam (circa 993 BC), Shishak invaded Judah with a formidable force of calvary, chariots, and foot soldiers including Libyans and Ethiopians. He captured many cities and even threatened Jerusalem. Because of Jehovah's mercy, Jerusalem was not left desolate; but its great wealth was handed over to Shishak (1 Kings 14:25–26; 2 Chron. 12:2–9). A relief on a temple wall at Karnak depicts Shiskak's campaign and lists numerous cities in Israel and Judah as having been captured.[1]

In about 967 BC, Zerah, the Ethiopian (or Cushite), led a huge army of a million men and 300 chariots from Egypt into Judah during King Asa's reign. Zerah and his army, which gathered in the Valley of Zephatah, Southwest of Jerusalem, were defeated and his fleeing forces were pursued and slaughtered as far as Gerar (2 Chron. 14:1, 9–15). Judah and Israel enjoyed respite from Egyptian attack for about two centuries until the rise of Assyria as the dominant world power.

CONQUESTS AND WARS

In the year 853 BC, the Arameans and the Israelites, inspired by Elijah the prophet, defeated Shalmanesser III of Assyria at the Battle of Qagar. Shalmanesser (858–824 BC) reorganized his army and later defeated the forces of Damascus and Israel. Indeed, as narrated in *The History of the World* by John Hall and John Kirk,[2] under Shalmanesser III, the Assyrian policy took on all the hallmarks of a grand design. The repeated hammer blows of his armies were directed with an almost single-minded dedication and persistence against Assyria's Western neighbors and brought about the first military confrontation between Assyria and Egypt. The earlier mentioned Battle of Qagar (circa 853 BC) pitted Shalmanesser III against a grant coalition of Western states, including Israelites, Arameans, Cilicians, Egyptians, Arabians, Ammorites, and Phoenicians. King Ahab of Israel contributed significantly to the infantry and, more especially, the chariotry on the allied side. Ahab died within the year, but the coalition survived major changes and met Shalmanesser three more times (849, 848, 841 BC). Only after the last of these encounters could the Assyrian king truthfully claim the subjugation of the Western allies. The triumphant march across a prostrate westland by Shalman was recalled more than a century later in an explicit biblical reference to the name of an Assyrian king (Hosea 10:14)—Shalman, short form of Shalmanesser. By 800 BC the Assyrian military power declined under successive weak monarchs and with it, Assyrian wealth.

Conquests, wars, and commercial interactions with various kingdoms and peoples exposed Israel to wholesome and unwholesome influences. In the course of the eighth century BC, prophets of the Old Testament—Amos, Hosea and Isaiah—began to castigate the moral decadence or turpitude of the Jewish rulers and their syncretic tendencies. The prophets rejected contemporary and foreign standards and urged other worldly ideas prophesying that the dilution of the old religion would lead to the fall of the kingdom of Israel. This prediction was fulfilled when the Assyrians reemerged under a new king, Tiglath-Pileser (ruled circa 744–727 BC), who restored Assyrian military power and established a strong and highly mobile standing army.

THE ASSYRIAN DOMINATION

Tiglath-Pileser III, Shalmanesser V (circa 726–722 BC), and Sargon II (circa 721–705 BC) changed the whole balance of power in the Near East, destroying Israel among other states and reducing the rest, including Judah, to vassalage. Tiglath-Pileser's second campaign to the West (734–732 BC), after his first campaign in the Northern and Eastern frontiers (circa 737 BC), was in response to Judah's call for assistance as recorded in 2 Kings 16:7. This campaign reduced Israel to a fraction of its former size as more and more of coastal and Trans-Jordan lands were either incorporated in the growing Assyrian Empire or reduced to vassal states. Within this period, Rezin, King of Syria, recovered Elath to Syria and drove the Jews from there (2 Kings 16:6).

Shalmanesser V (rule, circa 726–722 BC) and Sargon II (rule, circa 721–705 BC) followed Tiglath-Pileser's example. Shalmanesser V invaded Israel and laid siege on Samaria. The rump kingdom of Judah could not stand against Sargon's army and King Ahaz wisely heeded to Isaiah's counsels of caution. The advent of Hezekiah (circa 715–687 BC) brought back the anti-Assyrian coalition in Judah which led to the dispatch in 712 BC by Sargon of his commander-in-chief, Turtanu (the Tartan of Isaiah 20:1) against Ashdod, a city allied with Judah, which was captured.

Sargon's records speak of the deportation of 27,290 Israelites to a location in the upper Euphrates and Media. He was more successful against a coalition formed by the kings of Hamath and Damascus and other allies, gaining victory over them in a Battle of Karkar on the Orontes River. Second Kings 17:24 and 30 list people of Hamath among those whom the king of Assyria settled in the cities or Samaria in place of exiled Israelites. According to Sargon's records, in his fifth year he attacked and conquered Carchemish, a city of commercial and military importance on the upper Euphrates River. The standard Assyrian procedure of deportation of the city's inhabitants and of their replacement by foreign elements followed. In Isaiah's warning regarding the menace of the Assyrians (Isa. 10:5–11), Carchemish, along with Hamath and other cities, are cited as examples of the crushing power of Assyria. Later Sargon reports settling Arab tribes in Samaria.[3] Sargon's aggressive reign brought the Assyrian Empire to a new peak of power and produced the last great Assyrian dynasty.

Sargon's son and successor, Sennacherib (circa 705–681 BC), attacked the kingdom of Judah during King Hezekiah's fourteenth year on the throne of Judah (2 Kings 18:13; Isa. 36:1). Hezekiah had rebelled against Assyrian yoke because of the actions of his father, Ahaz. It should be recalled that rather than put faith in God, Ahaz, out of fear of the Syro-Israeli conspiracy, chose the shortsighted policy of bribing Tiglath-Pileser III of Assyria to come to his aid (Isa. 7:2–6; 8:12). The temporary relief the ambitious Assyrian king brought to Ahaz by defeating the Syro-Israeli coalition brought the heavy yoke of Assyrian domination, which Hezekiah sought to remove under Sargon's son Sennacherib (2 Kings 18:1–8).

Sennacherib reacted by sweeping through Judah, reportedly conquering forty-six cities and then from his camp in Lachish he demanded of Hezekiah a tribute of thirty gold talents (over eleven million dollars US) (2 Kings 18:13–16). Though this sum was paid, Sennacherib sent his officers and spokespersons to demand the unconditional surrender of Jerusalem. (See 2 Kings 18:17–25; 2 Chronicles 32:1–19.) As a result of Sennacherib's breach of agreement and arrogance and utter disregard for Jehovah, an angel of the Lord was sent and Sennacherib's armies, estimated at about 185,000, were annihilated in one night and the Assyrian king was forced to retreat to Nineveh (2 Kings 19:35–36). There he was assassinated by two of his sons and replaced on the throne by another son, Esar-haddon (2 Kings 19:37; 2 Chron. 32:21–22; Isa. 37:36–38).

THE FALL OF ASSYRIA, THE RISE OF BABYLON

The seizure of the Babylonian throne by Nabopolassar in about 645 BC marked an end of Assyrian suzerainty over Babylon and the establishment of a new dynasty, generally known as the neo-Babylonian or Chaldean dynasty. Although the Assyrian military machine continued to be highly effective instrument for almost two decades, Nabopolassar successfully defended Babylonian's independence. However, with the assistance of the Medes and Josiah of Judah (circa 639–629 BC), Assyria was finally eliminated as a dominant world power. The annihilation of the Assyrian capital and cities Nineveh, Kalah, Assur, and Dur-Sharrukin between 615 and 612 BC are attested in part by The Babylonian Chronicle and even more tellingly, in the archaeological evidences from these sites. One recounts the fall of Nineveh the capital of Assyria following a siege carried out by Cyaxares (632 BC): "The city was turned into ruin—hills and heaps of debris."[4] The impact on the contemporary world and lessons for the twenty-first-century nations can be measured with the prophecies of Isaiah, Jeremiah, Nahum, and Zephaniah. (See Isaiah 10:12; 24–26; 23:13; 30:30–33; 31:8–9; 44:27; 45:1–2, Jeremiah 50:38; 51:30–32; Nahum 3:1–19; Zephaniah 2:13.)

> The Lord…says: "I will punish the King of Assyria for the willful pride of his heart and the haughty look in his eye.…I removed the boundaries of nations…I subdue their kings. As one reaches into a nest, so my hand reached for the wealth of the nations; as men gather abandoned eggs so I gather all the countries, no one flapped a wing, or open his mouth to chirp."
>
> —ISAIAH 10:12–14, NIV

> He will stretch out his hand against the north and destroy Assyria, leaving Nineveh utterly desolate and dry as the desert.
>
> —ZEPHANIAH 2:13, NIV

> King of Assyria, your shepherds slumber; your nobles lie down to rest. Your people are scattered on the mountains with no one to gather them. Nothing can heal you; your wound is fatal. All who hear the news about you clap their hands at your fall, for who has not felt your endless cruelty?
>
> —NAHUM 3:18–19, NIV

Only Egypt remained loyal to Assyria, and Pharaoh Neco fought against Josiah at Megiddo where the Judean king was killed (circa 629 BC). The last remnants of Assyrian power, possibly under Assur-uballit (circa 611–609 BC), was finally defeated and the Assyrian history came to a sudden end (2 Kings 23:29–30).

EVENTS IN JUDAH: NEBUCHADNEZZAR AND THE BABYLONIAN EXILE

From 605–586 BC events in Judah moved swiftly following the death of Josiah. Pharaoh Neco seized the opportunity of his demise to interfere in Israel's domestic affairs by deporting Josiah's successor, Jehoahaz, and appointed the second son of Josiah, Jehoiakim, as king. Soon after, the Babylonian crown prince, Nebuchadnezzar II (circa 604–562 BC) defeated the Egyptian army in the Battle of Carchemish (605 BC) and consolidated the Babylonian empire. Nebuchadnezzar completed the restoration started by his father, Nabopolassar, and brought the city to its greatest glory. In Daniel 4:30, he boasted of his achievement with the question, "Is not this great Babylon, that I have built for a royal dwelling by my mighty power and for the honor of my majesty?" (NKJV). Under him the Chaldean empire assimilated and annexed most of Assyrian conquered territories and briefly regained for Babylonia the position of the third world power in the ancient world after Egypt and Assyria. Jehoiakim continued to pay tribute to Nebuchadnezzar for three years, after which he revolted. This culminated in rapid military responses from Nebuchadnezzar in form of small raids from Babylonians, Arameans, Moabites, and Ammonites. However, before the Babylonians could capture him, Jehoiakim died. His son Jehoiachin succeeded him. He quickly surrendered and was taken captive along with other nobility to Babylon in about 617 BC.

Nebuchadnezzar went on to appoint Zedekiah as king. He served as Israel's last king. In time Zedekiah also revolted; he refused to pay tribute to Nebuchadnezzar and Jerusalem was attacked and besieged for two and a half years. Facing starvation, Zedekiah, his royal household, and his army fled by night through the Arabah but were overtaken in the plains of Jericho (2 Kings 25:4). Zedekiah was captured and dragged off in chains to Riblah, where he saw his sons slaughtered before he was blinded and taken to Babylon. One month later Jerusalem was ransacked and laid desolate (circa 607 BC). Numerous high officials were executed, the temple furnishings were carried off, and the children of Israel were taken into exile to Babylon where they remained for seventy years in fulfillment of Jehovah's pronouncements. Under Nebuchadnezzar Babylon was a "golden cup" in the hand of the sovereign Lord of the universe and of nations to pour out His anger against apostate and unfaithful Judah and Jerusalem.

> So I took the cup from the LORD's hands and made all the nations
> to whom he sent me drink it: Jerusalem and the towns of Judah, its
> kings and officials, to make them ruin and an object of horror and
> scorn, a curse—as they are today.
>
> —JEREMIAH 25:17–18, NIV

> Babylon hath been a golden cup in the LORD's hand, that made all
> the earth drunken: the nations have drunken of her wine; therefore
> the nations are mad.
>
> —JEREMIAH 51:7

Nebuchadnezzar II died in October of 582 BC and was succeeded
by Awil-Marduk (Evil-Merodach). Evil-Merodach is recorded as
having showed kindness to captive King Jehoiachin (2 Kings 25:27–30).
Not much is known about the reign of Neriglissar, evidently the successor of Evil-Merodach and of Labashi-Marduk. Historians agree that
Nebuchadnezzar's conquest of Jerusalem and Judah with the exile of
Judean aristocracy to Babylon is the most famous of his triumphs.

GOD'S MIGHTY AND INVINCIBLE HAND

In His infinite wisdom, God uses leaders to achieve His purposes on
earth. He used Nebuchadnezzar to punish the intransigence and idolatry
of His chosen children of Israel and to fulfill Daniel's prophecy of the
seventy years of Jewish exile in Babylon. Similarly, He used Assyria to
show His indignation against the Israelites.

> O Assyrian, the rod of mine anger, and the staff in their hand is
> mine indignation.
>
> —ISAIAH 10:5

> "I will deliver Zedekiah king of Judah, and his servants, and the
> people, and such as are left in this city from the pestilence, from the
> sword, and from famine, into the hand of Nebuchadnezzar king of
> Babylon."
>
> —JEREMIAH 21:7

> For thus saith the LORD, That after seventy years be accomplished at
> Babylon I will visit you, and perform my good word toward you, in
> causing you to return to this place.
>
> —JEREMIAH 29:10

The End of Babylonian Power,
the Rise of Medo-Persians

Jeremiah's prophesied redemption of the children Israel after seventy years in Babylonian exile materialized when the Medo-Persian king, Cyrus the Great, triumphantly entered Babylon (circa 539 BC) and was led by the Marduk priesthood, who had turned against Belshazzar, the son of Nabonidus (circa 556–539 BC) left in the Babylonian capital as co-regent. In an easy conquest, Cyrus (559–530 BC) assumed control of all of Babylon and brought down the curtain on the last native Akkadian state in fulfillment of Isaiah's prophecy (Isa. 44:27–28). In brilliant strategy Cyrus's army engineers diverted the mighty Euphrates River from its course through the city of Babylon. Then down the riverbed the Persians moved up over the riverbanks to take the city by surprise through the gates along the quay. Quickly passing through the streets, killing all who resisted, they captured the palace and put Belshazzar to death. Babylon fell in one night, ending centuries of Semitic supremacy. (See Jeremiah 50:38, 51:30–33; Isaiah 45:1–2.) Cyrus the Great assisted the Jews to return to Jerusalem in 525 BC (Ezra 1:1–8), to rebuild the temple of Jerusalem as appointed by Jehovah, prophesied by Isaiah, and narrated by Ezra (Isa. 45:1, 13; Ezra 5:13; 6:14).

> Thus says the LORD to his anointed, to Cyrus, whose right hand I have holden....I have raised him up in righteousness, and I will direct all his ways: he shall build my city, and he shall let go my captives, not for a price nor reward, saith the LORD of hosts.
>
> —ISAIAH 45:1, 13

Cambyses (circa 530–522 BC) is presented by scholars as being made king of Babylon by his father, Cyrus the Great, soon after the conquest of Babylon. While Cambyses evidently did represent his father annually at the New Year's festival at Babylon, he seems to have resided at Sippar during the rest of the time. Research based on study of cuneiform texts indicates that Cambyses evidently did not assume the title king of Babylon until the year 530 BC, being made co-regent with his father, Cyrus, who was then setting out on military exploits that culminated in his demise. Following the death of Cambyses in about 522 BC while he was returning from Egypt, the Persian throne was occupied for a brief period by his brother Bardiva (or possibly by a Magian name Gaumata).[5]

DARIUS THE GREAT

Darius (circa 522–486 BC) seized the Persian throne after slaying the occupant of the throne with the aid of six other Persian nobles. He was faced with an empire in revolt upon assuming the kingship and considered to have spent the next two years subduing the insurrectionary elements throughout the empire. Egypt, which had thrown off the Persian yoke, was reconquered by Darius about 519–518 BC. He then extended the imperial borders into India in the East and into Thrace and Macedonia in the West. Darius is also credited for his efficient reorganization of the imperial administrative structure, for the establishment of an imperial law code, called the Ordinance of Good Regulations, and for having reopened the canal connecting the Nile River of Egypt with the Red Sea.

Darius Hystaspis or Darius the Great features in the Bible record with regard to the rebuilding of the Jewish temple at Jerusalem. The foundation of the temple was laid in about 536 BC, but was discontinued because of a ban in about 522 BC. It was not until the second year of the reign of Darius (circa 520 BC) that work resumed on the temple (Ezra 4:4–5, 24). It was at this time that the prophets Haggai and Zechariah inspired the Jews to renew the construction and work started again (Ezra 5:1–2; Hag. 1:1, 14–15; Zech. 1:1). The resumption of work on the temple elicited an inquiry resulting in the sending of a letter to King Darius by Tattenai, the governor representing the imperial interests in the region west of the Euphrates, and other officials. The letter, which advised Darius of the construction, also presented the Jews' argument for the legality of the project. It further requested an investigation in the royal archive to determine if there existed written evidence to support the Jewish claim (Ezra 5:3–17).

The book *Insight on the Scriptures* explains:

> The Jewish declaration that contrasted the action of the Chaldean Nebuchadnezzar, as the destroyer of the temple with the Persian Cyrus, as the one authorizing its construction, should have had an appropriate and felicitous effect on Darius, since, in the first years of his reign, he had to overcome two revolts by rebels taking the name Nebuchadnezzar (called Nebuchadnezzar III and Nebuchadnezzar IV by historians), claiming to be sons of Nabonidus and endeavoring to make Babylon independent of the Persian Empire.[6]

Bible historians record that by March 6 of 515 BC or by the third day of the lunar month Adar that is in the sixth year of the reign of Darius the Great, the temple work was successfully completed (Ezra

6:13–15). The success was made possible as a result of the cooperation of Darius and his officials as well as the continued encouragement of the prophets (Zech. 7:1; 8:1–9, 20–23). Darius was thus used by Jehovah to serve His purpose, though the Persian king was a devotee of the god Ahura Mazda, regarded as the greatest of all gods and protector of the just king. According to Zoroaster (circa 628–551 BC), religious reformer and founder of Zoroastrianism or Mazdaism, Ahura Mazda created the universe and the cosmic order he maintains.

Darius's invasion of Greece resulted in the defeat of his force at the battle of Marathon in about 490 BC. He died four years later in 486 BC and was succeeded by his son Xerxes, who was later succeeded by Darius III.

ALEXANDER THE GREAT, THE RISE OF THE GRECIAN EMPIRE

Alexander the Great, son of Phillip II of Macedonia, having consolidated his authority in Greece, moved against the Medo-Persian Empire led then by Darius III. He secured two decisive victories in Asia Minor against the Persians (the first at the Granicus River, the second on the Plain of Isus where a great Persian army, estimated at half a million, was utterly defeated). It is instructive that Jehovah used Nebuchadnezzar to fulfill prophet Ezekiel's prophecy, made centuries before its actualization, of the destruction of the island city of Tyre.

> Therefore, this is what the Sovereign LORD says: I am against you, Tyre, and I will bring many nations against you....From the north I am going to bring against Tyre Nebuchadnezzar, king of Babylon....They will plunder your wealth and loot your merchandise....When I make you a desolate city, like cities no longer inhabited, and when I bring the ocean depths over you and its vast waters cover you.
>
> —EZEKIEL 26:3, 7, 12, 19, NIV

It is therefore quite significant that Alexander took the rubble of the old mainland city of Tyre destroyed by Nebuchadnezzar some years before and built an 800 meters (0.5 miles) causeway out to the island city. The city of renown, peopled by men of the sea who were a power on the seas, was finally destroyed by Alexander in the month of July 332 BC. Indeed, nearly 200 years after Zechariah's prophecy was uttered it was fulfilled by Alexander (Zech. 9:3–4).

In about 330 BC Alexander rode triumphantly into Jerusalem and was warmly welcomed by the Jews. According to Flavius Josephus,[7] Alexander was shown the book of Daniels' prophecy, most likely the eighth chapter of Daniel, where a mighty Greek king would subdue and conquer the Persian Empire. As a result of the revelation made to him, Alexander, according to Josephus, spared Jerusalem and advanced south into Egypt where he was welcomed as a deliverer. In Egypt Alexander founded the city of Alexandria, named after him. He then moved eastward, returning from Egypt through Palestine, and at the Battle of Gaugamela defeated and overwhelmed a reorganized Persian army of about one million with just forty-seven thousand men. The Persian army lay at Alexander's feet. Darius III fled eastwards and was murdered by the Satrap of Bactria. In 327 BC he crossed to the Indus, but died prematurely in 323 BC. His plans to rebuild Babylon failed, not just because of his premature death from malaria attack and reckless lifestyle but because Jehovah had ordained his death and decreed the permanent desolation of Babylon as foretold by Daniel and Jeremiah. By 297 BC Alexander's vast empire had disintegrated into four parts; the Hellenistic kingdoms of Macedon and Thrace, the Seleucid dynasty of Spain, and the Ptolemaic in Egypt, whose invasion of Palestine in 301 BC revived old tensions with Syria. This was also in fulfillment of Daniel's prophecy.

Daniel had prophesied the rise of a kingdom that will destroy the Medo-Persia Empire in the following words:

> A goat with a prominent horn between his two eyes came from the west, crossing the whole earth without touching the ground. It came toward the two-horned ram I had seen standing beside the canal and charged at him at great rage.... The ram was powerless to stand against it; the goat knocked it to the ground and trampled on it, and none could rescue the ram from his power.... The two-horned ram that you saw represents the kings of Media and Persia. The shaggy goat is the king of Greece.
>
> —DANIEL 8:5–7, 20–21, NIV

As to the demise of Alexander and the disintegration of his empire into four, Daniel states,

> The goat became very great, but at the height of its power his large horn was broken off, and in its place four prominent horns grew up toward the four winds of heaven.
>
> —DANIEL 8:8, NIV

Jeremiah's prophecy that Babylon would never be rebuilt was foretold as thus:

> "So desert creatures and hyenas will live there, and there the owl will dwell. It will never again be inhabited or lived in from generation to generation. As I [God] overthrew Sodom and Gomorrah along with their neighboring towns," declares the LORD, "so no one will live there, no man will dwell in it."
>
> —JEREMIAH 50:39–40, NIV

HELENISTIC INFLUENCES

Before his demise, Alexander had introduced Greek culture and the Greek language into all parts of his domain. Common Greek (Koine) became the international language, hence the latter portion of the Bible was written in Koine rather than Hebrew. Alexandria, Alexander's created city, built in 332 BC became the principle city of Egypt; and under the Ptolemies, the Hellenistic kings of Egypt, Alexandria was made the Egyptian capital. It continued to serve as the administrative headquarter of Egypt on through the Roman conquest of 30 BC and the Byzantine epochs down to the Arabic conquest in the seventh century AD.

Alexander incorporated Israel into the international Hellenist culture. In the city of Alexandria, the Jews formed a sizable portion of the population. A good number of the Jews were descendants of the refugees who had fled to Egypt after Jerusalem's fall and destruction in 607 BC (or 586 BC). Alexandrian Jews produced the Greek Septuagint, the first translation of the Hebrew Scriptures, in Alexandria. Historical records show that this took place during the reign Philadelphus Ptolemy (II) (285–246 BC).

Following the partition of Greece among Alexander's generals, Judah became a border state between the Ptolemaic regime of Egypt and the Seleucid dynasty of Syria. First controlled by Egypt, Judah was seized by the Seleucids in about 198 BC. Greek religion, language, literature, and attire were promoted in an attempt to unite Judah and Syria in a Hellenic culture. Greek colonies developed in Palestine and Syria and throughout Jewish territory, including the colonies at Acco (Ptolemais), Bethshean (Scythoplies), and Samaria (thereafter called Sebaste). Greek colonies were also built on fresh sites, particularly east of the River Jordan. They flourished during the rule of the Seleucids of Syria and the Ptolemies of Egypt. However, the rise of the Maccabean-Jewish state beginning from about 168 BC greatly endangered the relative independence of these colonies, which, though heavily populated by Jews, had become centers of Greek culture and organization, very much out of step with the Maccabean worldview and objectives.

ENTER THE ROMANS

When the Roman general Pompey conquered and reorganized Palestine in about 63 BC, these Hellenistic cities were given Roman protection and a favored status. They were allowed to mint their own coins and to a large extent exercise self-government. However, they still owed allegiance to Rome and to the Syrian provincial government and were required to pay taxes and provide men for military service.

Julius Caesar rose to power after Pompey's victories had led to the annexation of Syria. He subdued Gaul, and after defeating Pompey became the imperial ruler; appointed dictator for ten years in about 46 BC. Civil wars ensued following Julius Caesar's assassination in 44 BC by a pro-senatorial conspiracy that feared he would become a dictator for life. After an interval in which a triumvirate attempted to hold the reins of power, Octavian (Augustus) Caesar finally became the sole ruler of the Roman Empire (circa 31 BC to AD 14). In 27 BC he succeeded in becoming emperor, having himself proclaimed "Augustus." He centralized power and prevented continued civil strife. Egypt became a Roman province in 30 BC, while Judea became a Roman territory in AD 6. It was during the rule of Augustus Caesar that Jesus Christ was born in 2 BC in Bethlehem in Judea (Luke 2:1–7).

The successor of Augustus, Tiberius (circa AD 14–37) was ruling during the glorious ministry of our Lord and Savior Christ Jesus. It was also during the reign of Tiberius and the Roman governor of Judea Pontius Pilate that Jesus was crucified (executed under Roman law and evidently on a charge of treason against the state goaded on by a Jewish crowd). Tiberius expanded the Roman Empire, instituted social reforms, and consolidated imperial power. Gaius (Caligula) succeeded Tiberius and ruled from about AD 37 to AD 41. Claudius (AD 41–54) came next and he issued a decree expelling the Jews from Rome (Acts 18:1–2). Emperor Nero's rule followed (circa AD 54–68), and it was to Nero that the apostle Paul appealed his case (Acts 25:11, 12, 21).

ISRAEL IN POST-CRUCIFIXION ERA

After the crucifixion of Jesus Christ in AD 30, the early Jewish Christian sect developed a unique emphasis on the resurrection of Christ the Messiah, the imminent transformation of the world, and the dawning of a millennium of universal love. Thus, Christianity emerged in Israel, the land of the Hebrews, and out of the religion of the Hebrews. Jesus Himself was a Jew, as were all His initial followers. The Messianic tradition was strong in Judaism as the findings from the Dead Sea scrolls reaffirm.

Paul of Tarsus, first century AD, who saw the death of Jesus Christ as a universal sign reflecting cosmic forces, spread Christian ideas throughout the Roman Empire. It required the apostle Paul, a brilliant Hellenized Jew, to break Christianity out of its Judaic shell. Paul's preaching to the Gentiles was indeed the turning point, and the idea that the church was independent of the synagogue was never again seriously questioned. The Pauline Epistles, preceding by several years the writing of the Gospels, were the foundation of Christian theology. Paul's tireless missionary activity and the voluminous messages stemming from a powerful intellect trained in both rabbinic laws and Greek learning made him by far the towering figure in the history of the early church. Contact with Hellenic thought turned Christianity into a world religion.

The Pharisees in Israel opposed the adoption of Hellenistic culture by their conservative Saducean rulers and were accused of arid formalistic legalism because of their emphasis on the regulation of the aspects of life in accordance with Jewish law. However, they enjoyed the allegiance of majority of the Jewish population because of their austere and ascetic lifestyles.

JERUSALEM'S DESTRUCTION: CHRIST'S PROPHECY FULFILLED

The earlier mentioned Roman emperor Nero rebuilt Rome after a devastating fire, which gutted much of the capital. The fire was blamed on Jews and Christians, who were unpopular within the empire because they refused to recognize the emperor's divinity. Paul and Peter were executed in the ensuing persecution (circa AD 64). The blood of the martyrs became the seed of the church. Galba (circa AD 68–69), Otho, and Vitellius (AD 69) ruled respectively and briefly after Nero.

In AD 69 Vespansian (AD 69–79) became emperor. The Jewish revolt against Roman rule attained its highest boiling point during this period (AD 66–70), culminating in the destruction of Jerusalem in AD 70, as foretold by Jesus Christ (Luke 19:42–44). It should be recalled that shortly before His crucifixion, death, and resurrection in AD 33. Jesus called Jerusalem the killer of the prophets and stoner of those sent forth to her (Matt. 23:37). The city as a whole followed the pattern of its past and rejected the Messiah, the Spirit-begotten Son of Jehovah. Christ foretold what would happen to Jerusalem, that the days would come upon her when her enemies would build around her a fortification with pointed stakes (Luke 19:43). He also warned:

> When you see Jerusalem surrounded by armies, you will know that its desolation is near. Then let those who are in Judea flee to the mountains, let those in the city get out, and let those in the country not enter the city.... They will fall by the sword and will be taken as prisoners to the nations. Jerusalem will be trampled upon by the Gentiles; until the time of the Gentiles are fulfilled.
> —LUKE 21:20–21, 24, NKJV

In AD 66, following a Jewish revolt, Roman armies under Cestius Gallus came against Jerusalem. Nevertheless, as the first century Jewish historian Flavius Josephus narrates in his *Jewish Antiquity*, Gallus suddenly recalled his troops and contrary to all expectations retired from the city. This provided Christians many opportunities to flee from Jerusalem, which they promptly did. Soon the Roman army under Titus returned. This time they built a fortification with pointed stakes—an encircling fence about 7.2 kilometers (4.5 miles) long (exactly, as Jesus had prophesied). After a siege of about five months, the city was taken, thoroughly destroyed, and the temple reduced to ruins.

Flavius Josephus wrote that eleven hundred thousand Judeans perished by famine and sword. Young men, tall and handsome, were preserved as war booty, those above seventeen years sent as prisoners to labor at mines in Egypt, while great numbers were distributed to the provinces to be destroyed by the sword or wild beasts in the theaters. Those under seventeen, according to Josephus, were carried away as slaves and these numbered over ninety thousand. A useful lesson to be learned from all this is provided by Josephus in the following words:

> Now if anyone consider these things, he will find that God takes care of mankind, and by all ways possible foreshows to our race what is for their preservation, but that men perish by their own miseries which they have madly and voluntarily bring upon themselves.[8]

Sixty-two years after the destruction of Jerusalem there was a new wave of Jewish revolts under the Roman rule of Emperor Hadrian (AD 132). Bar Kochba, supported by Rabbi Akiba, attempted to rally his compatriots around the Jewish flag of statehood. Three years later (AD 135) the revolt collapsed and the procurator Tinius Rufus had Jerusalem plowed under. On the site of the ancient Jewish temple, a new edifice was erected in honor of Capitoline Jupiter. By this time both the Jewish states of the Northern and Southern Kingdoms and the United Israeli Nation had lost all vestiges of national cohesion, strength, and glory.

The Roman Empire attained the zenith of her glory under Trajan (AD 98–117). It was under him that the empire reached its greatest limits. The boundaries under his reign extended far out in all direction—to the Rhine and the North Sea, the Danube, the Euphrates, the Cataracts of the Nile, the great African Desert, and the Atlantic to the West. Further expansion became impossible due largely to pressure from "barbarian" migration in the north and east, which brought increased economic and social instability to Rome.

CHRISTENDOM: CONSOLIDATION AND DISSENSIONS

The reign of Emperor Theodosius (AD 378–395) witnessed the beginning of close identification of the interests of the Christian church and the empire in the east. During the declining years of the Roman Empire, Constantine the Great was emperor (AD 306–337). After seizing control he transferred the capital to Byzantium (Constantinople). In the next century Rome fell, in AD 476, and the German overlord Odoacer became its first "barbarian" king.

After the death of Paul and Jerusalem's destruction, the Pauline version of Christianity with its transcendental significance became completely dominant. Composed narratives, the first of which was the Gospel of Mark, gradually replaced the oral tradition of early Christianity. The Christian emphasis on the individual conscience and on love brought further persecution in Rome, where religion was primarily a public or political concern. The early church clarified and developed a sophisticated theology in response to the attacks from religions whose origin lay outside the Judea–Christian tradition, including Gnosticism, Manicheanism, Montanism, and Mithraism. By AD 400 Christianity had been established as the religion of the Roman Empire; but with the barbarian invasion, a long struggle against paganism began. Missions were sent out to the Germanic tribes, and those who were converted largely adopted the Arian form of Christian faith, far apart from the Judaic tradition.

With its consolidation and the removal of the threat of alien ideas, the Christian church turned in upon itself and became engaged in a series of fierce internal doctrinal disputes centering on the many interpretations of the nature of Christ. This began in the age of Constantine (AD 325) with the so-called Arian controversy. The issue was whether Christ was the same or a different substance from that of God. The Nicaean Council, called by Constantine, decided against Arius and in favor of the Roman party, which claimed that God and Christ were of the same substance. Constantine and his successors moved increasingly in favor of the opposite interpretation; in other words, that Christ was both human and divine. The controversy continued unabated in a multiple of ways to the era of Justinian, when the so-called Monophysites—who held to the doctrine that in the incarnate Christ there is only one nature, not two—were suppressed in Byzantium and a single orthodoxy was imposed.

While matters of doctrine provided the excuse for ecclesiastical controversies, rivalries between jurisdictions within the Christian empire, compounded by ethnic and cultural differences, were at the root of most of the conflicts. The Council of Chalcedon in AD 451 had established five patriarchates (patriachal sees) of Rome: Alexandria (Egypt and Cyrenaica), Jerusalem (Palestine), Antioch (Syria), Constantinople (Thrace, Greece, Asia Minor), and Rome (the West). Under Pope Damasus, the Roman see claimed primacy over the patriachates, basing its claim on the Petrine text. However, this did not ensure unity since Rome and Alexandria continued to resent the way the Byzantine emperor influenced the church's stand on doctrinal issues. At the same time, Western monastism emerged with the founding of the Benedictine rule. The growing independence of the papacy and the new monastic movement made Christianity a powerful political weapon among the barbarian kingdoms, so that national conversion and suppression of "heresy" had a more than religious significance.

The mutual antagonism came to its climax during the twelfth and thirteenth centuries as the West, becoming increasingly potent militarily, thrust a series of Crusades against the Near East for the recovery of Palestine. This was the aftermath of a request from the Eastern emperor to Pope Urban. In AD 1095 the Eastern emperor Alexius I sent out an urgent appeal for help to Pope Urban II who proclaimed the first Crusade to regain the Holy Land. In a classic display of oratory at Clermont in Southern France, Pope Urban captured vividly an inspiring picture of a holy war. He blended the ideas of pilgrimage, restoration of domestic peace, remission of sin, self-interest through conquest, and recovery of the Holy Land into one flashing conception—Crusade. Pope Urban urged Christians to take up the cross and strive for a cause that promised not merely spiritual rewards but material gain as well:

> For this land which you inhabit…is too narrow for your large population, nor does it abound in wealth, and it furnishes scarcely food enough for its cultivators. Hence it is that you murder and devour one another.…Enter upon the road to Holy Sepulcher; Wrest that land from the wicked race, and subject it to yourselves.[9]

It has been chronicled that the inception of the Crusades ignited horrible attacks against the Jews and even fellow Christians, who were not exempt from rape and plunder. From the end of the eleventh century to the end of the thirteenth, Christian Europe, led by the Pope, launched seven major Crusades, as well as various small expeditions. This is treated later in this chapter.

THE RISE OF ISLAM

As Christendom consolidated and tore itself apart, Islam rose as a small sect in the seventh century AD and quickly became a powerful cohesive movement with an aggressive evangelical mission. In 622 Muhammad (AD 570–632) and a small following began the Muslim era with a flight from Mecca to Medina, after opposition and harassment in their native Mecca. Muhammad made Medina, where a Christian king accommodated him, his base for his jihad against his Mecca opponents. After eight years of desultory fighting and negotiation, he eventually obtained possession of Mecca in AD 630. He destroyed the pagan idols in Mecca and converted the site of the Ka'ba into a Muslim holy place.

By the time of Muhammad's demise in AD 632, his followers had demonstrated their ascendency over virtually all the major tribal groups of the Arabian Peninsula, and the broad framework of the Arabo-Muslim social and political relationships were being worked out. This included non-Muslims, among whom the Christians and the Jews acquired the status of "dhimmis" or protected communities while idolaters were regarded as beyond the pale. From this period there grew up the idea of a world divided into two—the Daral-Islam, consisting of the lands where Muslims could live secure in the practice of their religion and governed by their own law; and the Daral-Harb, the lands inhabited by infidels who one day, God willing, would be brought into the community of Islam.

After the death of Muhammad, divisions appeared in the Muslim Ummah over his successor. But in spite of the disunity, Caliph Umar (634–644) expanded the Islamic realm in the Near East. Umar proved to be one of the greatest Muslim rulers and was the first to assume the title Amiral-Mu'minin (commander of the faithful). In AD 633 the Arabs under Caliph Umar invaded Southern Palestine. In 634 Jerusalem was taken, and in 635 Damascus fell into their hands. The Byzantine surrender of Edessa in 636 rounded off the conquest of Northern Syria. The invasion of Egypt began in about AD 639 and was completed with the capture of Alexandria in 642. The Islamic jihadists forbade all other religions except Islam in the Arabian Peninsula. Elsewhere Christian and Jewish communities were left undisturbed so long as they paid the kharaj, or land tax, and the jizyeh, or poll tax. In time disputes about the authority and succession of the caliphate under Othman and Ali led to civil war which destroyed the unity of the Ummah and led to the establishment of the Umayyad dynasty at Jerusalem, circa 638.

Islamic jihadists continued to expand the frontiers of Islam with conquests through the Byzantine Empire across Africa into Spain. They mastered the entire peninsula, except for the far North; and by AD 732 they had penetrated into France as far as the country around Poitiers where they were repulsed in an engagement with the Frankish troops of Charles Martel. It was not until the Crusades that Christian kingdoms sought to check the meteoric expansion of the Islamic faith by conquest.

THE CRUSADES

The Christian Reconquista in Spain was the most successful and enduring part of the militant European response to the Islamic presence on its Southern and Eastern flanks. This response started in the eleventh century with the Norman conquest of Sicily in 1060 and of Malta in 1091. By AD 1099 Godfrey of Bouillon and his crusaders marched on Jerusalem, after what has been described as their brilliant and victorious march across Seljuq Anatolia. This first Crusade captured a long strip of territory along the eastern coast of the Mediterranean and created the feudal Latin kingdom of Jerusalem. With the success of the Crusade following the recovery of Jerusalem in the summer of 1099, many of the crusaders departed, leaving a relatively small garrison of defenders to hold a vastly overextended and therefore vulnerable Frankish kingdom of Jerusalem. The absence of any well articulated long-range planning or organization weakened the effectiveness and cohesion of the crusaders and opened the flanks for more cohesive "infidels" to reassert themselves. In AD 1144 the kingdom of Edessa fell, and when the kingdom of Jerusalem faced its first crisis, tottering on the brink of destruction in 1147, Bernard, the powerful mystic of Clairvaux, called for the second Crusade. This abortive Crusade organized to shore up the defenses of Jerusalem failed dismally. Louis VII, the king of France, and Conrad III, the German emperor, led armies to the Holy Land and sought to capture the city of Damascus. When they failed, they returned to Europe.

Saladin, the sultan of Egypt and Syria, brought fresh and vigorous leadership to the Muslims. In 1187 Jerusalem was captured by Salah al-Din (Saladin), the legendary ruler of the Saracens, and a third Crusade was organized. This time it was led by the three most powerful rulers of the West, Richard (the Lion-Hearted) of England, Phillip Augustus of France, and Frederick Barbarossa of Germany. Frederick died in Asia Minor, and differences between Richard of England and Phillip of France led to the abandonment of the Crusade to Richard. Saladin and Richard thus remained the chief protagonists. To create a united and strong Islamic front against the Christians, Salah al-Din proclaimed a jihad, or holy war. He is, however, acknowledged as a patient statesman and chivalrous warrior. His down-to-earth approach to peaceful settlement was manifested in his generous proposal that Richard should marry his sister and be given Palestine as a wedding present. Of course this proposal came as a shock to the Europeans. However, Richard and Salah al-Din finally agreed to a three-year truce and free access to Jerusalem for Christian pilgrims.

A fourth Crusade was grudgingly embarked upon by Frederick II (AD 1218–1250) of the kingdom of Sicily in 1227 under compulsion and threat of excommunication by Pope Gregory IX (1227–1241). His initial retreat from the Crusade earned him the Pope's excommunication, and under ban, went to undertake a "repeat" Crusade and was able to make peace with the "infidels," crowning himself "king of Jerusalem."

TURKISH DOMINANCE

Jerusalem was again lost to the Turks in 1244, and the seventh Crusade (1248–1250) achieved little. Louis IX of France (1226–1270) embarked on the seventh and last Crusade and died in Tunis with little accomplishment in spite of his crusading zeal. He is recorded as a ruler with a deep and sincere belief in the value of Christianity who attained canonization in 1297, twenty-seven years after his demise.

Mamluk Turks continued their dominance of the Mediterranean with a strong army and stable government in Egypt. One of their rulers, Rukn al-Baybars I (circa 1277), successfully wiped out the remaining Crusade enclaves and ensured the continued control of Jerusalem. Other crusaders marched and meandered east during those years, but none of their efforts could wrest the control of Jerusalem from Muslim control. The era of crusaders ended effectively in AD 1291. Acre, the last stronghold of the Christians in the land where Jesus walked, preached, and performed all the wonders, fell to those who denied His deity.

The tide changed briefly with the succession of Phillip II (1527–1598) to the Spanish throne. Under Him the Holy League, which united the naval forces of Spain, the Papacy, and Venice in 1571, scored a splendid victory against the Ottoman Turks. On the morning of October 7, 1571, the Catholic forces attacked the vast fleet of Ali Pasha in the Bay of Lepanto near the Gulf of Corinth and decisively defeated the Ottoman Turks. It was the last battle of the Holy League. At least thirty thousand Turks were reportedly killed, over 800 were captured, with 230 Turkish ships either destroyed or taken as war booties. In addition, the victors set free over fifteen thousand captured Christian slaves. After centuries of humiliation at the hands of the Turks, the Christians at last had scored a major military victory. The myth of Turkish invulnerability was shattered. Yet, in its moment of exultation, the Holy League failed to capitalize on its advantage. After the victory at Lepanto, it departed, and thus gave the Turks time to recuperate and once again achieve virtual mastery of the Mediterranean until 1918.

It is needful to recall that during the capture of Granada, the Moorish outpost by Spain in the fifteenth century, Jews were expelled from Spain in 1492. This took place under Ferdinand, the heir of Aragon and king of Sicily. This expulsion reemphasizes the great dispersals that took place among the Jews during the Crusades and the various wars for the control of the Mediterranean, and the most coveted trophy of all the laurels—the Holy City of Jerusalem. Indeed, ancient Jerusalem enjoyed a unique distinction as the city in which Jehovah God placed His name.

> I will give one tribe to his son so that David my servant may always
> have a lamp before me in Jerusalem, the city where I chose to put
> my Name.
>
> —1 KINGS 11:36, NIV

Napoleon Bonaparte's oriental ambition, beginning with his expedition to Egypt in 1798, marked the opening phase of the painful and protracted confrontation between European civilization and Islamic societies. There were also the European rivalries, and because of these rivalries spilling over into non-European world, the Ottoman Empire was drawn into the ever shifting and hardscrabble diplomatic coadunations with or against Britain, France, and Russia. Of course, in these, the Jews, the Israelites, were inescapably drawn into the historic drama.

POST FIRST WORLD WAR I PARTITIONS

The First World War, which began at the end of July 1914, and was triggered by the murder of the heir to the Harsburg throne in Sarajevo, the Bosnian capital, facilitated the end of the Ottoman Empire. It also redrew the map of the Mediterranean, the Middle East, and the status of the Jewish people. By 1917 the British had scored great success against the Ottoman Turks with offensives in Mesopotamia and Palestine. In the Palestine Campaign they secured the cooperation of Hashemite bedouin Arabs whose revolt against the Ottoman Empire was sustained by British gold and the intellectual and diplomatic prowess of Colonel T. E. Lawrence. Baghdad fell on March 11, 1917, and Jerusalem was captured by General Edmund Allenby on December 9, 1917. By October 30, 1918, the Ottoman Empire had signed an armistice with the British government. Aligned with Germany and Austria-Hungary, the Turks had suffered heavy defeats on several fronts and were left at the mercy of Great Britain.

The Treaty of Sevres, signed on August 10, 1920, dismembered the former Ottoman Empire and decreed the partition of Anatolia. The former Arabic-speaking provinces of the Ottoman Empire were confirmed as Tripolitania (Libya) an Italian colony and Egypt a British protectorate. Syria and Lebanon were allotted to France as League of Nations mandates and Mesopotamia (Iraq) and Palestine went to Britain. Sharif Husayn of Mecca had previously received British assurances (the McMahon Declaration, October 24, 1915) regarding the establishment of Hashemite Arab kingdom that would have embraced all the Arab-speaking lands of the Fertile Crescent and the Arabian Peninsula. These assurances were, however, jettisoned in the face of French pressure for a stake in the Middle East, as anticipated in the Anglo-French Sykes-Picot Agreement of May 1916. The Balfour Declaration of November 2, 1917, supporting the establishment of a Jewish homeland in Palestine, brought Jerusalem back to the front burner of world political discourse.

The declaration, ratified by fifty nations, was a big blow to the Arabs, which put an end to their dream of a united Arab kingdom from the Fertile Crescent to the Arabian Peninsula as envisaged in the McMahon Declaration.

However, the idea of the creation of a Jewish homeland in the Middle East was of age-old ancestry. It started with the focused and articulated objectives of the European Zionist movement in the 1880s. The first significant Jewish immigration into the region of Palestine began at this period. Throughout the 1920s and 1930s, while the British wrestled with the problem of what to do about the future of their Palestine mandate, Jewish immigrants continued to pour into the region. Tensions between the Jews and the Palestinians rose accordingly, leading to outbreaks of violence. For a while the British played around with the idea of the partition of Palestine into two states, but the idea never saw the light of day as it was rejected offhand by the Arabs. By 1939 British policy had begun to swing markedly in the direction of appeasement with the Arabs. A white paper released in 1939 proposed that Jewish immigration should be limited to 15,000 per year (about a quarter of its actual rate) until 1944. It was envisaged that after 1944 further Jewish immigration would be subject to Arab acquiescence, while very tough new restrictions were to be placed on Jewish land purchases in Palestine. The Jews flayed this development.

A NATION BORN IN A DAY

The advent of World War II prevented the proposed policy from being implemented, and the entire issue of Palestine remained in abeyance. After the end of Second World War in 1945, the proposed policy was revived following a massive new wave of Jewish immigration into Palestine due to Hitler's pogrom and the rise of anti-Semitism in Europe. It is estimated that by 1946 the proportion of Arabs to Jews in the region stood at about two to one—1.27 million Arabs to 678,000 Jews. The British had recognized by this time that the Palestinian question was beyond their solution and turned the whole problem over to the United Nations. In November 1947 the UN voted for partition of Palestine upon the expiration of the British mandate of May 1948 in the face of strident Arab opposition.

Thirty-three nations voted for partition: Australia, Belgium, Bolivia, Brazil, Byelorussia (white Russia), Canada, Costa Rica, Czechoslovakia, Denmark, The Dominican Republic, Ecuador, France, Guatemala, Haiti, Iceland, Liberia, Luxembourg, Netherlands, New Zealand, Nicaragua,

Norway, Panama, Paraguay, Peru, Philippines, Poland, Sweden, Ukraine, Union of South Africa, USSR, United States of America, Uruguay, and Venezuela. Countries that voted against partition include Afghanistan, Cuba, Egypt, Greece, India, Iran, Iraq, Lebanon, Pakistan, Saudi Arabia, Syria, Turkey, and Yemen.

The following countries abstained from voting: Argentina, China, Ethiopia, Great Britain, Honduras, Mexico, and Yugoslavia.

On the same day the British mandate ended, May 14, 1948, Israel proclaimed itself an independent state, fueling attack from the Arab states of Egypt, Iraq, Jordan, Lebanon, and Syria. After two thousand years of their dispersion, the Jewish State of Israel was reborn. Within hours, through President Harry Truman, the United States of America became the first of the nations of the world to accord recognition to the Israeli state. A prophecy made about 2,500 years ago was here fulfilled.

> Who has ever heard of such things? Who has seen things like this? Can a country be born in a day or a day be brought forth in a moment?
>
> —ISAIAH 66:8, NIV

Jerusalem again came under Jewish control for the first time in 2,573 years. The Arab states made good their threat to invade and destroy Israel before her rebirth, which led to the 1948 war, referred to as the war of liberation or independence by the Israelis. It ended with an armistice in January 1949. By the time of the cease-fire, Israel had increased her territorial holding by about 50 percent. Israel went on to create the institutions of a new state—a democracy with Chaim Weizmann as its president, David Ben-Gurion as its prime minister, and a parliament called the Knesset as it supreme legislative body.

On July 26, 1956, just weeks after negotiating a treaty with Britain and France over the future of the Suez Canal, the Egyptian president, Gamal Abdal Nasser, unilaterally nationalized the waterway. Angered by a joint US and British decision to withdraw financial support for the building of Aswan Dam, Nasser expelled British diplomats and businessmen from the country and nationalized the canal. Faced with the threat of being denied use of the canal, Britain, France, and Israel collaborated to attack Egypt. The second Arab-Israeli war, known in Israel as the Sinai Campaign and among the Arab as the Tripartite Aggression, began at noon of October 29, 1956. Israeli paratroopers landed in the Mitla Pass, twenty-four miles east of the Suez Canal, and by November 4 the Anglo-French armada joined in the invasion. The invasion, codenamed "Operation Musketeer" was a virtuosic military accomplishment. The Egyptian army was pulverized and three-quarters of the canal was repossessed. The attack provoked international condemnation, and under dual threat of American sanctions and Soviet missiles, Britain and France withdrew their troops. The Israelis, by contrast, controlling all of Sinai, Gaza, and the Straits of Tiran, maintained their positions and were not in a hurry to retreat. Israel eventually succumbed to demands from US and Russia to pull her troops from Sinai but not without guarantees for free passage through the Straits of Tiran and protection against border raids.

A multinational United Nations Emergency Force (UNEF) was finally then created to oversee the Anglo-French withdrawal from Egypt and Israel's withdrawal from Sinai. The two "good faith" agreements—one between President Abdal Nasser and UN Secretary General Dag Hammarskjold and the other between the US Secretary of State John Foster Dulles and Israel's foreign minister Golda Meir—paved the way for the entry of UNEF by March 11, 1957, and the withdrawal of Israel from Sinai.

Ten years of relative peace was broken in 1967. Throughout the early 1960s Nasser's behavior toward Israel became increasingly hostile. The "good faith" agreement fashioned by Dag Hammarskjold in 1957, upon which Egypt would confer with the general assembly and the UNEF advisory council before changing the force's mandate, was in no way sacrosanct or inviolable. Nasser's bellicosity and continued state of belligerency in the Middle East led to the expulsion of the UNEF that was stationed on the Egyptian side of the border and the closure of the Gulf of Aqaba, an international waterway to Israeli shipping. This ultimately led to the 1967 Arab-Israeli war. On June 5, 1967, Israel launched simultaneous preemptive air and ground attacks on Egypt, Syria, and Jordan. The war lasted six days and only urgent action by the UN Security Council prevented the Arabs from being completely routed. When a cease-fire was announced on June 10, Israel had taken from Egypt the Gaza strip, the whole Sinai Peninsula, and the east bank of the Suez Canal. They had also taken the West Bank of the Jordan River and the Arab sector of Jerusalem from Jordan and had seized the Golan Heights from Syria.

The fourth Arab-Israeli war broke out in 1973. On October 6, 1973, Egypt and Syria launched a massive surprise attack on Israel while she was celebrating the Jewish holy day of Yom Kippur. The Israelis suffered very high losses, signaling the possibility of total defeat for Israel.

But superior war tactics and command, assisted by timely infusions of emergency military aid from the United States, and over all the invincible hand of God ensured that Israel turned the tide on both their Northern and Southern fronts. The US went on to broker a cease-fire and attempted a failed peace conference in Geneva under the then Secretary of State Henry Kissinger. In November 1974 the Palestinian Liberation Organization (PLO), which had fallen under Yasser Arafat, was accorded recognition by the United Nations.

By the end of 1977, the Egyptian-Israeli peace negotiations took an astonishing turn when President Anwa al-Sadat, who had succeeded Nasser after the latter's demise in 1970, accepted an invitation by Israeli Prime Minister Menachem Begin to address the Knesset on the outstanding issues between the two nations. The US capitalized on this and President Jimmy Carter succeeded in bringing the two leaders together at Camp David in the United States in September 1978. In a marathon thirteen-day meeting, Carter persuaded Sadat and Begin to agree on a framework for the conclusion of a Peace Treaty between Israel and Egypt. After difficult negotiations the treaty was finally signed in March 1979, and Israel began to withdraw its troops from the Sinai in May.

Following the Israel-Egyptian accord, the PLO stepped up its attack against Israel. Israel began its policy of displacing the Palestinians in the West Bank by the building of Jewish settlements there. By this time Lebanon, a hodgepodge of fiercely contending ethnic, political, and religious groups, had become the PLO's principal base for staging attacks on Israel. In 1982 Israel launched a full-scale retaliatory invasion of PLO bases in Lebanon successfully destroying PLO strongholds in Tyre and Sidon as well as the PLO headquarters in East Beirut. This led to the evacuation of PLO members from Lebanon under international supervision. Israel's first major attack on Lebanon had taken place in 1978 in retaliation for a PLO raid that had left thirty civilians dead. By the late 1980s Israeli-Palestinian relations were dominated by the Intifada, the popular militant uprising against Israeli occupation.

In November 1988 the Palestinian National Council (PNC), the PLO's semi-parliament, reluctantly accepted the UN General Assembly Resolution 181 of November 29, 1947, calling for the creation of Jewish and Arab States in the territory of Palestine, and Security Council Resolution 242 issued in the wake of the Six-Day War of 1967 and recognizing Israel's right to exist.

In July 1992 Yitzhak Rabin was brought to power as prime minister of

Israel for the second time in twenty years on a straightforward peace plat-
form. The establishment of a new Israeli government under Rabin of the
Labor Party facilitated negotiations between the PLO and Israel leading
to secret talks in Oslo, Norway. On August 20, 1993, Israel and the PLO
signed a draft peace agreement at the Norwegian government's guest
house. On September 13, 1993, Israel's foreign minister Shimon Peres and
Arafat's second in command, Mahmoud Abbas, met in the White House
lawn in the United States and signed the Declaration of Principles on
Interim Self-Government Arrangements (DOP). The DOP provided for a
transitional period not to exceed five years, during which Israel and the
Palestinians would negotiate a permanent peace settlement. During this
interim period, the Palestinian National Council (PNC) elected through
free democratic franchise after Israeli military withdrawal from area of
the Gaza strip and the West Bank, would administer the territories.

In 1994 Prime Minister Rabin, Foreign Minister Shimon Peres, and
the PLO leader, Yasser Arafat, received the Nobel Peace Prize, even as
Jewish and Palestinian radicals resumed fighting and killing in the hope
of derailing the peace process. On November 4, 1995, a Jewish extremist
assassinated Yitzhak Rabin as he was leaving a peace rally. In January
1996 Arafat was elected president of the Palestinian Authority, and in
June 1996 Israel's labor government was replaced by the conservative
Likud Party whose leader, Benjamin Netanyahu, became the prime
minister.

On September 24, 1996, Israel opened a new entrance to an archaeological tunnel in Jerusalem dating to the Hasmonean era (second century to first century BC). The tunnel is located hundreds of yards from
religious holy sites, and the opening of a new entrance was to create on
exit at its northern end. Arafat kicked against the opening of the new
tunnel entrance and unleashed a mass call to riot. By the time fighting
was over on September 27, fifteen Israelis and fifty-eight Palestinians lay
dead, with hundreds more injured. In January 1997 the Netanyahu government signed the Hebron protocol stipulating the redeployment of the
Israeli Defense Force (IDF) from the last major Palestinian town. But
then peace remained elusive.

In September 2000 a new wave of Intifada escalated to an unprecedented level following the continued failure of the peace process. The
Palestinian Authority under Arafat began a move to transform his
security forces into a 100,000 strong army with the help of Egyptian
and Jordanian military experts. An embryonic division was reportedly

established in Gaza, while Egypt, Libya, Morocco, Pakistan, and Yemen provided military training, according to reports. Following Ariel Sharon's sweeping electoral victory, Arafat, in a televised address to the Palestinian Legislative Council on March 10, 2001, called for the resumption of negotiations with Israel, but not without a proviso. A predestined outcome to attain (Palestinian) national right to safeguard their holy Christian and Islamic sites and secure their rights to self-determination and the establishment of an independent state with holy Jerusalem as its capital.

The Palestinian insistence on Jerusalem and the status of Jerusalem remains a stumbling block to lasting peace in the region. It is apparent that relative peace in the Middle East would have to include mutual recognition of Israeli and Palestinian states in Palestine and mutually acceptable right over the control of Jerusalem. The word here is *relative* peace for that region and the world at large, since perfect peace for the universe can only be attained through Jehovah God's divine intervention at His fullness of time.

> The Son is the image of the invincible God, the firstborn over all creation. For in him all things were created…whether thrones or powers or rulers or authorities.…For God was pleased to have all his fullness dwell in him and through him to reconcile to himself all things whether things on earth or things in heaven, by making peace through his blood, shed on the cross.
>
> —COLOSSIANS 1:15–16, 20, NIV

Yes! This is the only perfect peace that the earth will ever know at Jehovah's fullness of time when all knees shall bow to the sound of Christ's name and all tongues will confess and proclaim that Jesus Christ is Lord and Savior to the glory of His Father, Jehovah of armies, and the Lord of hosts (Phil. 2:10–11).

Summary of Israel in World History from AD 70 to 1948

The Roman Period (AD 70–325)

The Byzantine Period (AD 325–614)

The Persian Period (614–634)

The Arab Period (634–1072)

The Seljuk Period (1072–1099)

The Crusaders Period (1099–1291)

The Mamluk Period (1291–1517)

The Turkish (Ottoman) Period (1517–1917)

The British Period (1917–1948)

Independent Israel (1948–Present day)

Chapter 2

DISPERSAL AND TRIBULATION HISTORY

I will scatter them among nations that neither they nor their
fathers have known, and I will pursue them with the sword
until I have made an end of them.

—JEREMIAH 9:16, NIV

THE DISPERSAL

THE SCATTERING OF the children of Israel resulting from God's
judgment of apostate Judah and Jerusalem as foretold by the
prophet Jeremiah shows the folly and vanity of trusting in their
own strength or wisdom, or the privileges of their circumcision, or anything but God's righteous judgment against the worship of the false gods
of their own fancy, the work of their hands, which Jehovah, the God of
their fathers, had repeatedly forbidden. The God of creation, of nations,
the King of kings, punishes those who treacherously depart from Him
and rebel against Him. Because of their rebellion, God decreed that their
dispersal abroad shall be their destruction. Since they set up gods which
neither they nor their fathers had known and had been corrupted and
debauched by their intimacy with the heathen, they would therefore lose
their liberty as God's ensign to nations, His chosen people, to these heathen. Though they will be scattered in such a manner that they will not
know where to find one another, the omnipotent and omnipresent God
will find them all. He will gather them back as His people under a new
covenant.

"Look, the days are coming"—this is the LORD's declaration—"when
I will make a new covenant with the house of Israel and with the

house of Judah.... I will put My teaching within them and write it on
their hearts. I will be their God, and they will be My people.... The
whole valley—the corpses, the ashes, and all the fields as far as the
Kidron Valley to the corner of the Horse Gate to the east—will be
holy to the LORD. It will never be uprooted or demolished again."
—JEREMIAH 31:31, 33, 40, HCBS

God warned King Solomon and the children of Israel in 2 Chronicles
7 that if they turned away from His statutes and commandments to serve
other gods, then He "will pluck them up by the roots out of my land
which I have given them; and this house, which I have sanctified for my
name, will I cast out of my sight; and will make it to be a proverb and a
byword among all nations" (v. 20).

However, before the great dispersals of the children of Israel to the
four corners of the earth following the Babylonian exile and the destruction of Jerusalem in 70 AD, there were waves of migration of the Jews
during the eighteen years domination of the Philistines and Amorites
in the eleventh century BC (Judg. 10:7) and the forty years overlordship
of Philistines (Judg. 13:1). Some dispersal also took place during the conquest of the Assyrians and the Egyptians following the idolatrous rule
of Jeroboam and Rehoboam's intransigence (1 Kings 12:11, 28). But the
Babylonian exile marked the beginning of the mass movement of the Jews
to nations outside the kingdom or nation of Israel, while the destruction
of Jerusalem in AD 70, in fulfillment of the prophecy of Jesus Christ, cli-
maxed the dispersal.

It should also be recalled that during the Babylonian captivity, into
which Nebuchadnezzar took the Judeans in 586 BC, the prophet Jeremiah
advised them in the following words:

Build houses and settle down; plant gardens and eat what they pro-
duce. Marry and have sons and daughters; find wives for your sons
and give your daughters in marriage, so they too may have sons and
daughters. Increase in number there; do not decrease. Also, seek the
peace and prosperity of the city to which I have carried you into
exile. Pray to the LORD for it, because if it prospers, you will prosper.
—JEREMIAH 29:5–7, NIV

When Cyrus the Great, the Persian monarch, in fulfillment of God's
design as foretold by the prophet Isaiah, (Isa. 44:28; 45:13), crushed
Nabonidus, the last Babylonian king, and permission was granted to
the Jewish captives in 538 BC to return home and rebuild the Jerusalem

Temple, not all of them returned. Many Jews had prospered and pro-
gressed in the stimulating environment of Babylon and choose to remain.
There were also Jews who had fled the Babylonian invasion into Egypt and
settled in Alexandria. These Alexandrians of Palestinian (Jewish) origin
choose to remain in Egypt and never returned to Jerusalem. Historical
records attest to the fact that when Ptolemy Lagi returned to Egypt after
the conquest of Judea in 320 BC, many Judeans accompanied him, and
that by 250 BC, Alexandria contained the largest number of Judaists in
the world (far outstripping Jerusalem).

The destruction of Jerusalem in AD 70 marked not just the end of the
Jewish state but also the zenith of Jewish Diaspora extending into our
so-called modern era. This development also heralded the period of the
"Holy" Roman Empire, which gave further impetus to Jewish dispersals.

However, biblical accounts attest to the fact that centuries before the
destruction of Jerusalem, the Jews had spread across the then Persian
Empire and formed a close-knit community to stimulate the envy and
hatred of Haman the Agagite to want the Jews eliminated from the
empire. The inspiring Book of Esther relates,

> Then Haman said to King Xerxes [Ahasauerus], "There is a certain
> people dispersed and scattered among the people in all the prov-
> inces of your kingdom who keep themselves separate. Their cus-
> toms are different from those of all other people, and who do not
> obey the king's laws; it is not in the king's best interest to tolerate
> them. If it pleases the king, let a decree be issued to destroy them,
> and I will put ten thousand talents of silver to the king's administra-
> tors for the royal treasury."
>
> —ESTHER 3:8–9, NIV

This would have been the first mass extermination of the Jews in
peacetime, should Haman's plot have succeeded. The timely intervention of Esther prodded on by Mordecai saved the Jewish population of
the Persian Empire (Esther 4:1–17; 5:1–14; 8:1–17). The Book of Esther
also reveals that the Jews were scattered throughout the 127 provinces of
the Persian Empire, stretching from India to Cush (Ethiopia), and that
people of other nationalities became Jews more out of fear than of conviction (8:17).

It is perhaps as from this period that Judaism became a tremendous
monotheistic proselytizing force in the pagan world attendant upon further dispersals of Jews from the Persian Empire. As the children of Israel

spread, the Judaic monotheistic faith also spread, as did Christianity and later Islam. Historical records show that there were converts among Yemenites and Greeks, the people of Adiabene (a Hellenistic state on the Tigris). Conversion in Rome had also carried Judaism through Italy into France, the Rhone Valley, and the Rhine Basin. Mass conversion of the Germanic tribes spread Judaism into Central and Eastern Europe, particularly Poland and Western Russia.

In the Indian Peninsula the kingdom of Cheras centered in Kerala, which was well known to both Greek and Roman traders and was reportedly visited by Saint Thomas, provided a haven for a small but prosperous Jewish community which was well rooted in the region by the fourth century AD.

Dispersal of the Jews and spread of Jewish faith got through to the Turko-Finish people or the Khazars of Europe in the eighth century AD. Jews, who had been banished from Constantinople by the Byzantine ruler Leo III (AD 717–741), settled among the pagan Khazars (or Khozars) and in competition with Mohammedan and Christian missionaries, won them over to the Judaic faith. Bulan, the ruler of Khazaria, became converted to Judaism around AD 740. Bulan's nobles and the Khazarian populations were later converted to the Jewish faith encouraged by their ruler's example.[1]

Heinrich Graetz, in his book *History of the Jews*, narrates that under the rule of Bulan's successor, who bore the Hebrew name Obadiah, Judaism gained further strength in Khazaria. Obadiah was, according to Graetz, the first to make serious efforts to further the Jewish religion. He established synagogues and schools to impart instructions in the Bible and the Talmud and also invited Jewish sages to settle in his dominions.[2]

In AD 969 the kingdom of Khazaria was invaded by the Russians and its capital fell to Sviatoslav of Kiev. Following the Russian conquest of Crimean portion of Khazaria in AD 1016, the Khazarian Jews were dispersed throughout the Russian Empire and Eastern European countries. Some were taken north where they joined the established Jewish community of Kiev. Others returned to Caucasus or went into Hungary. These Jews came to be known as the Ashkenazim Jews (Jews from Eastern Europe) and their population was swelled by Jews who fled from Germany at the time of Crusades and during the Black Death. Alfred Lilienthal contends that many of those Ashkenazim Jews "have little or no trace of Semitic blood in them."[3] This is understandable given the conversion of people of other nationalities to the Judaic faith and intermarriages.

Friedrich Hertz notes in *Race and Civilization* that in spite of all stumbling blocks, even in the Middle Ages and Modern Era, there have been occasional Judaic conversions in Slavic countries which accounts for the "unmistakable Slavic facial characteristics of Polish and Russian Jews."[4] Conversions to Judaism are reported in Hungary as late as 1229, as related in William Ripley's *Races of Europe*.[5]

From all indications we see the fulfillment of God's word in the prophecy of Jeremiah; "And I will cause them to be removed into all kingdoms of the earth, because of Manasseh the son of Hezekiah king of Judah, for that which he did in Jerusalem" (Jer. 15:4).

Manasseh, son and successor of King Hezekiah, greatly offended God because of his terrible idolatry. He practiced magic, employed divination, promoted spiritistic practices, made his sons pass through the fire, observed times, and turned the nation to the worship of all the starry hosts, for which Israel's dispersal to the kingdoms of the earth was foretold (2 Kings 21:2–9; 2 Chron. 22:2–9). Manasseh, who also became a loyal Syrian vassal, brutally crushed all opposition in Jerusalem. He married an Arabian princess, set aside his father Hezekiah's reforms, and installed ritual male prostitutes and the idols Baal and Asherah in his temple. He is also recorded to have promoted the sacrifice of children at the roaster, Tophet, in the Valley of Hinnom south of the city of Jerusalem.

Centuries of wars, conquests, and commercial and religious interactions had indeed scattered the Jews to the four corners of the earth. Through the centuries Jewish people dispersed into Baghdad, Cairo, Damascus, Fez, Kurdistan, throughout the coast of Africa, and deep into the countries of the Middle East. Jews were scattered into Hadhramaut into the Eastern protectorate. Jews lived in Bulgaria, Czechoslovakia, France, Greece, Italy, Romania, Yugoslavia, and Scandinavia. They migrated into Northern African countries where they dwelled in the Mellahs (Jewish quarters) of Algeria, Egypt, Morocco, Tunisia, and Yemen. They were found in South Africa, and for several centuries before the rebirth of Israel in 1948, had settled in China (K'ai-feng Jews in Honan province) and India. They were also in Australia, Argentina, Canada, and England. They similarly dispersed into Eastern European countries of Poland, Ukraine, Russia, and Germany. Indeed, they were in over seventy-four countries of the world and across all the continents.

Jews lived in ostracization for about 1,500 years from the main stream of French society until France became the first country in Europe to grant the Jews some rights of citizenship with some qualifications under

Napoleon Bonaparte. By the middle of AD 1800s, the Jews were well integrated into all walks of French life. They produced an array of exceptional scientists, lawyers, writers, poets, musicians, and brilliant doctors, who appeared to have justified the Napoleonic concept of assimilation.

Is this "scattering," the dispersals of the children of Israel, not a fulfillment of the earlier quoted prophecy of Jeremiah as he was led by Jehovah God to proclaim? We can learn very useful lessons for our future and the future of nations from its fulfillment as we can from another fulfilled prophecy of Jeremiah on the tribulations of the children of Israel as well as that of Jesus Christ on the fate of Jerusalem. Let us recall that the prophet Isaiah also talked of the gathering of the "dispersed of…Judah from the four corners of the earth" (Isa. 11:12, HCSB), thus signposting the dispersal of Jews to all continents of the earth. Let us now take a detailed look at the tribulation history of the children of Israel along the march of world history.

THE TRIBULATION

> This is what the LORD of Hosts says: "I am about to send against them sword, famine, and plague and will make them like rotten figs that are inedible because they are so bad. I will pursue them with sword, famine, and plague. I will make them a horror to all the kingdoms of the earth—a curse and desolation, an object of scorn and a disgrace among all the nations where I have banished them.
> —JEREMIAH 29:17–18, HCSB

With dispersal and banishment from their homeland, in fulfillment of God's words, came persecution, also in fulfillment of Jehovah's pronouncement. It is imperative to trace how and why the children of Israel got themselves into tribulation history to appreciate the judgment and justice of God. Let us also recall that Moses warned the children of Israel when they were in the desert of Arabah east of the Jordan of the dire consequences of disobedience to the commandments of Jehovah, calling heaven and earth to bear witness against them.

On the punishment for idolatrous living, Moses admonished them as thus;

> After you have had children and grandchildren and have lived in the land a long time—if you then become corrupt and make any kind of idol, doing evil in the eyes of the LORD your God and arousing his anger, I call the heavens and earth as witness against you this day

that you will quickly perish from the land that you are crossing the Jordan to possess. You will not live there long but will certainly be destroyed....A few of you will survive among the nations to which the LORD will drive you.

—DEUTERONOMY 4:25–27, NIV

The issue of the consequences for obedience or disobedience to the commandments and statutes of Jehovah God is a recurring theme in His dealing and relationship with the children of Israel. In Deuteronomy 28:1–68 God through Moses pronounced lengthy blessings to the children of Israel if they diligently obeyed His commandments and lengthier curses should they disobey Him. They eventually disobeyed, and this was apparently foretold including the terrible consequences, even to the siege of Jerusalem centuries before it happened. Their dispersal and the international opprobrium that will follow the dispersal are captured in Deuteronomy 28:37: "And thou shall become an astonishment, a proverb, and a byword, among all nations wither the LORD shall lead thee."

The earlier mentioned siege of Jerusalem was foretold in God's words written in Deuteronomy 28. We can also relate it to the siege of Samaria.

Because of the suffering that your enemy will inflict on you during the siege, you will eat the fruit of the womb, the flesh of the sons and daughters the LORD your God has given you. Even the most gentle and sensitive man among you will have no compassion on his own brother or the wife he loves or his surviving children, and he will not give to one of them any of the flesh of his children that he is eating. It will be all he has left because of the suffering your enemy will inflict on you during the siege of all your cities.

—DEUTERONOMY 28:53–55, NIV

In chapter 6 of 2 Kings, we read that there was a great famine in Samaria as a result of the siege brought upon the city by King Benadad of Aram. As a result, a woman boiled her son.

Then the king asked. "What's the matter?" She said, "This woman said to me. 'Give up your son, and we will eat him today. Then we will eat my son tomorrow.' So we boiled my son and ate him, and I said to her the next day, 'Give up your son, and we will eat him,' but she has hidden her son."

—2 KINGS 6:28–29, HCSB

The eating of human flesh is spoken of as commonly done among the Jews in the siege of Jerusalem by the Babylonians as we read from Lamentations 4:10: "With their own hands compassionate women have cooked their own children, who became their food when my people were destroyed" (NIV).

Moreover, in the last siege of Jerusalem by the Romans under Titus, first century Jewish historian Flavius Josephus tells us of a noblewoman that killed and ate her own child through the extremity of the famine, and when she had eaten one-half secretly that she could reserve the other half to herself, the mob, perceiving the aroma of meat, got into her house to whom she showed the other half inviting them to share with her if they so pleased. The mob horrified, declined and hurriedly left her to her meal.[6]

Even in the days of Abram, before he became known as Abraham, God's prophetic words to the patriarch had pointed the way to the beginning of great tribulations for the children of Israel in Genesis 15:13: "And he said unto Abram, Know of a surety that thy seed shall be a stranger in a land that is not theirs, and shall serve them; and they shall afflict them four hundred years."

This is God's prophetic pronouncement of their four hundred years of slavery in Egypt until Moses led them out of bondage towards the Promised Land of Canaan. The children of Israel continued in their unbelief, intransigence, and idolatry against Jehovah's righteous ordinances, even after the transcendent miracles He showed them in Egypt, on the Red Sea, and out of Egypt. He was therefore moved in righteous indignation to pronounce a forty years wandering in the wilderness upon His chosen people until all that failed to exercise faith in Him had died, except for Caleb the son of Jephunnah and Joshua the son of Nun.

> Doubtless ye shall not come into the land, concerning which I sware to make you dwell therein, save Caleb the son of Jephunneh, and Joshua the son of Nun....And your children shall wander in the wilderness forty years, and bear your whoredoms, until your carcases be wasted in the wilderness.
> —NUMBERS 14:30, 33

We have seen how the children of Israel suffered defeats and persecutions from wars in times of disobedience to God's ordinances and victories won at periods of obedience and true worship. We have also noted that the destruction of Jerusalem in AD 70, as foretold by God's prophets and presaged by Jesus Christ, marked the zenith of Jewish Diaspora, the loss of the Jewish nation, and their final dispersal to the four corners of the earth. It also heralded about one thousand nine hundred and thirty years of exile from their original homeland until the "one day" rebirth of a nation in 1948. These centuries of exile exposed the Jews to all forms of persecutions.

By the Middle Ages the early Christian church had developed a Christian antipathy, an instinctive feeling of hatred towards the Jews, which was borne out of the belief that Jews had murdered Christ. The great Christian writers of the first six hundred years of Christianity exhibited striking traits of anti-Judaism. For example, Origen (circa 185–254) said that the blood of Jesus falls on the Jews of all generations.[7] In the written words of the Syrian, St. John Chrysostom (AD 347–407), "The Synagogue is a brothel, a hiding place for unclean beasts....Never has any Jew prayed to God.... They are possessed by demons."[8]

At the first Council of Nicaea in AD 325, the Emperor Constantine ordained that Easter should not compete with the Jewish Passover. He declared,

> It is unbecoming that on the holiest of festivals, we should follow the customs of the Jews, henceforth, let us have nothing common with this odious people.[9]

Several imperial measures were decreed against the Jews, which include a ban on building of new synagogues, special levies and taxes, and outlawing of intermarriages between Jews and Christians.

Gregory of Nyssa (circa 540–604), called the Jews

> Murderers of the Lord, assassins of the prophets, Rebels against and haters of God, and rejecters of the faith of their fathers, Collaborators of the devil, race of vipers, informers, slanderers. With obscured brains, pharisaic yeasts, Sanhedrin of demons, accursed, despicable, stoners, enemies of all that is beautiful.[10]

In his classic work *Hitler and His God*, Georges Van Vrekhem also wrote of Martin Luther's anti-Semitic position, quoting Luther's own words:

> What shall we Christians do with this depraved, damned people of the Jews: their schools and synagogues should be burnt, their houses should be flattened, all their prayer books and Talmud should be

confiscated for they are full of idolatry, lies, malediction and cal-
umny. Their rabbis should be forbidden to teach on punishment of
death. They should be forbidden to walk freely on the streets, their
usury should be forbidden and all their valuable in gold and silver,
taken from them, the young and strong Jews of both sexes should
be forced to work in the sweat of their brows; they should compen-
sate for all the money fleeced from the Germans, and expelled from
the country.[11]

Paul Johnson in *A History of the Jews* asserts that Martin Luther's
pamphlet "On the Jews and Their Lies" published in Wittenberg "may be
termed the first work of modern anti-Semitism, a giant step towards the
road to the Holocaust."[12]

But as we can learn and discern from world history and the history of
the church, Christendom cannot be exonerated from the very "crimes"
Luther had accused the Jews of. More importantly, in all the accusations
and recommended punishments, where was Christ's doctrine of love?

Christ instructed His followers and listeners thus in Matthew 5:43–44;
"You have heard that it is said, 'Love your neighbor and hate your enemy.'
But I tell you love, your enemies and pray for those who persecute you,
that you may be children of your Father in heaven" (NIV). The apostle
John states in 1 John 4:18, 20 that "there is no fear in love. But perfect
love drives out fear, because fear has to do with punishment. The one
who fears is not made perfect in love.... Whoever claims to love God yet
hates his brother or sister, he is a liar" (NIV). In Romans 13:10, the apostle
Paul instructs, "Love does no harm to his neighbor. Therefore love is the
fulfillment of the law" (NIV). "For the entire law is fulfilled in one command: 'Love your neighbor as yourself'" (Gal. 5:14, NIV). Also Galatians
5:22 states that "the fruit of the Spirit is love, joy, peace, patience, kindness, goodness, faith, gentleness, and self-control" for which "there is no
law" (HCSB).

Was the absence of human love not the very reason why Christianity
itself fell under the sword of persecution? Indeed, the prevalence of
hatred and the dearth of love is the reason why Christians persecuted
and continued to persecute Christians in the name of doctrinaire differences. We are filled with the knowledge of this truth from the history of
the inquisition and the Crusades.

Let's recall that with the calling of the first Crusade by Pope Urban
II in 1095, leaders of the crusading mission and their followers went into
it with the belief that Jews killed Christ, the Son of God, and sought

therefore to revenge the death of Jesus Christ in Jewish blood. The following narrative by Van Vrekhem paints a picture of the atrocities of the crusaders against Jews.

> The first Jews were murdered at Rouen in the North West of France and the Judaic communities in that region sent warnings to their brothers in Germany for the Crusaders were expected to follow the Rhine upstream into Central Europe. But the communities in the Rhine Valley, well settled, prosperous and having acquired a special status, did not heed the warning to their regret.
>
> The first German victims were slaughtered in Speyer, then followed Worms, Mainz and several villages where Jews had sought refuge. The chief instigator of the killing was a German Count, Emicho Von Leisingen....
>
> The Bishop of Wurzburg collected butchered Jews, fingers, thumbs, feet, hands, and severed heads. He anointed these bloody pieces with oil and buried them in his garden. Count Emicho's Jerusalem farers marched along the Rhine to Cologne. Here as elsewhere, Israelites scattered, disguised themselves, some who were caught and refused to acknowledge 'the light of the world' were slain, their synagogues wrecked, burnt. And the hordes marched on singing of Jerusalem with many a rapturous 'hallelujah', robbing and destroying and leaving behind a trail of Jewish blood in Metz Trier, Regensburg, Bamberg, Praque, Nitra.[13]

Leon Poliakov in his *Histoire de l' antisemitisme* considers the slaughter of Jews by the crusaders as a capital moment in the history of Jewish people, wherein a heroic tradition was born by them to hold onto their beliefs, customs, and traditions, which would serve as an example to future generations of Jews.[14]

According to Georges Van Vrekhem, from the second half of the fourteenth century onwards the hatred against the Jews reached its climax. He asserts that this period can be fixed as the crystallization of anti-Semitism in its classical form, which later led to the celebrated statement of the Dutchman Erasmus Desiderius (1467–1536): "If it is the sign of a good Christian to hate the Jews, then we are all good Christians."[15]

The Jews were banished from Spain, France, and England, but Germany became the predominant country of anti-Semitism propelled by the activities of early German Christian fathers like Martin Luther and later Eugenio Pacelli, who became Pope Pius XII in whose watch Italian Jews were rounded up under the walls of the Vatican and transported to death camps. He exhibited patent anti-Semitism by his acquiescence to Hitler's final solution.

The Middle Ages turned out to be era of unprecedented persecution of the Jews, punctuated by occasional calls for restraint on the part of some humane and enlightened popes. The era was also marked by the development of the dangerous belief, starting probably in England in the twelfth century, that Jews tortured and sacrificed Christian children. This "blood label," as it was later referred to, spread rapidly with an associated myth that Jews stole consecrated hosts—the communion bread that had become the body and blood of Christ in mass—in order to perform abhorrent, odious, and horrid rites. Growing out of this myth was the widespread belief that Judaism involved the performance of magic aimed at undermining and ultimately destroying Christendom. This issue is extensively treated by Po-chia Hsia in his *Myth of Ritual Murder*.[16] Some European monarchs also took discriminatory actions against Jews. For instance, under King Edward of England (1272–1307) Jews were periodically expelled and their assets seized to fund the thirteenth century war between England and France. Phillip IV of France (1285–1314) also carried out similar measures against Jews in France.

The Black Death or bubonic plague which ravaged Europe for three years, from 1347 to 1350, and exterminated at least a third of its population was attributed to the Jews. Jewish communities were accused of employing magic acts to cause the Black Death. They suffered tremendous persecution as a result. At Strasbourg two thousand Jews were burned in their own cemetery and their possessions were distributed among the citizens. There were also mass killings in Cologne, Erfurt, Frankfurt, Hannover, Oppenheim, and Worms. The Hundred Years War of European powers, fought between 1337 and 1453, also created a fertile sociopolitical and economic setting for Jew baiting and persecutions. By the end of the fifteenth century, Jews had been expelled from nearly all of Western Europe, fleeing to Eastern Europe and countries around the Mediterranean.

Four hundred years of anti-Semitism attained a new height in 1648. In 1647 a new wave of peasant uprisings spread over Ukraine. The Cossacks were enraged by Polish occupation of the Zoporozhskaia Sech, which they saw as a threat to their very existence. Out of their revolt rose Bogdan Khmelnitski, who quickly became the arrowhead of a vast movement. In May 1648 he defeated the Polish army and Polish garrisons were forced out of Ukrainian towns. Meanwhile, the Jews had come into Ukraine with the blessings of the Poles. They settled as skilled artisans and merchants in Polish estates. But with the withdrawal of Polish forces, they were left at the mercy of Cossacks, who embarked on mass extermination of them. The extirpation took the lives of Jewish men, women, boys, girls, and children. According to several recorded reports, they were beheaded, burned alive, drowned, and hanged. Bizarre tales of cannibalism have also been painted of blood intoxicated Cossacks who dismembered Jewish children and ate their flesh in front of their parents—weird and unbelievable. The enormous tragedy of 1648 together with hundreds of years of continuous persecution created strange phenomenon within the Jewish ghetto walls and pale.

Russia, during this inglorious period, wallowed in the backwash of feudalism with grave exploitation by the aristocratic class. Consequently, the issue of bread, land, and reform was transformed into a movement for which the Jews played key roles resulting from the miserable state of many of them in the ghettos. Jews became the cannon fodder, the expendable old scapegoats, for the czarist regime, which made anti-Semitism a deliberate political weapon to divert the attention of the peasants who had hitherto harbored religious biases and hatred for Jews. The ignorant peasantry was again educated in the myth that Jews were magicians and witches and that they used Christian blood in their rituals.

Several decades of incessant persecutions in Russia attained their peak during the two years reign of Catherine I. A series of killings and anti-Jewish riots was unleashed against Jews who would not accept the Greek Orthodox religion. As a result of the refusal of Jews to convert, Catherine I expelled hundreds of thousands of Jews from Russia. Most of them emigrated to Poland. An era of war and conquest ensued in which Poland was conquered and reconquered, partitioned and repartitioned. During this period the earlier expelled Jewish population who went to Poland were inherited by Empress Catherine II (circa 1729–1796) following the sharing of eight-nine thousand square miles of Poland to Russia—a territory inhabited by over three million people. This event is said to have led directly to the establishment of Jewish Pale of Settlement.

Under the reign of Czar Nicholas, Jews were in 1827 driven ruthlessly from the smaller villages into an already overcrowded Jewish quarter in the larger cities. In the same year, Nicholas instituted a law compelling a quota of Jewish youths to be turned over each year to the army for twenty-five years of military service. Earlier, in 1821, the Russian theorist P. I. Pestel had in his book *"Russkaia Pravda"* (Russian Justice) advocated among other things, that Jews should be assimilated or expelled from Russia.[17]

When on March 13, 1881, Czar Alexander II (1818–1881) was assassinated, one of the convicted rebels was a Jewish lady. This volatile political development paved the way for further Jewish persecutions. Under the intellectual tutor Konstantin Pobiedonostev, who became the power behind the successor of Alexander II, Czar Alexander III (1881–1894), a plan for the extermination of Jews was put in place. Pobiedonostev was the procurator of the Holy Synod and was secretly supported by the Orthodox Church. His plan involved the annihilation of one-third of the Jewish population through government sponsored killings, starvation, and other forms of murder. One-third would go through expulsion and exile, while one-third would be forcefully converted. In Easter week 1881, the plan was put into action. The massacres reached new heights in 1882. The Jews of France and most of Western Europe lived in relative peace and prosperity compared to the Jews of Eastern Europe after the massacres and expulsions of the Middle Ages and post Middle-Age era. The gruesomely bloody sites of Jew hating and anti-Semitism abated in both England and France. As previously noted, with the advent of Napoleon Bonaparte (1769–1821) and the French revolution, a new dawn of literary and scientific achievements emerged for the Jews in France, while France became the first country in Europe to grant Jews rights of citizenship.

Napoleon Bonaparte's position that Judaism was a region not a nationality enhanced further the status of Jews in France. But Napoleon also demanded unalloyed loyalty to France and the recognition by Jews that Judaism was only a region to guarantee them unfettered equal rights. Thus, in spite of the continued existence of discreet form of anti-Semitism in France, Napoleon's revolution drastically reduced the opprobrium and grave unpleasantries associated with being Jewish.

However, by the close of the nineteenth century, the situation in France changed once again for ill against the Jews. By 1894 the anti-Semitic sentiments that had remained dormant for some decades was revived with the agelong "death to the Jews" protest call.

The plight of the Jews in Russia remained deplorable and was compounded by growing anti-Semitic sentiments. By 1903 matters reached a new low in the city of Kishinev where Jews were charged once again with using Christian blood for their rituals and the Russian government secretly encouraged the wanton killings of Jews, which left the ghettos of Kishinev desolate.

It was at height of the 1897 Jewish persecutions, which attained new heights in Austria, France, Germany, Poland, Romania, and Russia, that a parliament of world Jewry was held in the town of Basle, Switzerland. Jewish leaders at the conference called for a return of Jews to their ancient historic homeland, and out of the convention rose the Zionist movement.

The twentieth century heralded for the Jews their greatest tribulation, as we read from events in Germany following the ascendency of Adolf Hitler to which we now focus our attention.

Chapter 3

HITLER'S FINAL SOLUTION: THE JEWISH HOLOCAUST

> Christians say Holocaust is part of the evil of
> humanity. It isn't the evil of humanity. It's the evil of
> Christendom....Hitler was brought up to hate the Jews,
> particularly to hate Jews as the people of the Devil....I don't
> blame Germany for the Holocaust; I blame Christendom for
> the Holocaust.
>
> —HYAM MACCOBY[1]

IN HIS BOOK *The Holocaust*, Leni Yahil asserts that the Holocaust "was a general human catastrophe," and that the Jew, not for the first time in history epitomized man's fate in a time fraught with peril. He opines that Hitler created a fissure in the moral dam of religion and culture through which a flood of violence and cruelty, stemming from man's most sinister impulses burst forth and that the most prominent and shocking manifestation of this "age of violence was the extermination camp, where violence was raised as a banner and became the emblem of the age."[2]

In many ways Adolf Hitler's atrocities against the Jewish people was stimulated by the events of history dating back to the systematic elimination of the Jews in medieval Europe, the massacres of "Christian" crusaders, and more directly, the anti-Semitic works of early German Christian fathers like Martin Luther and the Catholic French aristocrat Joseph de Gobineau (1816–1882), who wrote and expressed his views of Jews in the following words:

> If with the help of his Marxist faith the Jew is victorious against the people of this world, then his crown will be a dance of death of humanity and this planet, empty of human beings, will again wander through space for millions of years. Eternal Nature avenges inexorably the trespassing of her laws. This is why I believe that today I act in conformity with the intention of the almighty creator: in acting against the Jews I fight for the work of the Lord.[3]

Perhaps, the greatest direct anti-Semitic influence on Hitler came from one of the most potent inductors of the anti-Jewish sentiment, Richard Wagner (1813–1880). His fame as a composer spread beyond Germany to virtually every city in Europe, while he had a tremendous influence on Hitler. Wagner's art helped in spreading his anti-Semitism, which intensified over the years to the point where he confidently declared,

> I hold the Jewish race to be the born enemy of pure humanity and everything noble in it. It is certain that it is running us Germans to the ground, and I am perhaps the last German who knows how to hold himself upright in the face of Judaism, which already rules everything.[4]

The German author Joachim Kohler wrote in his book *Wagner's Hitler* that "nobody will take from Wagner the merit of having been the first in German history to contribute with his writings to the advent of the 'disappearance' of the Jews."[5] Of course Martin Luther's anti-Semitic writings predate Wagner's.

However, in the year 1933 a horrific disaster befell the Jewish people in Germany. Hitler, who had followed closely the anti-Semitic descent from the Christian crusaders to Martin Luther and down to Wagner and others, moved first against the Jewish professionals—doctors, artists, lawyers, writers, and scientists, among others. Among the first Jewish intellectuals to leave Germany were the philosopher Walter Benjamin, who left for Paris on March 18, 1933; novelist Leon Feuchtwanger, who went to Switzerland; and the conductor Bruno Walter, who fled after being told that the hall of the Berlin Philharmonic would be burned down if he conducted a concert there. On April 6, 1933, the *Frankfurter Zeitung* explained that Walter and fellow conductor Otto Klemperer had been forced to flee because the government was unable to protect them against the "mood" of the German public, which had been "provoked by Jewish artistic liquidators." The Jewish scientist, theoretical physicist, and mathematician, Albert Einstein (1879–1955), whose special and general theories of relativity led to the development of the atomic bomb, left Germany for the United States on January 30, 1933, and never returned to Germany. His German citizenship was rescinded, and he later became an American citizen. Several other Jews also left Germany and many sought sanctuary in Poland.

In 1935, precisely September 15, Hitler introduced the Nuremberg Laws, which prohibited Jews from marrying Aryans, annulled existing marriages between Jews and Aryans (the law of the protection of German blood and German honor), prohibited Jews from serving as civil servants, stripped German Jews of their citizenship, and deprived them of all civil rights. In his speech introducing the laws, Hitler opined that if the Jewish problem remained unsolved by the laws, it may then be handed over by law to the National Socialist Party for a final solution (*Die Endlosung*).

The "Aryanisation" policy of the German economy under Hitler promoted the deliberate and systematic pauperization of the Jews through exclusions from employment as well as restrictions in business and professional engagements. For example, in July 1938 about 3,000 practicing Jewish doctors were prohibited from their professional engagements, while 709 were permitted to practice as "medical practitioners" and only to Jewish patients. In September of the same year only 172 lawyers were allowed to practice as "legal counsels" and were also restricted to Jewish clients.[6]

On November 7, 1938, a Jewish minor, Herschel Gruspan, assassinated Nazi German diplomat Ernst Von Rath in Paris. This incident was used by the Nazis to initiate the transition from legal repression to large-scale violence against Jewish Germans. The attendant massacres became known as November Pogroms, the Night of Broken Glass, or *Reichskristallnacht*. Over 7,000 Jewish shops and 1,688 synagogues were damaged or utterly destroyed. An estimated 30,000 Jews were sent to concentration Camps in Dachau, Sachsenhausen, Buchenwald and Oranienburg.[7]

Hitler did not hide his hatred for the Jews. In his author biography *Mein Kampf* (*My Battle*), he portrayed the Jews as mortal enemies who betrayed German people during the First World War and "battered the REICH for thirty pieces of silver."

> How can we explain the fact that up to 1918, the Jewish press championed the policy of the British Government against the German REICH and then suddenly began to take its own way and showed itself disloyal to the Government?...It was not in the interest of Great Britain to have Germany annihilated, but primarily a Jewish

interest.... The great leaders of Jewry are confident that the day is near at hand when the command given in the Old Testament will be carried out and the Jews will devour the other nations of the earth.[8]

He also wrote that "the personification of the devil as the symbol of all evil assumes the living shape of the Jew."[9]

From 1938 onward Hitler gave his total backing and encouragement to the organization of a brutal and sadistic reign of terror against the Jews. The gypsies, homosexuals, and mental defectives were not left out of Hitler's crazy pursuit of the purification of his German Aryan race through the mass extermination of the Jews and other "subhumans." The Jews became the center of this massive demographic revolution in Europe, beginning in Eastern Europe. The Third Reich under Hitler embarked upon the first stupendous massacres, a carefully planned operation of mass murder and the systematic killings of Jews as opposed to expulsion, forced conversion, assimilation, or random cruelty.

The German historian Eberhard Jackel wrote as thus of the Jewish Holocaust in 1986:

> The slaughter was systematically conducted in virtually all areas of Nazi-occupied territory in what are now 35 separated European countries. It was at its worst in central and Eastern Europe which had more than 7 million Jews in 1939. About five million Jews were killed there; including 3 million Jews in occupied Poland and over 1 million in the Soviet Union. Hundreds of thousands died in the Netherlands, France, Belgium, Yugoslavia and Greece.[10]

Indeed, in planning the pogrom of Jews in Europe, Hitler envisaged total victory in the Second World War and world dominance. He thus programmed the annihilation of Jews wherever they were found in Europe and other continents of the earth. In November 28, 1941, Hitler discussed the anticipated military offensive across the Caucasus into the Middle East with the Arab Mufti Amin al-Husseini wherein he explained that Germany's main objective in the area would be the extermination of the Jews in the Middle East. Earlier, in September 1941, Hitler had decreed that all German Jews must wear the yellow star, already in use in Poland. The yellow star became a stigma on Jews, which had a demoralizing effect on them. Christian Jews were not exempted from the humiliation and stigmatization

The purification of the Germanic Aryan race required that by any means possible, the Jews must disappear from the face of the earth. In the summer of 1941 after the failure of the scheme to expel all Jews to the French-owned Island of Madagascar, made impracticable by British sea power, Hitler gave Himmler the green light for the final solution of the Jewish question (*Endiosung der Judenfrage*). Hitler institutionalized a program whereby Jews and other victims of mass murder would be exterminated by a special murder squad (*Einsatzkommandos*) attached to conquering German armies. In the same vein, peaceful Jews—civilians; men, women, boys, girls, children, and the aged—who were to be killed, would be assigned to special murder commandos called *Einsatzgruppen*. Hitler instructed Himmler, head of the SS, to establish these units in March 1941.

By the winter of 1941–1942, the *Einsatzgruppen* had wantonly murdered an estimated five hundred thousand people. But this gruesome massacre was not systematically far-reaching for Adolf Hitler, who had by this period inherited about 10 million Jews within his European dominion and had already used gas for the annihilation of over seventy thousand of the handicapped and mentally ill in Germany as part of a campaign of generic purification. Castration was also widely practiced on the supposedly genetically impaired.

The success of the program for Jewish pogrom required the continuing involvement of several German government agencies. As a result, representatives of such agencies were summoned to a conference held on January 20, 1942, at Wannsee. At the Wannsee Conference the nature and implementation of the pogrom against the Jews of Europe was reviewed at length for the benefit of the agencies to be mobilized for the exercise. The range of the pogrom spelled out included not only Jews in German controlled and influenced areas but also Jews in England, Spain, Sweden, and Portugal—countries Hitler assumed would ultimately fall under German suzerainty. The various agencies of government not already participating became involved immediately after the conference. The foreign ministry was saddled with the responsibility of obtaining Jews from territories under German influence but not absolute control. It was decided to begin with France from where the first shipment left for Auschwitz, one of the major centers for killing on March 27, 1942.

However, the systematic murder of Jews, first in the newly occupied portion of the USSR and then in the rest of German-controlled Europe, was first initiated in the summer of 1941. In the following years the vast majority of those Jews who had not been able to leave pre-war Germany were deported and killed and their emptied homes turned over to others, even as the welfare organization distributed their furniture and vast quantities of confiscated clothes to the German population.

A major concern of the government apparatus from the fall of 1941 on was to obtain the cooperation of the various governments allied with or subordinate to Germany in turning over their Jewish citizens to Germans for deportation and killing. On this score the Germans got substantial help from the government of Vichy France, the stooge regimes of Croatia and Slovakia, and at least for some time, the government of Romania. The Italians were explicit in their repudiation to collaborate with the Germans. They offered shelter for Jews, not only in Italy itself but in the portions of France, Greece, and Yugoslavia occupied by the Italian army. Most Jews in these area survived until after the Italian surrender of September 1943 opened them to German control and hence to the application of the then commonly employed routines of collection, deportation, and murder. Only in the immediate vicinity of Rome was minimal attention paid to possible objections from the Vatican.

As the tide of war turned against the Axis, Romania began to resist German pressure for the turning over of its Jewish population, while Bulgaria had resisted from the start and the Danes had helped evacuate their Jewish neighbors to Sweden when the Germans planned to round them up. Until 1944 Hungary had also resisted German demands, including those voiced personally by Hitler and Von Ribbentrop that its well over half a million Jewish citizens be handed over. It was again after the occupation of the country by German troops that the process of deportation to the murder factories began. The international uproar occasioned by these events in the summer and fall of 1944 led to a delay which saved the lives of many.

Following the conquest of Greece in 1941, Jews in Greece were deported to German murder factories; and by the time of German withdrawal from Macedonia and Salonika on October 10, 1944, practically all Greece's Jewish population had been deported to the slaughter chambers.

As the country in Europe with the longest record of treating Jews decently, Holland was not the country to acquire popularity as a deporter of its Jewish citizens to be murdered in Hitler's death camps, crematorium, and gas chambers. The first measures to implement this program provoked the first major strike in German-occupied Europe, that of February 1944. In spite of Dutch resistance and some secret sheltering of individual Jews, vast majority of Dutch Jews, over one hundred thousand out of about one hundred forty thousand, were killed by the Germans. General Alexander Von Falkenhausen proceeded to run what has been described as the least oppressive of all the German occupation administrations, yet oversaw the murder of between twenty-five and forty thousand Belgium Jews.

Following German control of Hungary and with the enthusiastic aid of the puppet regime of Ference Szalasi and the Arrow Cross, the deportation to slaughter Hungary's over six hundred thousand Jews were effected. Hungary, the last refuge for Jews in German-controlled Europe, provided the last large contingents of victims until pressure from the Allies and the advance of the Russian Red Army combined to halt the deportations. According to a study by the Holocaust scholar David Cesarani, between May 15 and July 7, 1944, 437,000 Jews were rounded up and sent to the concentration and extermination complex at Auschwitz-Birkenau in Upper Silesia. Of the fraction selected to work, only a few thousand survived.[11]

In its push into Poland, the Russian Red Army reached two places of special significance in late July. They came to Majdanek, the easternmost and first of the larger death camps established by the Germans. The labor and extermination camp was the only one in the immediate vicinity of a large city, Lublin, and had served for years as a central site for forced labor and mass killing of Jews and of other people primarily from Poland and the Soviet Union. Over three hundred thousand had been murdered there. It was liberated by the Red Army before the Germans could destroyed the barracks, crematoria, gas chambers, and other vestiges of what would became the major monuments to the penetration of German culture into Eastern Europe. Here, pictures would first be taken and circulated around the world of huge piles of shoes, enormous quantities of human hair, and grinding machines for crushing bones into fertilizer.

At the end of a three-week-long trip into the occupied Ukraine in 1943, a German reporter expressed part of his findings in the following words:

> We heard entirely clear and explicit announcements about the Jewish question. Among the 16 million inhabitants of the area controlled by the civilian administration in Ukraine, there used to be 1.1 million Jews. They have all been liquidated....One of the higher officials of the administration explained the execution in the words, "the Jews are exterminated like roaches."[12]

A roll call of Hitler's human agents of torture, murder, and mayhem in Leon Uris' classic literature *Exodus* include but are not limited to the following:

> Ilsa Koch, who won infamy by making lampshades out of human tattoo skins, Dieter Wisliczeny, who played the role of stock-yard goat leading the sheep to slaughter; Kramer who sported in horse-whipping naked women, Adolf Erichman, the German Palestinian who spoke fluent Hebrew and was the master of genocide; SS Haupsturmfuehrer Fritz Gebauer, who specialized in strangling women and children barehanded and who liked watching infants die in barrels of freezing water; Heinen, who perfected a method of killing several people in a roll with one bullet, always trying to beat his previous record; Frank Warzok, who liked to bet on how long a human could live hanging by the feet; Obersturmbannfuehrer Rokita, who ripped bodies apart; Steiner who bore holes into prisoners' heads and stomachs and pulled fingernails, gouged eyes and like to swing naked women from poles by their hair; General Franz Jaeckeln, who conducted the massacres of Babi Yar, a suburb of Kiev, in which 33,000 Jews were in two days rounded up and shot to the approval of many cheering Ukrainians.[13]

Not only did the Germans display sadistic and utter disregard for the sanctity of human lives through gruesome mass murders and torture, people were used extensively as guinea pigs for scientific experiments. Extensive use of human subjects by German physicians was carried out at Auschwitz, Dachau, Buchenwald, Ravensbruck, Sachsenhausen, and Natzweiler concentration camps. The most infamous of these physicians was Dr. Josef Mengele, the "omnipotent arbiter of life and death" who worked in Auschwitz. His experiment included placing subjects in pressure chambers, testing drugs on them, freezing them, attempting to change eye color by injecting chemicals into children eyes, various amputations, and other brutal surgeries.[14]

Professor Hirt's Anatomical Institute at Strasbourg was involved in using women for experiments. At Dachau Scientific Centre, described as one of the biggest by Leon Uris, Dr. Heisskeyer injected children with tuberculosis (TB) germs and observed their death. Dr Schultz is known to have been interested in blood poisoning, while Dr. Racher's experiments involved the simulation of high altitude conditions in which human guinea pigs were frozen to death while they were carefully observed through special windows. This was aimed at finding ways of saving the lives of German pilots. There were other experiments in what the Germans referred to as truth in science, which reached its zenith, perhaps, in the attempted implantation of animal sperm in human females.

The gas chambers, concentration, and death camps were many. There were Buchenwald, Dachau, and Chelmno, where an estimated one million people were killed and Majdanek where 750.000 died. There were Belzec, Treblinka, and Sobidor, where there was first major revolt and escape by Jews and other prisoners. There were Trawniki, Poniatow, Krivo, and Krasnik with its death pits; Klooga with its crematorium; Diedzyn with its dogs; and Stutthof with its torture chambers. There were concentration camps at Choisel, Dora, Neuengamine, Gross-Rosen, Janowska, and Danzig, where bodies were melted to fat in the manufacture of soap. There were Danagien, Eivari, Goldpilz, Vievara, PortKunde, Kivioli, Varva, Magdeburg, Plaszow, Szebnie, Mauthausen, Sachsenhausen, Oranienburg, Landsberg, Bergen-Belsen, Reinsdorf, Bliziny, Fossenberg, Ravensbruck, Natzweiler, and the deadliest of all the concentration camps, Auschwitz, which stands even today as a monument and reminder of the Jewish Holocaust.

It was at Auschwitz that an estimated three million Jews and other people were exterminated and the bones of the cremated broken up with sledge hammers and pulverized so that there would never be a trace of death. It was at Auschwitz that the gold teeth of dead Jews were methodically pulled and melted down for shipment to Himmler's science institute and finely shaped human skulls were preserved as paperweights. At Auschwitz were found warehouses filled with eye glasses, boots, clothing, pitiful rag dolls, and human hair for the manufacture of mattresses.

Yehuda Bauer, Raul Hilberg, and Lucy Dawidowicz maintain that from the Middle Ages onward "German society and culture were suffused with anti-Semitism and the works of godless anti-Christian criminals." They posit that the Jewish Holocaust would not have been possible without the almost two thousand years of pre-history of Christian anti-Judaism.[15]

After the defeat of Hitler and Nazi Germany, the atrocities and grisly news and stories of the horrors committed by the Third Reich got to the reading public of the Western allied nations. The Red Army had overrun some of the horrific murder factories earlier and pictures had been printed in the United States and Great Britain, but somehow it did not strike the right cord or galvanize the Western world to concerted condemnation and action.

However, on April 12, 1945, General Dwight Eisenhower, Omar Bradley, and George Patton, all of the United States, toured the town of Gotha in Thiringia and Ohrdruf. They saw the gallows, the dead, and the still dying while Signal Corps photographers took pictures which would stun the American public. German civilians as well as GIs were instructed to see these camps or others like it. In the following days, American and British troops liberated other far larger and infamous camps. Hitler left a legacy of Europe in ruins, a ravaged and profoundly traumatized Jewish people, and a German people forced to face up to accusations of heartless and cruel complicity in its support of such horrendous and brutal crimes against humanity.

The London Conference held from June 26 to August 8, 1945, agreed on the establishment of an international tribunal and the procedures it would follow which led to the Nuremberg Trials. This was the culmination of the 1943 Moscow Declaration on German atrocities in occupied Europe.

After the Hitler-led Jewish Holocaust, the defeat of Germany, and the death of Hitler (after committing suicide along with his wife, Eva Braun, on April 30, 1945), the Jews still did not find a permanent respite. After the Second World War Russia remained uncomfortable with the Jews. Jewish intellectuals were sharply attacked and frequently arrested. Jewish cultural institutions were suppressed, publications in Yiddish were prohibited, the Yiddish theater was closed, and discrimination was exercised against all Jewish citizens applying to universities and for all important posts. In 1950 several prominent Jews were arrested on the pretext that they had planned to make the Crimea a homeland for the Jews, even after Israel had become a nation in 1948. Another spate of arrests of Jews in Georgia at the end of 1951 was attributed to bourgeois nationalism, thus underscoring the protection of national economic interest against alien or foreign domination as represented by the Jews. The number of arrests increased tremendously after the nineteenth party Congress of the Russian Communists of October 1952. Death sentences were passed against economic functionaries in the Ukraine, most of them Jews.

What scriptural and prophetic lessons can we learn from centuries of Jewish persecutions leading to the Holocaust and indeed their general history? The lessons are essentially threefold. First we learn that the Scripture, as the inspired Word of God, is beneficial for teaching, for reproving, for setting things straight, for disciplining in righteousness; that the man of God may be fully competent, completely equipped for every good work (2 Tim. 3:16–17). Secondly, we learn that Jehovah is a

God of living history and of nations, and that before Him all nations are as nothing and less than nothing (Isa. 40:15). And thirdly, we learn that all that befell the Israelites serve as examples and were written for a warning to Christians "upon whom the ends of the world are come" (1 Cor. 10:11). The tribulations of the children of Israel and the Holocaust against the Jews also remind us of Isaiah's prophetic warning to them:

> What will you do on the day of punishment [visitation] when devastation [desolation] comes from far away? Who will you run to for help? Where will you leave your wealth [glory]? There will be nothing to do except crouch among prisoners or fall among the slain.
>
> —ISAIAH 10:3–4; HCBS

In the book *The Historian and History*, Page Smith writes,

> [The Hebrews] were as pitiless to their heroes as to their villains, to themselves as to their adversaries, because they were writing under the eye of God and had nothing to gain and much to lose by dissembling.... Alongside the tedious chronologies of the warrior kings of Syria or Egypt, the account of the tribulations and the triumphs of a people chosen by God...make(s) an enthralling story. The Hebrew chroniclers had discovered one of the most essential elements of history—that it is enacted by real people, with all faults and blemishes.[16]

The archaeologist William Albright states, "The profound moral and spiritual intuitions of the Bible, which form a unique revelation of God to man through the channels of human experience, are just as true today as they were two or three thousand years ago."[17]

Israel, through the march of world history and tribulation history, is a living testimony of what has come to pass and what is yet to come from Bible prophecies. And what is yet to come is both frightful and hopeful, and indeed good news to all those who fear God and worship Him in spirit and in truth (John 4:24).

The prophet Ezekiel was divinely inspired by God to proclaim the judgment and justice of Jehovah on apostate Israel. While Israel inhabited their God-given land, they defiled it with their conduct and actions. Their behavior was likened to the impurity of a woman during menstrual period, which in the days of the Old Testament shut her out from the sanctuary and made whatever she touched ceremoniously unclean (Ezek. 36:17).

Jehovah, in righteous indignation, poured out His anger on them because of the blood they had shed on the precious land He gave to them after wiping out the idolatrous nations that had hitherto occupied them. They treated Jehovah's love and unsurpassed benevolence with contempt. Consequently, God dispersed them among the nations and scattered them among countries. Almighty Jehovah judged them according to their conducts and actions.

Ezekiel 36:18–19 reads,

> Wherefore I poured out my fury upon them for the blood that they had shed upon the land, and for their idols wherewith they had polluted it: And I scattered them among the heathen, and they were dispersed through the countries: according to their way and according to their doings I judged them.

The good news is that God will redeem Israel because of the everlasting covenant of grace He has with His chosen people, His banner to all nations. Indeed, the restoration of Israel is not for the sake of Israel but because Jehovah has to honor the holiness of His great and awesome name which Israel has profaned among the nations they were dispersed into. God-fearing and obedient mankind and nations are expected to benefit from the everlasting covenant with Israel.

Ezekiel proclaims God's word:

> Thus saith the Lord God; I do not this for your sakes; O house of Israel, but for mine holy name's sake, which ye have profaned among the heathen [nations], whither you went.... And the heathen [nations] shall know that I am the Lord ... when I shall be sanctified in you before their eyes.
>
> —Ezekiel 36:22–23

In this sanctification of God's name, nations will share in the Israel of God, for salvation is for the Jew first and then also for the Gentiles (the rest of the world) (Rom. 1:16). Only after God's faithfulness to the fathers of old has been established does the Lord extend His domain to include Samaritans and Gentiles. The apostle Paul proclaims in Acts 28:28: "Therefore I want you to know that God's salvation has been sent to the Gentiles, and they will listen!" (NIV).

The Gentiles (the rest of mankind) have become in all respects equal with the Jews as "heirs together with Israel, members together of one body, and sharers together in the promise in Christ Jesus" (Eph. 3:6, NIV). Christ, according to Paul from divine inspiration, has eradicated the distinction between Jewish and non-Jewish people, because His ransom blood makes atonement for the sin of *all* believers with equal access to God. God's covenant with Israel (to be their God and for them to be His people) now extends to all who are in Christ Jesus the Salvator Mundi, Savior of the world. Let's now examine the nature of this covenant, Israel, and nations in covenantal relationship with Jehovah and how this positively affects all of God's created humans and nations.

ANNIHILATION OF JEWISH POPULATION OF EUROPE BY (PRE-WAR) COUNTRY

Country	Estimated Pre-War Jewish Population	Estimated Jewish Population Annihilated	% Killed
Poland	3,300,000	3,000,000	90
Baltic Countries	253,000	228,000	90
Germany and Austria	240,000	210,000	90
Bohemia and Moravia	90,000	80,000	89
Slovakia	90,000	75,000	83
Greece	70,000	54,000	77
Netherlands	140,000	105,000	75
Hungary	650,000	450,000	70
Byelorussian SSR	375,000	245,000	65
Ukrainian SSR	1,500,000	900,000	60
Belgium	65,000	40,000	60
Yugoslavia	43,000	26,000	60
Romania	600,000		
Norway	2,173	890	41
France	350,000	90,000	26
Bulgaria	64,000	14,000	22
Italy	40,000	8,000	20
Luxembourg	5,000	1,000	20
Russian SFSR	975,000	107,000	11
Denmark	8,000	52	1
Finland	2,000	22	1
Total	8,861,800	5,933,900	67

VICTIMS KILLED

Victim	Killed
Jews	5.9 million
Soviet POWs	2.3 million
Ethnic Poles	1.8–2 million
Romani	220,000–1,500,000
Disabled	200,000–250,000
Freemasons	80,000
Homosexuals	5,000–15,000
Jehovah's Witnesses	2,500–5,000

Source: Holocaust, Internet

YEARLY ESTIMATES OF JEWS KILLED

Year	Jews Killed
1940	Under 200,000
1941	1,100,000
1942	2,700,000
1943	Over 500,000
1944	Over 600,000
1945	Under 200,000

Source: Holocaust. Internet

Len Yahail provides some figures of the extermination of the Jews sourced from the research of Russian materials by Wila Orbach from his work on "The Destruction of the Jews in the Nazi-occupied territories of the USSR."[18]

VICTIMS OF THE
EINSATZGRUPPEN AKTIONEN IN THE USSR

	Ationen		Victims		Total	Aktionen	Total	Victims
Date	No.	%	No.	%	No. per year	Overall Annual%	No. of Victims Annually	Annual %
1941								
Jul.	13	8.1	6,254	1.4				
Aug.	35	21.7	53,770	12.2				
Sept.	40	24.9	192,663	43.8				
Oct.	32	19.9	74,998	17.1				
Nov.	21	13.0	72,099	16.4				
Dec.	20	12.4	40,042	9.1				
Total	161	100.0	439,826	100.0				
					161	64.7	439,826	71.2
1942								
Jan.	18	25.4	47,057	28.8				
Feb.	12	16.9	27,840	17.0				
Mar.	11	15.5	22,086	13.5				
Apr.	9	12.7	4,480	2.7				
May	7	9.9	12,740	7.8				
Jun.	2	2.8	1,660	1.0				
Jul.	5	7.0	46,021	28.2				
Aug.	3	4.2	1,086	0.7				
Sept.	2	2.8	338	0.2				
Oct.	-	-	-	-				
Nov.	2	2.8	80	0.1				
Dec.	-	-	-	-				
Total	71	100.0	163,388	100.0				
					71	28.5	163,388	26.4
1943	8	3.2	1,815	0.3				
Undated	9	3.6	13,060	2.1				
Total	249	100.0	618,089	100.0				

REPORT ON THE EXTERMINATION OF THE JEWS OF KOVNO BY EINSATZ KOMMANDOZ COMMANDED BY SS STANDARTEN FURHRER KARL JAGER

Date	Men	Woman	Children	Total	Place	Note
Jul. 4	416	47		463	Fort 7	Carried out on Joger's orders by Lithuanian Partisans
Jul. 6				2,514		
Jul. 9	21	3		24	Fort 7	Carried out by Ensatzkommando and partisans
Jul. 19	17	2		19		I + 7 Communists I
Aug. 2	171	34		205	Fort 4	+ 4 Communists
Aug. 9	484	50		534	Fort 4	
Aug. 18	698	402				
	771 (intellectuals)			1,811	Fort 4	+ 1 Polish Woman
Sept. 26	412	615	581	1,608	Fort 4	
Oct. 4	315	712	818	1,845	Fort 9	Punitive action
Oct. 29	2,007	2,920	4,273	9,200	Fort 9	
Total	7,766	4,785	5,672	18,223		Including 1 male and female US nationals.

Chapter 4

ISRAEL AND NATIONS IN COVENANTAL REVELATION

T HE BIBLE REVEALS that God is a covenant-making, covenant-keeping, and covenant-revealing God. As a covenant-making God, we read of His covenant with Noah in Genesis 6:18: "But with thee will I establish my covenant"; with Abraham in Genesis 15:18 and 17:2: "In the same day the LORD made a covenant with Abraham," "And I will make my covenant between me and thee, and I will multiply thee exceedingly"; and with David in 2 Samuel 23:5: "Although my house be not so with God; yet he hath made with me an everlasting covenant." He told Solomon at the consecration of the Temple of Jerusalem (circa 950 BC) that if he (Solomon) walked before Him as David did, "Then will I stablish the throne of thy kingdom, according as I have covenanted with David thy father" (2 Chron. 7:17–18).

Jehovah God also promised to make a new covenant with the house of Israel and the house of Judah: "Behold the days come, saith the LORD that I will make a new covenant with the house of Israel, and with the house of Judah" (Jer. 31:31).

He also spoke of an everlasting covenant. In Isaiah 55:3 He said, "Incline your ear, and come unto me: hear, and your soul shall live; and I will make an everlasting covenant with you, even the sure mercies of David." Isaiah 61:8 states: "For I the LORD love judgment, I hate robbery for burnt offering; and I will direct their work in truth, and I will make an everlasting covenant with them." The psalmist in Psalm 111:9 declared, "He sent redemption unto his people: he hath commanded His covenant for ever."

Jehovah's covenant with the children of Israel is like the covenant to Aaron's priesthood (the priesthood of the Levites) as pronounced by Jehovah unto Aaron: "It is a covenant of salt for ever before the LORD unto thee and to thy seed with thee" (Num. 18:19). This unbreakable promise of immutable permanence was declared unto Jeroboam and all Israel by King Abijah on Mount Zemaraim: "Ought ye not to know that the LORD God of Israel gave the kingdom of Israel to David for ever, even to him and to his sons by a covenant of salt?" (2 Chron. 13:5). The expression "covenant of salt" denotes enduring and imperishable nature of the covenant, as we discern from the Abrahamic covenant.

As a covenant-keeping God, Jehovah reveals His firm adherence to whatever He is bound by duty or promise (His faithfulness and trustworthiness): "Know therefore that the LORD thy God, He is God, which keepeth covenant and mercy with them that love him and keep his commandments to a thousand generations" (Deut. 7:9).

King Solomon declared: "O LORD God of Israel, there is no God like thee in the heaven, nor in the earth, which keepest covenant, and showest mercy unto thy servants, that walk before thee with all their hearts" (2 Chron. 6:14).

As a covenant-keeping God, He has promised under the rainbow covenant not to destroy all flesh by means of a flood. The rainbow covenant made between Jehovah God and all flesh (human and animal), as represented by Noah and his family in about 2369 BC in the mountains of Ararat, endures forever—as long as mankind lives on earth. The rainbow is seen today by discerning Christians as a reminder of God's covenant with Noah, and all humans.

> And God said, "This is the sign of the covenant I am making between me and you and every living creature with you, a covenant for all generations to come: I have set my rainbow in the clouds, and it will be the sign of the covenant between me and earth. Whenever I bring clouds over the earth and the rainbow appears in the clouds, I will remember my covenant between me and you and all the living creatures of every kind. Never again will the waters become a flood to destroy all life. Whenever the rainbow appears in the clouds, I will see it and remember the everlasting covenant between God and all living creatures of every kind on earth."
>
> —GENESIS 9:12–16, NIV

We must, however, note the very important truth that Jehovah God did not promise that the earth will no longer be destroyed, but that it will not be destroyed with flood. The Book of Revelation gives us literary, symbolic, and allegorical insights as well as a frightening yet hopeful holistic picture of the coming firestorm destruction of the earth (Rev. 16:1–20).

As the human Creator and the Creator of the heavens and earth, God had to enter into covenant with humans as the work of His hands. He needed to have a binding sense of commitment to mankind and develop a mutual relationship hinged on His statutes and commandments and by so doing transform man as the vehicle of the expression of His existence, His will and purpose for man. Jehovah God wants to fulfill His will and purpose through this covenantal relationship not just with the children of Israel but with mankind as the work of His hands. The Edenic, Adamic, Noahic, Abrahamic, Mosaic (Sinaitic), Davidic, new (universal), and the everlasting covenants were made to fulfill the aforementioned purpose. The covenantal relationship with Israel extends to all humans, climaxing in mankind's salvific history through the emergence of the promised Seed, Christ Jesus, and fulfillment of the new and everlasting covenants.

The covenantal relationship began with the Edenic covenant in which Jehovah God prohibited the eating of the fruits from the tree of knowledge of good and evil which constituted the test of faith and obedience (Gen. 2:16–17). The first human parents, Adam and Eve, choose to disobey, prodded by Satan (the great serpent and father of lies). Emanating from their disobedience is the first Bible prophecy of the battle of ages between the "seed of the woman" and the "seed of the serpent" and the promise of blessing through the triumph of the woman's seed, Christ Jesus: "And I will put enmity between you and the woman, and between your offspring and hers; he will crush your head, and you will strike his heel" (Gen. 3:15, NIV).

The Genesis, 3:15 prophecy sets the theme for the whole Bible, including Revelation. By tempting Eve to disobey God and by presenting Jehovah as a liar whose commandment could be jettisoned without any dire consequences, Satan challenged His supreme rulership and insinuated that humans could attain perfection by rejecting Jehovah's sovereignty (Gen. 3:1–5). The Book of Revelation describes how the righteous Judge, Jehovah God, uses the kingdom rule of His Spirit–begotten Son, Jesus Christ, to vindicate His everlasting sovereignty and exculpate all admonishment from His name (Rev. 12:10). Jesus is that "seed" of the woman (heavenly Jerusalem), the foretold Messiah, the King-designate of the heavenly kingdom that would restore rulerships over the earth in Jehovah God's name. This will settle once and for all the battle of all ages between

Satan (Beelzebub), "the ruler of the demons," and God's Spirit-begotten Son, Jesus Christ. The issue involving government or sovereignty over humans and the earth will be resolved permanently "for we wrestle not against flesh and blood, but against principalities, against powers, against the rulers of darkness of this world, against spiritual wickedness in high places" (Eph. 6:12).

> Know and understand this: From the time the word goes out to restore and rebuild Jerusalem until the Anointed One, the ruler, comes, there will be seven "sevens" and sixty-two "sevens." It will be rebuilt with streets and a trench, but in times of trouble. After the sixty-two "sevens," the Anointed One will be put to death and will have nothing. The people of the ruler who will come will destroy the city and the sanctuary. The end will come like a flood: War will continue until the end, and the desolations have been decreed.
> —DANIEL 9:25–26, NIV

Vital to this study from the aforementioned verses of Daniel is the prophecy of the "Seed," the anointed One. And before a brief examination of this prophecy, it should be pointed out that "seven 'sevens' and sixty-two 'sevens'" has been deciphered by Bible scholars as 490 years of allotted time.

Matthew Henry's commentary states: "The times here determined are somewhat hard to be understood. In general, it is seventy weeks that is seventy times seven years which makes just 490 years. The great affairs that are yet to come concerning the people of Israel and the city of Jerusalem will lie within the compass of these years."[1]

Adam Clarke in his commentary writes, "Seventy weeks are determined—The Jews had sabbatical years (Lev. 25:6), by which years were divided into weeks of years, as in this important prophecy, each week containing seven years. The seventy weeks containing seven years. The seventy weeks therefore here spoken of amount to 490 years."[2]

The "seventy weeks" or "seventy sevens" then speak of seventy times seven equals 490 years in which certain things must take place in the plan and purpose of God, not only for Judah but that which involves the whole inhibited earth. The 490 years is a period of time in which God will work out His divine purposes in the realm of redemption. It is a distinctive period of time in human history.

But back to the prophecy of the anointed One, it is apparent that there were general promises of the coming of the Messiah made to the patriarchs. The preceding prophets had often spoken of Him as One that should come, but never was the time fixed for His coming until Daniel's prophecy. He came in consonance with the Abrahamic and Davidic covenants, and even far back in fulfillment of the Edenic covenant and promise, not only as the Propitiator of the sins of Jews but of the sins of the whole world.

> He came first to finish transgression, to restrain it, to break the power of it, to bruise the head of that serpent that had done so much mischief to take away the usurped dominion of that tyrant, and to set up a kingdom of holiness and love in the hearts of men, upon the ruins of Satan's kingdom, that where sin and death had reigned, righteousness and life through grace might reign.[3]

This brings us to Jehovah's covenant with Abraham and the promise that through him humankind will be blessed. Abraham proved to be a man of faith in God, even as his forebearers Shem and Noah; and as a result, he earned the reputation of the father of all those having faith while uncircumcised (Rom. 4:11). Abraham displayed an unshakeable faith and a radiant hope in Jehovah God.

ABRAHAMIC COVENANT

In Genesis 17:4–7 God appeared to Abram when he was ninety years old and established an everlasting covenant with him while changing his name to Abraham (meaning father of a multitude). He also revealed to Abraham in Genesis 15:13 that his descendants would be afflicted for a period of 400 years, even taken into slavery. They would be servants; and so they were in the horror and darkness of Egyptian slavery as we read in Exodus 1:

> So they put slave masters over them to oppress them with forced labor, and they built Pithom and Rameses as store cities for Pharaoh. But the more they were oppressed, the more they multiplied and spread; so the Egyptians came to dread the Israelites and worked them ruthlessly. They made their lives bitter with harsh labor in brick and mortar and with all kinds of work in the fields; in all their harsh labor the Egyptians used them ruthlessly.
> —EXODUS 1:11–14, NIV

In fulfillment of Jehovah's promise to Abraham, the Israelites continued to grow in population in spite of the harsh condition and death toll under Egyptian slavery. God's first prophecy to Abraham was that He would transform him into a great nation:

> As for me, behold, my covenant is with thee, and thou shalt be a father of many nations...for a father of many nations have I made thee. And I will make thee exceeding fruitful, and I will make nations of thee, and kings shall come out of thee. And I will establish my covenant between me and thy seed after thee in their generations for an everlasting covenant, to be a God unto thee, and to thy seed after thee.
>
> —GENESIS 17:4–7

To carry out His promise to Abraham, God laid the foundation for a nation by establishing a special covenant with Abraham's descendants. Abraham became the forefather of Isaac, Jacob, and Jacob's twelve sons, who became the leaders of Israel. Abraham also fathered other nations of the ancient world. Apart from Saria's (Sarah) maid, the Egyptian slave girl Hagar, who bore Ishmael (father of some Arab nations) to Abraham on the prompting of the then barren Sarai, Abraham married Keturah (after Sarah's death) who had six children with him. His inheritance went to Isaac (Gen. 25:1–6).

God's promise to make Abraham's name great is fulfilled in the fact that Abraham is revered not only as one of Judaism's great patriarchs but also in the Muslim faith and in Christianity. Jehovah's final statement to Abraham that through him (Abraham) all peoples on earth would be blessed (Gen. 12:3) embraces all that God has provided for our mortal earth through Abraham's posterity. From Israel came the great prophets of God. From Israel emerged all known writers of the Old and New Testaments. And from Abraham's descendants came the twelve apostles and supremely, Jesus Christ Himself. The death of Christ on the cross provides salvation for the entire human race and great blessings that come through the divine grace and favor of God.

Thus, God revealed the purpose and accomplishments of the Abrahamic covenant saying that through Abraham the Seed of promise (Jesus Christ) would come and this seed would possess the gates of his enemies "and in thy seed shall all the nations of the earth be blessed" (Gen. 22:18). This was Jehovah's promise to Abraham after he (Abraham) had proved his faith by obeying God's command to offer his only son, Isaac, as a sacrifice. Just as he was about to sacrifice his son, an Angel of Jehovah Jireh the great Provider, offered a ram for the sacrifice He was directing that Abraham should not lay his hand upon his only son, for Jehovah had seen the fear and love of Abraham towards Him (Gen. 22:2–12).

In 1 Corinthians 15:23–28 we read that God will put everything under the feet of the seed of Abraham, Jesus Christ, who must reign until He has put all his enemies under His feet. When God has put everything under Christ, then Christ Himself will be made subject to God who put everything under Him, so that God may be all in all. Thus, the Abrahamic covenant is a covenant to time without limit, boundless and endless. Its terms demand an extension through the ages until the accomplishment of the destruction of all the enemies of God and the worldwide blessing of the human family.

An important revelation was made by the apostle Paul regarding the Abrahamic covenant—the unilateral nature of the covenant in the sense that it was in reality a promise for which Jehovah God set no conditions that Abraham must meet in order for the promise to be fulfilled. Unlike the law covenant which was bilateral, the Abrahamic covenant needed no mediator.

> Brothers and sisters, let me take an example from everyday life. Just as no one can set aside or add to a human covenant that has been duly established, so it is in this case. The promises were spoken to Abraham and to his seed. Scripture does not say "and to seeds," meaning many people, but "and to your seed," meaning one person, who is Christ. What I mean is this: The law, introduced 430 years later, does not set aside the covenant previously established by God and thus do away with the promise. For if the inheritance depends on the law, then it no longer depends on the promise; but God in his grace gave it to Abraham through a promise.
> —GALATIANS 3:15–18, NIV

Indeed, the Abrahamic covenant set the stage for God's election of Israel as His ensign, His banner, His model nation through which His redemptive purposes, His nature, and His character will be divinely revealed to all nations

The Mosaic or Sinaitic covenant made 430 years after the Abrahamic covenant by the mountain of Sinai, as recorded in Exodus 19:5–6, made Israel a nation of *cohanim*, a priestly kingdom. Their priesthood was intended as an everlasting priesthood through which all nations would be blessed. As a kingdom of priests, they ought to preserve God's knowledge and nations should seek instruction from them because they are the messengers of the Lord Almighty. For God to maintain the everlasting covenant, just like that of the priesthood of Levi, He had to admonish them for their sins.

> "And you will know that I have sent you this warning so that my covenant with Levi may continue," says the LORD Almighty. "My covenant was with him, a covenant of life and peace, and I gave them to him; this called for reverence and he revered me and stood in awe of my name. True instruction was in his mouth and nothing false was found on his lips. He walked with me in peace and uprightness, and turned many from sin."
>
> —MALACHI 2:4–6, NIV

Israel's election, like that of the priesthood of Levi, also called for reverence and total respect and submission to Jehovah. If they failed to live up to the expectations of Him, then they would not only be admonished but punished.

God's reaffirmation of His everlasting covenant with Abraham with a sworn oath was the reward of his total subservience and submission on Mount Moriah where he willingly offered Isaac, his only son, as a sacrifice. Jehovah told him,

> I swear by myself…that because you have done this and have not withheld your son, your only son, I will surely bless you and make your descendants as numerous as the stars in the sky and as the sand on the seashore.
>
> —GENESIS 22:16–17, NIV

Through mankind's acceptance of the promised Seed, Christ Jesus, Jehovah has fulfilled the promise of the numerical strength of Abraham's descendants. All those living and dead through all generations that have received Christ "are as the stars in the sky and as the sand on the seashore." Besides, God's promise to him that "in thy seed shall all the nations of the earth be blessed" (Gen. 22:18) attests to the universality of the Abrahamic covenant. The promise affects all of God's created humans of all races, tribes, nations, and linguistic and dialectic groups who have received Christ, the promised Seed, and have by so doing been given the power to be called the sons of God.

> Yet to all who did receive him, to those who believed in his name, he gave the right to become children of God—children born not of a natural descent, nor of human decision or a husband's will, but born of God.
>
> —JOHN 1:12–13, NIV

Palmer Robertson presents a pertinent picture of the universal application of the Abrahamic covenant. He contends that when God first instituted the covenant sign that designated Abraham as His chosen vessel for communicating blessings to nations, God specifically indicated that "any Gentile could become a full-fledged Jew by professing the God of Abraham and being circumcised.... No racial barrier existed to keep Gentile [other nations] from becoming full participants in the covenant promises."[4]

The apostle Paul asked; "Is God the God of Jews only? Is he not the God of Gentiles too? Yes, of Gentiles too, since there is only one God, who will justify the circumcised by faith and the uncircumcised through that same faith" (Rom. 3:29–30, NIV).

Paul gives further clarification on the issue of justification (eternal salvation) by faith for everyone who exercises faith in the Seed of Abraham (Christ Jesus) just as Abraham was justified by faith in Jehovah when he was in uncircumcision.

> It was not through law that Abraham and his offspring received the promise that he would be heir of the world, but through the righteousness that comes by faith. For if those depend on by law are heirs, faith means nothing and the promise is worthless, because law brings wrath. And where there is no law there is no transgression. Therefore, the promise comes by faith, so that it may be by grace and may be guaranteed to all Abraham's offspring—not only to those who are of the law but also to those who are of the faith of Abraham. He is the father of us all. As it is written "I have made you a father of many nations."
>
> —ROMANS 4:13–17, NIV

MOSAIC COVENANT

The Mosaic or Sinaitic covenant, successor to the Abrahamic covenant, was principally a covenant with Israel made in about 1513 BC. It had its distinct features from all other covenants because it was, in the first instance, a constitution for the nation of Israel. It contains instructions for

Israel's socioeconomic and judicial system as well as religious and moral obligations. The temple system, the priesthood and sacrifices, were given great prominence under the Mosaic covenant. Unlike the Abrahamic and Davidic covenants of promise, the Mosaic covenant was rooted in law and was temporal until Christ's redemptive atonement leading to the new covenant. However, nations and obedient humans could still learn a great deal from the principles of social justice, business ethics, honesty, and daily moral living found in the Mosaic Law covenant.

Christ Himself said that He did not come to destroy the Mosaic Law covenant but to fulfill it.

> Do not think that I have come to abolish the Law or the Prophets; I have not come to abolish them but to fulfill them. For truly I tell you, until heaven and earth disappear, not the smallest letter, not the least stroke of pen, will by any means disappear from the law until everything is accomplished.
>
> —MATTHEW 5:17–18, NIV

The perfect accomplishment of the Mosaic Law covenant for universal salvation was found in the Lord Jesus Christ through the redemptive atonement of His blood on a torture stake. He thus abolished the ceremonial and external aspects of the Mosaic Law, which was exclusive to Israel. What the Mosaic Law could not achieve, being limited by flesh (the perpetual sinful ways of man), Jehovah did by condemning sin in the flesh through the sacrifice of His own Son as a sin offering in order that the law's requirement would be accomplished in everyone who walks according to the Spirit and not according to the flesh (Rom. 8:1–4). Indeed, for every human from all demographics who have received Christ there is no more condemnation because the spirit's law of life in Christ has set them free from the law of sin and death. The Mosaic covenant given to Israel was in fulfillment of the Abrahamic covenant given 430 years before and a roadmap to the Palestinian, Davidic, new, and everlasting covenants. Some of the key purposes of the Mosaic covenant include making the transgressions of all men manifest (Gal. 3:17–19), leading Jews to Christ (v. 24), and protecting the line of the seed of Abraham for universal salvation (vv. 19, 22).

As we read from Exodus 12, the Mosaic Law covenant extended benefits to non-Jews, thus laying the foundation for the Israel of God in the coming Seed of promise in the earlier Abrahamic and latter Davidic covenants.

A foreigner residing among you who wants to celebrate the LORD's
Passover must have all the males in his household circumcised; then
he may take part like one born in the land.... The same law applies
to the native-born and to the foreigner residing among you.

—EXODUS 12:48–49

We should recall that before the Mosaic covenant requirement for
circumcision for non-Israelites to share in the covenant, Abraham had
received circumcision as a seal of the righteousness he had by the faith
he exhibited while in his uncircumcised state. Through this he became
the father of all those having faith while in uncircumcision (Jews and
Gentiles) in order for righteousness to be counted to them (Rom. 4:11).

PALESTINIAN COVENANT:
PROPHETIC IMPORT TO NATIONS

Before examining the Davidic covenant, let's take a brief look at the
Palestinian covenant because it reveals a lesson in God's prophetic pronouncements on the wages of disobedience on the part of Israel extending
to other nations and from which they could learn useful lessons. Like the
Mosaic Law covenant, Moses was the mediator of the Palestinian covenant made exclusively with Israel in the land of Moab. It was given at
the end of the forty years of wanderings in the wilderness and just before
they entered the Promised Land about 1,473 years before our common
era (1473 BC). The essence of the covenant was to encourage faithfulness
to Jehovah and to make necessary adjustments and set forth certain laws
necessary for the children of Israel as they switched from a life of wandering to a settled life in the Land of Promise.

The covenant involved the allotment of the Promised Land to the children of Israel in fulfillment of one of the promises of the Abrahamic
covenant. This was the land God chose for Himself from all the lands
on earth. God told the Israelites, "The land is not to be permanently sold
because it is Mine, and you are only foreigners and temporary residents
on My land" (Lev. 25:23–24, HCSB).

The children of Israel were thus occupants of the land of promise
as Jehovah's stewards. The Palestinian covenant was made with eleven
promises of blessings if they remained obedient to the law covenant and
fourteen curses if they become disobedient as we read from Deuteronomy
28:1–68.

In times of obedience they enjoyed the promises of great blessings as we read from 1 and 2 Samuel, 1 and 2 Kings, 1 and 2 Chronicles, Judges, and Ruth, but were also gravely punished for disobedience and uprooted from the land of promise

One of the fulfilled curses, God's pronouncements for disobedience, involves the dispersal of the Israelites to other nations of the earth after the military conquest of their land, as we read from Deuteronomy 28:

> Then the LORD will scatter you among all nations, from one end of the earth to the other....Among those nations you will find no repose, no resting place for the sole of your foot. There the LORD will give you an anxious mind, eyes weary with longing, and a despairing heart. You will live in constant suspense, filled with dread both night and day, never sure of your life. In the morning you will say, "If only it were evening!" and in the evening, "If only it were morning!"—because of the terror that will fill your hearts and the sights that your eyes will see.
>
> —DEUTERONOMY 28:64–67, NIV

Surely, if God has chosen a nation and a people from all His created nations and people as His banner, His light through which He wants His glory illuminated to the rest of mankind and nations, that special and exclusive election must be hinged on the unflinching obedience of His statutes and commandments and serious and fatal consequences for disobedience; as was pronounced in the Edenic covenant—disobedience engendered death.

The fulfillment of the Palestinian covenant curse in the ejection of Israel from the land of promise and their dispersal is a clear manifestation of Jehovah's supremacy over all His created humans and nations. If it happened to His chosen people, His chosen nation, then no nation on the face of the earth is immune from His admonition and punishment.

THE DAVIDIC COVENANT

The Davidic covenant established by Jehovah to King David as representative of his family (1070–1038 BC) forty years after Saul's reign was a covenant of everlasting kingship upon God's throne, as we read from 1 Chronicles 29:23, "So Solomon sat on the throne of the LORD as king in place of his father David" (NIV).

The everlasting and unconditional covenant of kingdom and kingship through the lineage of David was bestowed upon him by Jehovah's promise made in 1 Chronicles as conveyed through the prophetic vision of Nathan.

> I declare to you that the LORD will build a house for you: When your days are over and you go to be with your ancestors, I will raise up your offspring to succeed you, one of your sons, and I will establish his kingdom. . . . I will establish his throne forever. . . . I will set him over my house and my kingdom forever; his throne will be established forever.
>
> —1 CHRONICLES 17:10–12, 14, NIV

Jehovah chose to send His only and Spirit-begotten Son to earth as the Son of Man and God in man through the earthly descent (lineage) of Abraham and David so that through His Son, Christ Jesus, His theocratic kingdom will be established for the eternal salvation of all humans.

The prophet Isaiah was led by the Holy Spirit of God to prophesy that of the princely rule of Christ and to the peace that His rule will establish "there shall be no end upon the throne of David, and upon his kingdom, in order to establish it firmly and to establish it with judgment and with justice from henceforth even for ever" (Isa. 9:6–7).

Zechariah also prophesied that, "The LORD will be king over the whole earth. On that day there will be one LORD, and his name the only name" (Zech. 14:9, NIV).

The covenants with God were both a guarantee of God's blessings and a reminder of His commandments. Indeed, the history of the children of Israel shows how the joy and sadness of a people and of nations depends on the acknowledgement of eternal moral and spiritual imperatives ordained by Jehovah. God's covenantal relationship with Israel bestows benevolently to the world His Son, Christ Jesus, who has through his life, death, and resurrection performed deeds of salvation that have fundamentally as well as retroactively to the beginnings of human history altered humanity's situation to the good. Walbert Bühlmann, author of *The Coming of the Third Church* and *God's Chosen Peoples*, presents a lucid and pertinent statement on the salvation work of Christ for humanity.

> In Him the way to the father now stands open to every human being. In Him every hidden hope is not only guaranteed but surpassed. On His account we can be sure that our longing for ultimate fulfillment is not a lifelong illusion, to be snuffed out in the stillness of death, but a justified certitude, for we have truly been assumed

into God in life, in death, and thereafter.... The more fully human beings achieve their self-identity, in history as in future, the further they will penetrate history's deepest mystery—and see themselves in Jesus Christ, to the glory of God the father.[5]

Just as His Father and our Father, Jehovah, Jesus Christ is also a God of living history whose salvific and historic relevance flows into the new and everlasting covenants which involve and affects all humans, to which we now direct our attention.

THE NEW COVENANT

The prophet Jeremiah was in the seventh century BC divinely inspired to foretell Jehovah's promise concerning the new covenant, as we read in Jeremiah 31:

> The days are coming, says the LORD, when I will make a new covenant with the house of Israel and with the house of Judah.... This is the covenant I will make with the house of Israel after those days, says the LORD: I will put My law in their minds, and write it on their hearts; and I will be their God, and they shall be My people.
> —JEREMIAH 31:31, 33, NKJV

The new covenant is not like the law covenant which Israel broke, and it completes the cycle of covenantal revelation leading to the everlasting covenant. On the night before His crucifixion, Jesus Christ established the celebration of the Lord's evening meal and announced the new covenant, which was ratified and confirmed by His ransom sacrifice.

> And he took bread, gave thanks and broke it, and gave it to them, saying, "This is My body which is given for you; do this in remembrance of Me." Likewise He also took the cup after supper, saying, "This cup is the new covenant in My blood, which is shed for you."
> —LUKE 22:19–20, NKJV

Jesus Christ is thus the mediator of the new covenant, a universal covenant extending to Gentiles, being the primary Seed of Abraham through whom all obedient humans will find salvation *ad majorem Dei gloriam*—for the greater glory of God. His blood maketh atonement for the soul.

> The blood of goats and bulls and the ashes of a heifer sprinkled on those who are ceremonially unclean sanctify them so that they are

outwardly clean. How much more, then, will the blood of Christ, who through the eternal Spirit, offered himself unblemished to God, cleanse our consciences from acts that lead to death, so that we may serve the living God! For this reason Christ is the mediator of a new covenant that those who are called may receive the promised eternal inheritance—now that he has died as a ransom to set them free from the sins committed under the first covenant.

—HEBREWS 9:13–15, NIV

Charles Spurgeon (1834–1892) captures the efficacy of the atonement blood of Christ in the following words during one of his numerous sermons:

Ten thousand times ten thousand are the souls for whom Jesus shed His blood. He, for the sins of all the elect, hath a complete atonement made. For every man of Adam born, who has believed or shall believe on that, or who is taken to glory before being capable of believing, Christ has made a complete atonement; and there is none other plan by which sinners can be made at one with God, except by Jesus' precious blood. I may make sacrifices; I may mortify my body; I may be baptized; I may receive sacraments; I may pray until my knees grow hard with kneeling; I may read devout words until I know them by heart; I may celebrate masses; I may worship in one language or in fifty languages; but I can never be at one with God, except by blood; and that blood, "the precious blood of Christ."[6]

In establishing the new covenant with its new priesthood, new sanctuary, and new sacrifice, Christ entered into the heavenly tabernacle in God's presence once and for all in perfect, unblemished atonement presentation of His shed blood, obtaining eternal redemption for all believing humans, everyone that has received Him and given the power to be called the sons of God. (See Hebrews 9:11–12; Galatians 3:26–27; John 1:12–13.)

The intent of the new covenant is to draw out a people from all nations as part of Abraham's seed for the glory and exalted name of Jehovah. The covenant bestows the blessings of resurrection and eternal life for every one exercising faith in Christ Jesus. Indeed, through our Lord Jesus Christ, all of God's created humans are assured of eternal life because He showed clearly during His earthly ministry that He is the resurrection and life who has conquered death for all mankind. The fact that He healed all manner of sicknesses, performed all manner of miracles, raised the dead, and was Himself resurrected from the dead confirmed His authority; and control over the elements by calming the stormy sea reveal the glory and perfection of His coming kingdom—an end to all human problems and sorrows. We can through complete faith in Him experience spiritual resurrection from our death in transgressions and sins and come to a full experience of the blessedness of the physical and spiritual resurrection.

Christ confirms in the John 5:24 and 28–29 that whoever believes in His Father, Jehovah, who sent Him, has eternal life and has crossed from death to life. He also pointed to the time when all who are in their graves will hear His voice and come out, those who have done good rising to live and evil ones rising to condemnation. Christ has proclaimed with the authority of His Father, Jehovah of armies, that He is the living one who lives for ever and ever and holds the keys to Death and Hades. He is the one who will make everything new. He is the one that will ensure that nations will no more war against nations and that they will turn their weapons of mass destruction into pruning hooks and plowshares (Isa. 2:4). He is the one that will ensure that the wolf, the lamb, the leopard, the goat, the lion, and the calf will lie down together eating straw, while the infant will play near the hole of cobra and a young child will put his hand into the viper's nest without any harm to him. He is the Prince of Peace who will bring the elusive peace to all nations, for man is incapable of creating a peaceful world without His divine intervention (Isa. 11:1–9).

The new covenant carries with it the accomplishment of the kingdom of God under Christ's kingship, as Christ told His apostles to proclaim the good news of the kingdom, the foundation of which was built on the church—the body of Christ. "And this gospel of the kingdom will be preached in the whole world as a testimony to all nations, and then the end will come" (Matt. 24:14, NIV).

Christ is the King who will pass judgment on wicked nations, for the wrath of God is constantly being revealed from heaven against all the godlessness and wickedness of men who suppress the truth by their wickedness. These are men and nations who ignore and deny God's invincible qualities, His eternal power, and His divine nature which have been in existence since the creation of the universe, to which no man can justifiably claim ignorance (Rom. 1:18–20).

If nations recognize earthly rulers, presidents, prime ministers, kings, and queens and do obeisance to them who are but mortal men and women, it should, therefore, not be too difficult for intelligent humans to discern or at least appreciate the possibility of the heavenly and earthly kingship of Jesus Christ. For those led by the Spirit of God, the Spirit of truth, Christ's coming kingdom is a *fait accompli*—a certitude at God's own appointed time when the enthroned Christ carries out judgment over the earth with angelic support. The words and prophecies of Jehovah as presented in His manual for life—the Holy Bible confirms a new world order under Christ's kingship that will put an end to all of man's earthly problems, troubles, imperfections, wars, diseases, famine, natural disasters, and man's inhumanity to man. The new covenant bestows this kingdom to all those who have received Christ and have been given the power to be called the sons of God.

The eternal crown for all overcomers in Christ Jesus made in the everlasting covenant is made possible by the new covenant which also has as its greatest promise, the fullness of eternal life brought by faith in the righteousness of Christ.

> For God so greatly loved and dearly prized the world that He [even] gave up His only begotten (unique) Son, so that whoever believes in (trusts in, clings to, relies on) Him shall not perish (come to destruction, be lost) but have eternal (everlasting) life.
>
> —JOHN 3:16, AMP

ISRAEL AND NATIONS IN EVERLASTING COVENANT

The words of Jehovah as revealed in the Holy Bible clearly show that before the Abrahamic covenant God had established an everlasting covenantal relationship with all humans and the inhabited earth with her associated plant and animal life. This is the rainbow covenant promised Noah after the worldwide deluge, which destroyed the whole earth as it was then in Noah's day. Genesis 9:11–16 reads,

> And I will establish my covenant with you, neither shall all flesh be cut off any more by the waters of a flood; neither shall there anymore be a flood to destroy the earth. And God said, This is the token of my covenant between me and you and every living creature that is with you, for perpetual generations: I do set my bow in the cloud, and it shall be for a token of a covenant between me and the earth. And it shall come to pass, when I bring a cloud over the earth, that the bow shall be seen in the cloud: And I will remember my covenant, which is between me and you and every living creature of all flesh; and the waters shall no more become a flood to

destroy all flesh. And the bow shall be in the cloud; and I will look upon it, that I may remember the everlasting covenant between God and every living creature of all flesh that is upon the earth.

So we are assured by the everlasting rainbow (Noahic) covenant that the entire inhabited earth will no longer be destroyed by flood. Yes, no matter how great the flood or no matter how extensive is the destruction of the tsunami, it may destroy vast areas, but not the entire inhabited earth as was the flood of Noah's generation. The rainbow stands to this day as a sign or reminder of God's everlasting covenant to mankind. Through the prophet Isaiah Jehovah compared His covenant of peace with the children of Israel with the rainbow covenant.

> For this is as the waters of Noah unto me: For as I have sworn that the waters of Noah should no more go over the earth; so have I sworn that I would not be wroth with thee, nor rebuke thee.
> —ISAIAH 54:9

The flood was certainly not a myth nor a fable but a true historical occurrence that was also mentioned by Jesus Christ, who was an eyewitness of the event from His heavenly realm long before He took up human flesh for His earthly ministry. Christ referred to the prophetic significance of the flood in the prophecy of His second coming and the conclusion of the present chaotic and imperfect human system of things, as we read from Matthew chapter 24:

> As it was in the days of Noah, so it will be at the coming of the Son of man. For in the days before the flood, people were eating and drinking, marrying and giving in marriage, up to the day Noah entered the ark; and they knew nothing about what would happen until the flood came and took them all away. That is how it will be at the coming of the Son of man.
> —MATTHEW 24:37–39, NIV

Luke 17:26–28 also records Jesus' prophetic reference to the flood of Noah's day and the destruction of Sodom in pointing to His second coming.

The "everlasting salvation" promised Israel in Isaiah 45:17 extends also to all humans through the sacrificial blood of Christ and His incoming everlasting kingdom, which accommodates everyone who receives and exercises faith in Him for "Israel will be saved by the LORD with an everlasting salvation; you will never be put to shame or disgraced to ages everlasting" (NIV).

Jehovah Himself through His inspired words upon the prophet Isaiah called on all nations to embrace His redemption plan necessitated by man's inglorious fall in Eden. Isaiah 45:22 reads, "Turn to me and be saved all you ends of the earth; for I am God, and there is no other" (NIV).

The everlasting covenant promised David and Israel is for the witnessing of God's glory and redemption work for all peoples and nations and their accommodation in Jehovah's salvific plan for mankind through the "leader and commander" (Christ Jesus), as we read from Isaiah 55:

> Give ear and come to me; listen, that you may live. I will make an everlasting covenant with you, my faithful love promised to David. See, I have made him a witness to the peoples....Surely you will summon nations you know not, and nations you do not know will come running to you.
>
> —ISAIAH 55:3–5, NIV

Gentiles, the rest of the nations, God's created humans from all demographics are also called upon to embrace His everlasting covenant so that they will be bestowed with an everlasting name. Isaiah chapter 56 is very instructive, and it reads,

> Let no foreigner who has bound himself to the LORD say, "The Lord will surely exclude me from his people." And let not any eunuch complain, "I am only a dry tree." For this is what the LORD says: "To the eunuchs who keep my Sabbaths, who choose what pleases me and hold fast to my covenant—to them I will give within my temple and its walls a memorial and a name better than sons and daughters; I will give them an everlasting name that will endure forever. And foreigners who bind themselves to the LORD to minister to him, to love the name of the LORD, and be his servants, all who keep the Sabbath without desecrating it and who hold fast my covenant—these I will bring to my holy mountain and give them joy in my house of prayer. Their burnt offerings and sacrifices will be accepted on my altar; for my house will be called a house of prayer for all nations.
>
> —ISAIAH 56:3–7, NIV

The coming of Christ, the Messiah, is proclaimed to all nations as Isaiah's prophetic words reveal: "The Lord has made proclamation to the ends of the earth: 'Say to Daughter Zion, "See your savior comes! See his reward is with him, and his recompense accompanies him"'" (Isa. 62:11, NIV).

The Scripture talks about the blood of the everlasting covenant— Christ's atonement blood, shed on the cross of Calvary as an everlasting covenant of eternal life to all humans who exercise faith in Him and His atonement blood.

> May the God of peace, who through the blood of the eternal covenant brought back from the dead our Lord Jesus, that great Shepherd of the sheep, equip you with everything good for doing his will, and may he work in us what is pleasing to him, through Jesus Christ, to whom be glory for ever and ever. Amen.
> —HEBREWS 13:20–21, NIV

It is apparent that as an all-knowing (omniscient) God with unchanging (immutable), all-powerful (omnipotent), everywhere present (omnipresent) attributes, Jehovah, foresaw the fall of man from His creative purposes and the entrance of sin into the world, having given man a free will. He therefore prepared an everlasting covenant of redemption for mankind, which was to be made manifest by the blood of the everlasting covenant shed by His only-begotten Son, Christ Jesus. This everlasting covenant was not made with man but made between Jehovah God, Jesus Christ, and the Holy Spirit in heaven. Jehovah declared the Spirit and letters (words and terms) of the covenants; Jesus, the mediator of the covenant, is the sacrificial lamb who serves as both "offering and offerer, sacrifice and priest"; while the Holy Spirit serves as the executor and the seal, sign, and token. This preexistent everlasting covenant in heaven between the person of the eternal Godhead, the Father, Son, and Holy Spirit, made possible all other covenants of creation and redemption on earth, which involves all of God's created humans and through which everyone exercising faith in Christ Jesus and His atonement blood is assured of everlasting life. Israel is the banner, God's ensign, of these covenants to all nations. It is through Israel, God's chosen people, that these covenants extend to all of God's created humans.

It is therefore given unto all men to receive the promise of Jehovah pertaining to the everlasting covenant in which a "new heart" will be planted into all His children who have received Christ and the power to be called the sons of God and have become heirs of God and joint heirs with Christ in His coming kingdom. Jehovah, through the prophet

Ezekiel, speaks of this new heart in an everlasting covenantal relationship of peace with Israel and nations.

> I will give a new heart and put a new spirit in you; I will remove
> from you your heart of stone and give you a heart of flesh. And I
> will put my Spirit in you and move you to follow my decrees and be
> careful to keep my laws.
>
> —EZEKIEL 36:26–27, NIV

Ezekiel chapter 37 reads,

> I will make a covenant of peace with them; it will be an everlasting
> covenant....I will put my sanctuary among them forever. My
> dwelling place will be with them; I will be their God, and they will
> be my people. Then the nations will know that I the LORD make
> Israel holy, when my sanctuary is among them forever.
>
> —EZEKIEL 37:26–28, NIV

It is this message to nations, the road to eternal salvation, that the
tortuous and turbulent history of Israel in covenantal relationship with
God leads other nations and peoples into. It is through Israel that mankind's final destiny in covenantal relationship with God finds fulfillment
in the atonement blood of His only and Spirit-begotten Son, Christ Jesus.
It is through Israel that Jehovah's grand plan for nations and peoples for
a new heavens and earth under the divine kingship of Jesus, the King
of kings and the Lord of lords, will be accomplished. Thus, Christ pronounced the Great Commission to His disciples to cover all nations, all
the nooks and crannies of the inhabited earth, as we read in Matthew:

> All authority in heaven and on earth has been given to me. Therefore
> go and make disciples of all nations, baptizing them in the name of
> the Father and of the Son and of the Holy Spirit, and teaching them
> to obey everything I have commanded you. And surely I am with
> you always, to the very end of the age.
>
> —MATTHEW 28:18–20, NIV

With the Great Commission, salvation comes within the embrace of
all humans willing to avail themselves of the loving and clasping arms
of the Savior, Christ Jesus, and accept willingly His sacrificial blood—
the seed of our eternal salvation. Through the Great Commission, Christ
asserts His universal dominion as mediator of the new covenant. He

sends His disciples, pastors, ministers, teachers, and prophets across all generations, to whom He is ever present in Spirit, to preach the good news of His coming kingdom. He has commissioned His followers, as leader and commander, King of kings and Lord of lords, to set up His kingdom here on earth, to prepare the way for His second coming.

Just as in His first coming, Israel will play a pivotal role in His second coming and in the final redemption of nations when the enthroned Christ carries out judgment with angelic support. Let us now examine how God's Word reveals this eternal truth, and how Christ will establish a kingdom of priests from every tribe, language, people, and nations who will serve Jehovah and reign on earth (Rev. 5:9–10) and how Israel is central to the fulfillment of this redemption plan.

Chapter 5

ISRAEL IN THE FINAL
REDEMPTION OF NATIONS

How is Israel central to the fulfillment of Jehovah's redemption plan for mankind? What pivotal role will Israel be made to play in the salvation of nations and the entrance of all peoples and nations within God's theocratic governance of righteousness and justice under Christ's Messianic kingdom rule?

We have seen through the march of world history that mankind's earthly journey through all ages and generations has been filled with wars, famine, pestilences, and natural and man-made disasters, including man's inhumanity to fellow man. Through this man's remarkable capacity for selfless love and great scientific, technological, and medical achievements are all endangered and unsustainable because of man's inability to live in perfect peace. Indeed, the capacity of mankind to show selfless love is limited, largely by the preponderance of human wickedness and atrocities perpetrated and perpetuated by a powerful few.

We have also seen that in spite of all trials, tribulations, and persecutions of the Jewish people, such as no other people or nation on planet Earth has experienced, Israel has carried with her the special gift of God as His chosen people and has bestowed upon the world great blessings in virtually all of human endeavor. Apart from spiritual and eternal blessings through the lineage of the patriarch Abraham to nations through the Jewish Jesus and the selfless service of Jewish disciples and apostles in the salvific ministry of Christ (the Great Commission to all mankind), Israel has made invaluable contributions to the world in science, technology, medicine, law, banking and finance, literary and fine arts, as well as in other fields.

It is a historical fact that a quarter of all the Nobel Prizes won by Germans in the first quarter of the twentieth century were won by

German Jews. Over twenty Jewish Nobel Prize winners emigrated from Germany in 1933. Jews made outstanding contributions as doctors, chemists, physicists, mathematicians, philosophers, historians, philologists, writers, stage directors, musicians, and in several other professions.

The works of the following Jewish born Nobel Laureates are still utilized and appreciated today: Albert Einstein (1879–1955), Michelson Albert Abraham (1852–1931), Isaac Bashevis Singer, Elie Wiesel, Thomas Mann (1875–1955), Mossbauer Rudolf Ludwig, Urey Harold, Willstatter Richard, Frank James (1882–1964), Waksman Selman Abraham (1883–1973), Agnon Shmuel Yusef (1888–1973), Bethe Hans Albrecht, Korad Emil, Cori Carl Ferdinand (1896–1984), Gerty Theresa Radnitz (1896–1957), John Franklin Enders (1897–1985), Flory Paul John (1910–1985), Garbor Dennis (1900–1979), Friedrick August Von Hayek (1899–1922), Herzberg Gerhard, Kuznets Simon (1901–1985), Sir Krebs Hans Adolf (1900–1981), Landsteiner Karl (1868–1943), Leontief Wassily, Maria Geoppert (1906–1972), Perutz Max Ferdinand, Root Elihu (1845–1937), Sachs Nelly (1891–1970), Chaim Weizmann (1949–1952), Robert Aumann, and many more.

German, Austrian, Russian, Polish, Italian, French, English, and American nationals of Jewish descent have also made great contributions in the fields of music, physics, archaeology, graphic arts, literature, sculpturing, painting, aerospace engineering, mathematics, medicine, psychoanalysis, electronic and computer inventions and development, biochemistry, psychology, journalism, anthropology, philosophy, theology, pharmacology, and so on.

The list of such Jewish great minds include Emil Nolde (1867–1951), Kathe Kollwitz (1867–1945), Felix Mendelssohn, Buber Martin (1878–1965), Winkelmann Johann Joachin (1717–1768), Arthur Miller, Camille Pissaro, Efrem Zimbalist, Leonardo da Vinci, Michael Dell, John Kemeny, Jonas Salk, Sigmund Freud (1856–1939), Emile Berliner, Albert Sabin, Barenboim Daniel, Asimov Isaac, Cham Nachman Bialuk (1873–1934), Boas Franz, John Eberhard Faber (1822–1879), Otto Loewl (1873–1961), Herzl Theodre (1860–1904), Alexander Prokofuff (1822–1879), Zworykin Vladimir Cosma (1889–1982), Isaac Mayer Wise (1819–1900), among others.

In listing the names of Nobel Prize winners of Jewish descent, we must not forget the invaluable contributions of nationals of other nations of the world who have equally won the Nobel Prize.

We should remember the likes of Agnes Gonxha Bojaxhiu, better known as Mother Teresa, (1910–1997). She was the diminutive Yugoslav born Roman Catholic nun, who lived a life of selfless service to humanity and founded the Missionaries of Charity, tending to the sick, the poor, and needy of society. We also note the Irish-born British playwright, critic and reformer, Sir George Bernard Shaw (1856–1950); Russian chemist, Semenov Nikolai (1896–1983); Swedish physicist, Karl Mann George Siegbahn (1886–1778); Polish author, Sienkiewicz Henrykl (1846–1911); English chemist, Soddy Frederick (1877–1956); English Physicist, Sir Joseph John Thomson, (1856–1940); English mathematician and philosopher, Sir Betrand Arthur William Russell (1872–1970); and American physicians Richard Dickinson Woodruff (1895–1973) and Robbins Frederick Chapman.

The long list includes the Russian physicist, Prokhomar Alexander Mikhailovich; American physicist, Purcell Edward Mills; French poet and diplomat, Perse St. John (1881–1979); Soviet poet and novelist, Pasternak Boris (1890–1960); German physical chemist, Nernst Hermann (1864–1941); German journalist, Carl Von Ossietzky (1889–1935); German chemist, Ostwald Wilhelm (1853–1932); American chemist and physicist, Edward Williams (1838–1923); English zoologist, Sir Medawar Peter Brian (1915–1957); the American general and statesman, chief of staff of the United States Army in World War II, Marshall George Catlett (1880–1959); English mathematician and physicist, Paul Adrien Maurice Dirac (1902–1984); Italian poet, Glosue Carducci (1835–1949); Norwegian author, Sigrid Undsel (1864–1949); American biologist, George Wald; and Irish physicist, Ernest Thomas Sinton Walton (1903–1995).

Mention should also be made of the American geneticist, Barbara McClintock; Dutch physicist and author, Lorentz Hendrik Antoun (1853–1926); French microbiologist, Lwoff Andre (1902–1994); nuclear physicist from the United States, Willis Eugene Jr.; the Icelandic author, Halldór Kiljan Laxness (1902–1998); French physician, Charles Louis Alphonse Laveran (1845–1922); American statesman, Frank Billings Kellogg (1851–1937); Czechoslovakian chemist, Jaroslav Herovsky (1890–1967); Swedish statesman and secretary general of the United Nations, Dag Hammarskjold (1905–1961); South African author, Nadimer Gordimer; Nigerian playwright, poet, and essayist, Wole Soyinka; and German surgeon, Frossman Werner (1904–1979).

Let us equally remember the English nuclear physicist, Sir John Douglas Cockcroft; British nutritionist and agricultural scientist, Boyd Orr Lord (1880–1971); German chemist and industrialist, Carl Bosh (1874–1940); Spanish poet, Vicente Alexandre (1878–1984); Guatemalan author and diplomat, Miguel Angel Asturias (1899–1974); German chemist, Adolf

Von Boeyer (1835–1917); American biochemist, James Dewey Watson; China–born American physicist, Chen Ning Yang; Scottish physicist, Charles Thomson Rees Wilson (1867–1959); Irish poet, playwright, and essayist, William Butler Yeats (1865–1935); and Nobel Peace Prize winners like Nelson Mandela, Bishop Desmond Tutu, Yitzhak Rabin, Shimon Peres, and many more.

It is important to point out that a closer and deeper study of the lives of the aforementioned Nobel Laureates reveal that the genealogy of many of them can be traced to Jewish ancestry through the maternal or paternal lineage, thus reemphasizing a dominant Jewish contribution to world development in fulfillment of Jehovah's Abrahamic covenant: "In your seed all the nations of the earth be blessed" (Gen. 22:18, NKJV). But these are all ephemeral mortal blessings as compared to the blessings of all nations through the Jewish Jesus, blessing of everlasting life.

ISRAEL: GOD'S PASTURELAND, INSTRUMENT OF GOD'S JUSTICE AND VICTORY

Since its formation as a nation, Israel, God's pastureland, has been under incessant attacks and foreign domination. On account of the attacks from surrounding hostile nations such as Amalek, Ammon, Assyria, Babylon, Edom, Egypt, Ethiopia, Moab, Philistia, and Syria, the psalmist King David cried out to Jehovah,

> O God do not remain silent....See how your enemies growl.... "Come," they say, "let us destroy them as a nation, so that Israel's name is remembered no more."...They form an alliance against you—the tents of Edom and the Ishmaelite, of Moab and the Hagrites, Byblos, Ammon and Amalek, Philista, with the people of Tyre. Even Assyria has joined them to reinforce Lot's descendants. Do to them as you did to Midian....Make their nobles like Oreb and Zeeb, all their prince like Zebah and Zalmunna, who said, "Let us take possession of the pasturelands of God."...Let them know that you, whose name is the LORD, that you alone are the Most High over the earth.
>
> —PSALM 83:1–2, 4–9, 11–12, 18, NIV

Let us recall that, as we read from Judges 7:24–25, and 8:3–5, Oreb and Zeeb were in the Midianite 135,000 strong army of kings Zebah and Zalmunna that Gideon and his 300 men, through Jehovah's direction and mighty hands, put to flight. The two princes were captured and put to death by men of Ephraim and their heads were brought to Gideon.

Under Saul's kingship (circa 1077–1037 BC) or (circa 1051–1011 BC cited by some scholars), the Israelites living East of River Jordan defeated the Hagrites, as we read from the 1 Chronicles 5:10. They took about one hundred thousand Hagrites captive as well as war booties of thousands of asses, camels, and sheep.

During the reign of King Eglon of Moab, who oppressed Israel for eighteen years because of their apostasy (Judg. 3:12–15), the Ammonites, in collaboration with the Amalekites, attacked Israel. Eglon was head of the coalition of Moab, Amalek, and Ammon in their military invasion of Israel. Not only did the Ammonites terrorize the Israelites of Gilead, they also tormented the tribes of Benjamin, Ephraim, and Judah as narrated in Judges 10:6–10. First Samuel 11:1–4, 11–15 narrates how Saul defeated the Ammonites under the Ammonite king Nahash leaving only a few survivors of the latter's army.

Under King Manahem of Israel (circa 790–781 BC), the Assyrian king Tiglath-Pileser III moved against Israel; and Manahem quickly sought Tiglath-Pileser's favor by offering a tribute of a thousand talents, estimated at current value of over six million United States dollars. Tiglath-Pileser responded with a temporary withdrawal of the Assyrian army (2 Kings 15:19–20).

King Pekah of Israel (circa 778–758 BC), who took over kingship of Israel in Samaria after assassinating King Pekahiah (780–778 BC) under whom he served as adjutant, formed a military alliance with King Rezin of Damascus against King Ahaz (Jehoahaz) of Judah (circa 761–746 BC) (2 Kings 15:25–27). In spite of the divine assurance of the prophet Isaiah to King Ahaz that the military coalition of Pekahiah and Rezin would be defeated, Ahaz in faithlessness went on to induce the Syrian king Tiglath-Pileser III with tribute in exchange for protection against the force of Pekahiah and Rezin. Tiglath-Pileser responded with a swift invasion of Israel, conquering and overcoming the regions of Galilee, Gilead, Naphtali, and several northern cities as related in 2 Kings 15:29 and 1 Chronicles 5:6, 26. Damascus was also conquered and its king, Rezin, assassinated. King Ahaz's Damascus visit to Tiglath-Pileser III after the conquest is narrated in 2 Kings 16:10.

Indeed, Tiglath-Pileser became the "hired razor" prophesied by Isaiah to shave the kingdom of Judah, highlighting further the imperative of prophecy and obedience of Israel: "In that day the Lord will use a razor hired from beyond the Euphrates River—the king of Assyria—to shave your head and private parts, and to cut off your beard also (Isa. 7:20, NIV).

From the period of the divided kingdom (circa 997 BC) to Nebuchadnezzar's first conquest of Jerusalem (circa 605 BC), Jerusalem and Israel became increasingly vulnerable to attacks. King Shishak of Egypt attacked the kingdom of Judah during the fifth year of Rehoboam, Solomon's son and successor (circa 993 BC). Shishak captured the fortified cities of Judah and entered into Jerusalem, carting away as booties the temple treasures and other valuables. However, Jehovah prevailed, and through the counsel of the prophet Shemaiah, Rehoboam and the princes of Judah humbled themselves and Jerusalem was saved from destruction. Second Chronicles 12:1–12 relates the story.

King Baasha (circa 975–953 BC) of the Northern Kingdom of Israel invaded Jerusalem during the reign of God-fearing and God-loving King Asa of Judah. First Kings 15:16–22 and 2 Chronicles 16:1–6, relates how Baasha waged war against Judah and how King Asa induced the Assyrian king to harass Baasha from the Northern flank, thus giving him (Asa) the leeway to raze Baasha's fortified city of Ramah, which was then undergoing some construction.

We can also recall the invasion of Jerusalem by the Assyrians during the reign of Judean king Hezekiah and how 185,000 Assyrian troops were miraculously and supernaturally annihilated in fulfillment of Jehovah's promise to faithful Hezekiah to "defend this city, to save it, for my own sake, and for my servant David's sake" (2 Kings 19:34).

At the close of King Josiah's reign (circa 659–629 BC), Pharaoh Neco led his Egyptian army northward in support of the Assyrians. Josiah's attempt to turn the Egyptian forces back at Megiddo resulted in a mortal injury and his death (629 BC). All Judah and Jerusalem mourned Josiah's death as narrated in 2 Chronicles 35:20–25 and 2 Kings 23:29–30. In spite of Josiah's faithfulness and undiluted love for Jehovah, the Lord went on to pronounce His rejection of Judah and Jerusalem because of the idolatry and wickedness of King Manasseh.

> Nevertheless, the LORD did not turn away from the heat of his fierce anger, which burned against Judah because of all that Manasseh had done to arouse his anger. So the LORD said, "I will remove Judah also from my presence as I removed Israel, and I will reject Jerusalem, the city I chose, and this temple, about which I said, "My Name shall be there."
>
> —2 KINGS 23:26–27, NIV

The socioeconomic and political situation in God-rejected Judah deteriorated sharply after the demise of faithful Josiah. Four apostate kings followed each other in quick succession culminating in the oppressive reign of King Jehoiakim (circa 628–618 BC or circa 608–598 BC cited by some scholars). Under Jehoiakim Judah became a vassal to Babylon. His revolt against Babylon's suzerainty provoked a successful Babylonian siege and occupation of Jerusalem as well as the pillaging of the city's treasures.

At the age of eighteen, Jehoiachin succeeded his father Jehoiakim and ruled for just three months. He surrendered to the superior military might of the Babylonian king, Nebuchadnezzar. King Jehoiachin, his mother, his wives, his officials, the leading men of Judah, a seven thousand force of fighting men, and a thousand craftsmen and artisans were deported to Babylon (2 Kings 24:1–16; 2 Chron. 36:5–10).

As narrated earlier in chapter 1, "Israel in World History," Babylonian king Nebuchadnezzar appointed Zedekiah, Jehoiachin's uncle, king over Judah, and he became a loyal vassal of Babylon (circa 618 BC). Zedekiah's elevation fulfils prophet Jeremiah's prophecy that Jehoiakim would have no heir to the throne of David in Jerusalem: "Therefore this is what the LORD says about Jehoiakim king of Judah: He will have no one to sit on the throne of David" (Jer. 36:30, NIV).

Zedekiah's attempt to shed off the Babylonian overlordship and tax burdens led ultimately to an eighteen-month siege of Jerusalem and the destruction and desolation of the city in 607 BC (some scholars cite 586 BC) under the command and direction of Nebuchadnezzar's army chief, Nebuzaradan. Zedekiah and virtually all of Jerusalem were taken captive and exiled to Babylon. This was the beginning of the seventy years of desolation prophesied by Jeremiah (circa 625–586 BC), as pointed out earlier in chapter 1: "This whole country will become a desolate wasteland, and these nations will serve the king of Babylon seventy years" (Jer. 25:11, NIV).

Precisely seventy years after the Babylonian exile (circa 607–537 BC), Cyrus the Great, king of Persia, issued a decree freeing the exiled Jews and giving them permission to return to Jerusalem. In about 520 BC Cyrus' successor, Darius Hystaspis, gave permission to the Jews to rebuild the temple of Jerusalem (Ezra 1:1–4; 4:4–5, 24). In about 515 BC, the rebuilding of the temple was completed under the leadership of Zerubbabel, the first governor of the repatriated Jews, who had in about 537 BC led a Jewish remnant back to Jerusalem and Judah. Zerubbabel was the one Jehovah had promised He would make His "signet ring" through the prophet Haggai:

> The word of the LORD came to Haggai a second time.... "Tell Zerubbabel governor of Judah that I am going to shake the heavens and the earth. I will overturn royal thrones and shatter the power of the foreign kingdoms.... And I will make you like my signet ring."
> —HAGGAI 2:20–23, NIV

Following the successful completion of the temple, more exiles returned to Jerusalem with the priest scribe Ezra in about 468 BC, bringing with them additional treasures to beautify the temple of Jehovah in Jerusalem. The Ezra-led return of the exiles was carried out with the cooperation of King Artaxerxes Longimanus (Ezra 7:1–28).

The tortuous history of disintegrated Israel and Judah, with the attendant diasporas, continued after the Babylonian desolation, exile, and return from exile through the successive domination and overlordship of the Ptolemies of Egypt (circa 336–166 BC), the Seleucids of Syria, the Hasmoneans (Maccabeans), and the Romans, under whom Jerusalem was once again destroyed in AD 70, as our Lord and Savior, Christ Jesus, foretold.

It ought to be apparent to all discerning sons and daughters of God that His election of Israel represents hope for mankind. God chose to demonstrate historically and authentically through Israel how much He loves them and expects their obedience, as well as the submission of all His created humans. Israel forms God's resting place on earth, and deservingly so as He has not abandoned the earth or His created humans; for He "so loved the world that He gave His only begotten Son, that whoever believes in Him should not perish but have everlasting life (John 3:16, NKJV). We are all chosen people in Christ Jesus.

> From one man he made all the nations, that they should inhabit the whole earth; and he marked out their appointed times in history and the boundaries of their lands. God did so they would seek him and perhaps reach out for him and find him, though he is not far from any one of us.
> —ACTS 17:26–27

Clearly, Israel, where God chose to spring forth the "root of Jesse [Jesus Christ], which shall stand for an ensign of the people; to it shall the Gentiles [nations] seek: and his rest shall be glorious" (Isa. 11:10) is central to the redemption and salvation of nations. Jerusalem will be the epicenter, the earthshaking point of the second to the final battle of nations—the war of the great day of almighty God (Armageddon).

Indeed, Jerusalem is amply presented in the inspired words of God as a pivotal point in the final battles between the forces of good and evil, as represented by Jehovah God, Christ our Savior, and the angelic hosts of heaven with faithful earthly servants; and Satan and his fallen demonic spirits and their earthly followers. In his summation of the epicentral place of Jerusalem in God's redemption plan for mankind, Pastor John Hagee reminds us that "in the eternal counsel of Almighty God, He has determined to make Jerusalem the decisive issue by which He will deal with the nations of the earth."[1]

Let's examine some of these biblical revelations of the imperative of Jerusalem in Jehovah's redemption and salvation plan for mankind and the nations of the earth.

THE HOLY CITY, GOD'S CHOSEN CITY

Jerusalem is of great significance in the secular and spiritual history of the human race. The secular and biblical history of Jerusalem epitomizes the ravaging secular and spiritual history of mankind. Why so? It is because it is the city where Jehovah chose to engrave His holy name—His omnipresent, omnipotent, and omniscient nature, though He is never far from all nations and people. Jerusalem is the city where God chose to show His glory to all nations. In tearing the united kingdom of Israel into two—the ten Northern tribes of Israel with Samaria as its capital and the two Southern tribes of Judah with Jerusalem as capital—Jehovah, through the prophet Ahijah, spoke as thus about Jerusalem: "I will give one tribe to his son so that David my servant may always have a lamp before me in Jerusalem, the city where I chose to put my Name" (1 Kings 11:36, NIV).

As narrated in Genesis 14:18, Jerusalem, which in Hebrew means the "foundation or possession of a twofold peace," was originally known as Salem. Salem was an ancient city where Melchizedek was king and priest of the Most High God. The word *salem* has been incorporated in the name Jerusalem and is referred to in Psalm 76:1–2 as Zion: "In Judah God is known; His name is great in Israel. In Salem also is His taber-nacle, And His dwelling place in Zion." In Hebrews 7:2 Paul the Apostle states that Melchizedek king of Salem means "king of peace."

First century Jewish historian Flavius Josephus relates that the first person to build Jerusalem was Melchizedek:

> But he who first built it (Jerusalem) was a prudent man among the Canaanites, and is in our own tongue called (Melchezedek), the righteous king for such he really was on which account he was (there) the first priest of God, and first built a temple (there) and called the city Jerusalem which was Salem.[2]

Regarding the origin of Jerusalem, Josephus also narrates,

> It was David therefore who first cast the Jebusites out of Jerusalem and called it by his own name, the city of David. For under our forefather Abraham, it was called (Salem) or Solyma, but after that time, some say that Homer mentioned it by name of Solyma (for he named the temple Solyma) according to the Hebrew language which denoted security.[3]

Jerusalem is thus referred to as the "secured" city, the city of peace. The prophet Isaiah described Jerusalem as the city of Jehovah: "all who despise you will bow down at your feet and will call you the city of the LORD, Zion of the Holy One of Israel" (Isa. 60:14, NIV).

Before the dedication of the temple of Jerusalem and after the placement of the ark of the Lord's covenant to its place in the inner sanctuary of the temple's Holy of Holies (Hebrew, *qodesh ha-qadashim*) beneath the wings of the cherubim, Solomon reminded the children of Israel of God's choice of Jerusalem as His city.

> Since the day I brought my people out of Egypt, I have not chosen a city in any tribe of Israel to have a temple built so that my Name might be there.... But now I have chosen Jerusalem for my Name to be there.
>
> —2 CHRONICLES 6:5–6, NIV

After the consecration of the temple, Jehovah appeared to King Solomon at night and affirmed His choice of the temple of Jerusalem: "I have chosen and consecrated this temple so that my Name may be there forever" (2 Chron. 7:16, NIV).

Jesus Christ described Jerusalem as the city of the great King, Jehovah, the almighty God: "But I say to you, do not swear at all: neither by heaven, for it is God's throne; nor by the earth, for it is His footstool; nor by Jerusalem, for it is the city of the great King" (Matt. 5:34, NKJV).

The psalmist referred to Jerusalem as the city of the great King where God dwells, the city of the Lord Almighty (Ps. 48:2, 8).

From the narrative in Nehemiah 11:1, we learn that the leading men of Israel settled in Jerusalem and had to cast lots among the rest of the people, one out of every ten of them so as to bring them to live in Jerusalem, the Holy City.

The status of Jerusalem as the Holy City is further confirmed in Isaiah 52:1, through the divinely inspired words of the prophet: "Awake, awake, Zion, clothe yourself with strength! Put on your garments of splendor, Jerusalem, the holy city" (Isa. 52:1, NIV). The status of Jerusalem as the Holy City is in fact recognized by peoples of different religious beliefs and persuasions from all over the world including Arabs who refer to the city as *el quds*—the Holy City.

Jerusalem also epitomizes the turbulent and ravaging history of mankind because it has from one generation to another been the object of conquests by war generals and dominant world powers as well as ambitious political and religious leaders. Jerusalem is the city of war and peace.

In his enthralling and masterfully written book, *Jerusalem*, Simon Sebag Montefiore asserts that the history of Jerusalem is the history of the world and that the fact that Jerusalem was once regarded as the center of the world is in our present day truer than ever. He points out that "the city is the focus of the struggle between the Abrahamic religions, the Shrine for increasingly popular Christian, Jewish and Islamic fundamentalism, the strategic battlefield of clashing civilizations."[4]

According to Montefiore, as "the meeting place of God and man," Jerusalem is where man seeks "a greater force than himself to find answers to the fragile joys and perpetual anxieties that mystify and frighten humanity." Jerusalem "is where these questions are settled at the Apocalypse—the end of days when there will be war, a battle between Christ and Antichrist, when the Kaaba will come from Mecca to Jerusalem, where there will be Judgment, resurrection of the dead and the reign of the Messiah, and the kingdom of Heaven, the New Jerusalem."[5]

While in every nation of the world men who genuinely seek God find Him and, as a result, also make their nations meeting places between them and God, Jerusalem does have a unique place in God's eternal plan for nations and this appears to be the crux of Montefiore's statement.

Indeed, Jerusalem is a city of war. The unending struggle for Jerusalem, the savage warfare, egregious disorders, sieges, catastrophic and terrorist wars that was and are still associated with it makes the city a city of war. Jerusalem is as much a city of peace. That the city had also known and seen peace in ages past and will become the future center of world peace, when God makes wars to cease throughout the ends of the earth and when nations will beat their swords into plowshares and their spears into pruning hooks (Ps. 46:9; Isa. 2:4), makes Jerusalem the city of peace.

Let us now take a fairly detailed look at Jerusalem, the city of wars and conquests.

JERUSALEM: CITY OF WARS AND CONQUESTS

> Now the glory of God of Israel went up from above the cherubim, where it had been, and moved to the threshold of the temple. Then the LORD called to the man clothed in linen who had the writing kit at his side and said to him, "Go throughout the city of Jerusalem and put a mark on the foreheads of those who grieve and lament over all the detestable things that are done in it."...Then he said to them, "Defile the temple and fill the courts with the slain. Go!" So they went out and began killing throughout the city.
>
> —EZEKIEL 9:3–4, 7, NIV

The removal of the appearance of the divine glory from over the cherubim signifies God's departure from the house of Israel and Judah, leaving their house desolate with a pronouncement of war over Jerusalem. This was fulfilled in the death of multitudes by famine and pestilence especially by swords of the Chaldeans and in the last destruction of Jerusalem by the Romans in AD 70 (prophesied by Jesus Christ), as in several wars fought over the city.

Those who remained faithful through their works of grace are recognized by God with a symbolic mark upon their foreheads and usually escape God's wrath, as in the last destruction of Jerusalem when the Christians were all secured in a city called Pella and did not perish with the unbelieving Jews because they believed in Christ, the Messiah, and heeded His warning (Luke 21:20–24).

As a city disowned by God, Jerusalem became a city of war knowing no peace and was conquered and reconquered over twenty-seven times in all her history. It is thus the most conquered city on earth.

Let's once again recall the attack on Jerusalem by Shishak, the Egyptian king, about 910 BC and how he carried away the treasures of the temple of the Lord and those of the royal palace (1 Kings 14:25–26). There was an attempted attack on Jerusalem by Hazael, king of Aram, during the reign of Judean king Joash (circa 835–796 BC) as narrated in 2 Kings 12:17.

Sometime in 826 BC, Jehoash, also known as Joash, king of Israel, attacked Judah, destroyed the walls of Jerusalem, captured the Judean king Amaziah at Bethshemesh, plundered the temple treasures, and carried them to Samaria (2 Kings 14:13–16).

In about 701 BC (some scholars cite 711 BC), Sennacherib, king of Assyria (circa 704–681 BC), attacked all the fortified cities of Judah, capturing them. As a result of this invasion, King Hezekiah of Judah was forced to surrender all the silver in the temple of Jerusalem and gold of the temple door as tributes to the Assyrian king to save Jerusalem from destruction. Sennacherib's insistence to conquer Jerusalem despite the tribute he received from Hezekiah failed dismally as a result of God's intervention (2 Kings 18:15–16; 19:35–37).

From about 607 BC the Babylonian invasion of Jerusalem began with the rise of Nebuchadnezzar as king of Babylon. During his forty-three-year rule (circa 624–582 BC), Nebuchadnezzar thrice conquered Jerusalem. His invasion of 586 BC left in its wake a massive destruction of Jerusalem and the temple (2 Kings 25:2–7). Nebuchadnezzar's final invasion of Jerusalem took place in about 582 BC with virtually no resistance and the resultant exile of an additional 745 Jewish elites to Babylon. Indeed, the traditional date for the destruction of the temple of Solomon in Jerusalem is the 9th of Ab, August 16, 586 BC.

> On the seventh day of the fifth month, in the nineteenth year of Nebuchadnezzar king of Babylon, Nebuzaradan commander of the imperial guard, an official of the king of Babylon, came to Jerusalem. He set fire to the temple of the LORD, the royal palace and all the houses of Jerusalem.…Nebuzaradan the commander of the guard carried into exile the people who remained in the city.
> —2 KINGS 25:8, 11, NIV

The prophet Jeremiah provides further detail of the number of Jewish exiles:

> So Judah went into captivity away from her land. This is the number of the people Nebuchadnezzar carried into exile: in the seventh year, 3,023 Jews; in Nebuchadnezzar's eighteenth year, 832 people from Jerusalem; in his twenty-third year, 745 Jews taken into exile

by Nebuzaradan the commander of the imperial guard, there were 4,600 people in all.

—JEREMIAH 52:27–29, NIV

Let's briefly digress and recall that the Northern Kingdom of Israel with Samaria as its capital ceased to exist under Jewish kingship after the last king, Hoshea (circa 758–740 BC), a contemporary of Ahaz, king of Judah. In about 737 BC, Shalmaneser V, king of Assyria, began his three-year siege on Hoshea's Samaria following the latter's renunciation of his vassal status to Assyria and political romance with the Egyptian king named So. Finally in the nineth year of Hoshea, Shalmaneser captured Samaria and deported the Israelites to Assyria settling them in Halah, in Gozan on the Habor River, and in the towns of the Medes (2 Kings 17:1–6).

It should be pointed out that apart from the 4,600 exiles recorded by Jeremiah, a batch of 10,000 Jews, made up of officers and fighting men, craftsmen, and artisans, as well as King Zedekiah, his mother, wives, his officials, and leading men of Jerusalem, were carried into captivity as narrated in 2 Kings 24:14–15.

Alexander the Great, son of Phillip II of Macedonia (circa 356 BC), made his incursion in Jerusalem in 332 BC. According to the Jewish historian Flavius Josephus, Alexander was shown the Book of Daniel's prophecy, perhaps the eighth chapter, where a mighty Greek king would subdue and conquer the Persian Empire for which he spared Jerusalem from plunder and destruction.

> And when the book of Daniel was shown him wherein Daniel declared that one of the Greeks should destroy the Empire of the Persians, he supposed himself was the person intended. And as he was then glad, he dismissed the multitude for the present, but the next day, he called them to him and directed them to ask what favors they pleased of him.[6]

Daniel's fulfilled prophecy states,

> In the third year of King Belshazzar's reign, I, Daniel had a vision....I looked up, and there before me was a ram with two horns....I watched the ram as it charged towards the west and the north and south. No animal could stand against him, and none could rescue from his power....As I was thinking about this, suddenly a goat with a prominent horn between his eyes came from

the west, crossing the whole earth without touching the ground.... I
saw him attack the ram furiously, striking the ram and shattering
his two horns. The ram was powerless to stand against it; the goat
knocked it to the ground and trampled on it, and none could rescue
the ram from its power. The goat became very great, but at the
height of its power, its large horn was broken off, and its place four
prominent horns grew up toward the four winds of heaven.... The
two-horned ram that you saw represents the kings of Media and
Persia. The shaggy goat is the king of Greece, and the large horn
between his eyes is the first king. The four horns that replaced the
one that was broken off represent four kingdoms that will emerge
from his nation but will not have the same power.

—DANIEL 8:1, 3–5, 7–8, 20–22, NIV

Let us be reminded that Daniel's prophecy reemphasizes the commanding presence and direction of Jehovah God in the affairs of nations
and the importance of fulfilled and yet to be unfulfilled prophecies in the
continued march of human history as well as the need to be concerned
and well-informed about Bible prophecies.

In the spring of 334 BC, Alexander won his first battle against the great
Persian king Darius III at the Granicus River in the northwest corner of
Asia Minor (now Turkey), completely defeating Darius' army of about
half a million men with thirty thousand foot soldiers and five thousand
calvary men.

As God's prophet Daniel foretold, Alexander's vast kingdom broke up
into four after his demise at the age of thirty-two on June 13, 323 BC.
By the year 301 BC, four of Alexander's generals established themselves
in power over the empire he left behind. Indeed, "four horns" replaced
the "one broken horn." From Alexander's vast empire rose four Grecian
or Hellenistic kingdoms. General Lysimachus took possession of Asia
Minor and Thrace. General Cassander took charge of Macedonia and
Greece. Seleucus I Nicator was given the control of Mesopotamia and
Syria, while Ptolemy Lagus, Ptolemy I, ruled Egypt and Palestine.

Daniel also foretold that none of Alexander's four broken empires
would be inherited by his descendants (Dan. 11:4). Accordingly, within
fourteen years after Alexander's sudden death, his legitimate son
Alexander IV and his illegitimate son Heracles were assassinated.

In about 168 BC, the Seleucid king Antiochus IV Epiphanes (circa
175–164 BC) passed through Jerusalem on his way to Syria after a successful battle against Ptolemy VI at Pelusium. He invaded and plundered

Jerusalem with the help of Meneleus, also known as Onias, of the priesthood in Jerusalem. Antiochus also defiled the Jerusalem temple by entering the Holy of Holies (*qodesh ha-qadashim*). In 167 BC he established a Seleucid garrison in Jerusalem after the destruction of the city's fortification. Towards the end of 167 BC, the Seleucids introduced religious reforms which included the construction of a pagan altar in the temple.

Flavius Josephus gave the following account of Antiochus' atrocities:

> King Antiochus returning out of Egypt for fear of the Romans made an expedition against Jerusalem.... And the king came to Jerusalem and pretending peace, he got possession of the city by treachery.... He left the temple bare and took away the golden candlesticks, and the golden altar (of incense) and the table (of shew bread), and the altar (of burnt offering). He also emptied it of its secret treasures and left nothing at all remaining; and by this means cast the Jews into great lamentation for he forbade them to offer those daily sacrifices which they used to offer to God, according to law.... And when the king had built an idol altar upon God's altar he killed swine upon it and so offered a sacrifice neither according to law, nor the Jewish religious worship in that country. He also compelled them to forsake the worship which they paid their own God, and to adore those whom he took to be gods, and make them build temples and raised idol altars in every city and village and offer swine upon them every day. He also commanded them not to circumcise their sons and threatened to punish any that should be found to have transgressed his injunction.... They also strangled those women and their sons whom they had circumcised, as the king had appointed, hanging their sons about the necks as they were upon the crosses. And if there were any sacred book of the law found, it was destroyed, and those with whom they were found miserably perished also.[7]

Simon Montefiore also paints the following picture of Antiochus' cruelty:

> Antiochus forbade any sacrifices or services in the temple, banned the Sabbath, the law and circumcision on pain of death and ordered the temple to be soiled with pig's flesh. On 6 December, the temple was consecrated as a shrine to the state god Olympian Zeus, the very abomination of desolation. A sacrifice was made to Antiochus, the god king, probably in his presence at the altar outside the Holy

of Holies. The temple was filled with riot and reveling by Gentiles who dallied with harlots, fornicating in the holy places. Menelaos acquiesced in this, people processed through the temple wearing ivy crowns and offer prayers. Even many of the priests descended to watch naked games at the gymnasium.

Those practicing the Sabbath were burned alive or suffered a gruesome Greek import, crucifixion. An old man perished rather than eat pork; women who circumcised their children were thrown with their babies off the walls of Jerusalem. The Torah was torn to shreds and burned publicly. Everyone found with a copy was put to death. Yet the Torah like the temple was worth more than life. These deaths created a new cult of martyrdom and stimulated expectation of the Apocalypse. Many of them that sleep in the dust of the earth shall awake and come to everlasting life in Jerusalem. Evil would fail and goodness triumph with the arrival of a Messiah—and a son of man invested with eternal glory.[8]

Antiochus V Eupator continued with Seleucid domination and over-lordship of Jerusalem. In 162 BC he and his ally, Lysias, scored a temporary victory over rebelling Jewish Zealot Judas Maccabeus. Antiochus Eupator killed Maccabeus' younger brother Eleazar and gained access to the Temple Mount. Judas Maccabeus led a successful Jewish revolt against the Seleucids between 165 and 160 BC, when he was killed in a battle near Elasa against a Seleucid army led by Bacchides, Demetrius Soter's army general.

Judas Maccabeus' two brothers Simon and Jonathan carried his body back to Modein where they buried him in the family tomb of Mattathias, credited with being the spurrer of Jewish opposition to Greek efforts to force Jews in Judea and Jerusalem to accept Hellenistic religious and civic practices.

Indeed, the story of the Maccabean revolt against Antiochus IV Epiphanes started with Mattathias in Modein, northwest of Jerusalem, where he was a civil leader and served also as a priest. An envoy from Antiochus IV Epiphanes ordered Mattathias to offer a sacrifice in the imported tradition of the Greeks. To Mattathias not only would this have been a grave betrayal to Jehovah God but it would have also constituted a direct affront to the centrality of the temple in Jerusalem, which after the reform of Josiah became the only place sacrifice could officially be conducted.

When Mattathias bluntly refused to obey, another Jew hasted forward to perform the ritual, but he was killed along with Antiochus Epiphanes' envoy before any sacrifice could be performed. Mattathias tore down the altar and issued a clarion call for all faithful Jews in Modein to support him. He then led them into the wilderness (the Gophna Hills) to find refuge in anticipation of retaliatory action from King Antiochus Epiphanes. Mattathias was accompanied by his five sons—John, Simon, Judas, Eleazar, and Jonathan. Judas, who was labeled the "Maccabee," a term meaning "hammer," perhaps because of his power, became the most famous of the lot and the label "Maccabee" eventually came to be applied to the entire Maccabeus family.

Simon and Jonathan continued with the revolt after the demise of their brother Judas Maccabeus, who held sway between 166 BC and 160 BC. His father, Mattathias, controlled the struggle from 167 BC to 166 BC, when he died. Jonathan led the Maccabean army against Demetrius II Nicator's Seleucid army at Cadasa (Kedesh) in upper Galilee in 144 BC and then at Hamath in Coele-Syria (Lebanon) in 143 BC. On both occasions the Jewish Maccabean force won decisively.

In about 67 BC Aristobulus besieged Jerusalem and substituted pig for sheep sacrifice in an attempt to end Jewish temple worship of Yahweh. This was successfully resisted by the Jews on the 17th of Tammuz (the fourth Jewish month of the sacred calendar, the 10th of the secular calendar (October).

In 63 BC the Roman general and emperor Pompey conquered Jerusalem. Internal sectarian dissension had grown in Jerusalem which factionalized Judea and drove the Maccabean (Hasmonean) kingdom into civil war. Acrimony between the two contenders to the throne, John Hyrcanus II who had the backing of the Pharisee party and Aristobulus II who was supported by the Sadducee party, had reached its zenith when Pompey forced a truce between the two factions. Aristobulus II eventually surrendered his force to Pompey who then advanced his army towards Jerusalem along the way capturing Jericho. When he arrived in Jerusalem, loyalists of John Hyrcanus II opened the gates of the upper city to Pompey. But those loyal to Aristobulus II took refuge on the Temple Mount. The Romans built a ramp and went on to destroy the walls and towers that separated the temple area from the city proper. The assault was successful and an estimated twelve thousand Jews died in the aftermath. In the same year, 63 BC, Pompey reinstalled John Hyrcanus II as ethnarch (prince) and high priest and used him as a Roman client king to administer Judea. He served from 63 to 40 BC when he was executed by Herod the Great after the latter's instatement by Marcus Antonius

(Anthony) as king of Judea. The year 63 BC marked the end of the Maccabean (Hasmonean) dynastic rulership of the state of Judea which began in 167 BC.

Following the annexation of Judea and its formation as a Roman province in AD 6, Roman procurators were appointed to administer the province. Pontius Pilate, who dealt with Jesus, was one such procurator and he governed the province from about AD 28 to AD 37.

In AD 70 Titus the Roman general conquered Jerusalem in response to the first Jewish revolt against Roman policies, such as the increased Romanization of Judea and the worship of Roma and Augustus. The Roman Emperor Vespasian left his son Titus in charge of the Jewish war. From February in AD 70, Titus besieged Jerusalem as the Lord Jesus foretold, and in August of the same year the city capitulated. Jerusalem was razed to the ground. Most of the city's dwellers were deported to be killed as games in the arenas as part of the triumphal celebrations associated with Roman victory. The temple's sacred symbols, the great Menorah and the sacred books, were carted away. Over two hundred twenty-two Jews and others died as a result of the war.

In the latter part of AD 73, the last stronghold of Jewish resistance and revolt, Masada, was conquered under the command of Flavius Silva. Masada became famous as a symbol of Jewish resistance where about one thousand Jews held out against Roman infantry; many committed suicide rather than be taken prisoner by the Romans.

In AD 130 the Roman emperor Aelius Hadrian visited Jerusalem and started the construction of a city to replace the one destroyed in AD 70, which included the construction of a Roman temple to Jupiter. The city was named Aelia Capitolina. In AD 132 Hadrian outlawed circumcision, which led to widespread resentment among the Jews and the rise of a Jewish national leader, Simon Bar Kochba, who received popular support of the Jews and led guerrilla warfare against the Romans. For three years Simon Bar Kochba and his men controlled the rural areas of south of Jerusalem and the agricultural land on which the city of Jerusalem was dependent. This caused considerable problems for the Roman governor of the province of Judea, Tinius Rufus, who called for reinforcements to deal with the rebellion. Emperor Hadrian responded by sending some of his best generals to deal with the Bar Kochba-led rebellion. Among them were the governors of Arabia, Britain, and Syria.

By the end of AD 135, the numerous guerilla bands of Simon Bar Kochba's army had been all but destroyed and a final siege by the Romans took place at Bethar. Bar Kochba and his mutineers refused to give up their arms but chose to die of disease and lack of water. When the siege was finally put under complete control, Simon Bar Kochba's corpse was found among the deceased and his head was severed from his body and taken to Emperor Hadrian. Hadrian then proceeded to deal ruthlessly with Judaism and Judean nationalism. He forbade the teaching of the Mosaic Law and renamed the province of Judea as Syria Palestina. Simon Montefiore provides the following narrative of Hadrian's new city, Aelia Capitolina:

> Now in Jerusalem, on the wreckage of the Jewish city, he planned a classic Roman town built around the worship of Roman, Greek and Egyptian gods. A splendid three gated entrance, the Neapolis (today's Damascus Gate), built with Herodian stones opened into a circular space, decorated with a column, whence the two main streets, the cardines-axis led down to two forms, one close to the demolished Antonia fortress and another South of today's Holy Sepulchre. There Hadrian built his temple of Jupiter with a statute of Aphrodite outside it, on the very rock where Jesus had been crucified, possibly, a deliberate decision to deny the Shrine of Jewish Christians. Worse, Hadrian planned a shrine on the temple Mount, marked by a grandiose equestrian statute of himself. Hadrian was deliberately eradicating Jerusalem's Jewishness.[9]

Montefiore also present the following picture of the aftermath of Hadrian's onslaught on Simon Bar Kochba and the fate of Judea, citing Cassius Dio, a Roman writer and historian:

> Fifty of their outpost and 985 villages were razed to the ground. 585,000 were killed in battles and many more by starvation, disease and fire. Seventy five known Jewish settlements simply vanished. So many Jews were enslaved that at Hebron slave market, they fetched less than a horse. Jews continued to live in the countryside but Judea itself never recovered from Hadrian's ravages. Hadrian not only enforced the ban on circumcision but banned the Jews from approaching Aelia on pain of death. Jerusalem had vanished. Hadrian wiped Judea off the map, deliberately renaming it Palestina after the Jew's ancient enemies, the Philistines.[10]

In AD 614 about twenty thousand Jews from Antioch and Tiberias joined the Persian commander Shahrbaraz (the Royal Boar) to invade

Jerusalem. The Jews gave their support to the Persians in protest against Byzantine persecutions.

Some twenty-three years later, in about AD 637, the Muslims conquered Jerusalem. The triumphant Muslim leader and commander, Caliph Omar Ibn el-Khattab, was taken to the Temple Mount and the site of the rock by the Greek intellectual and patriarch of Jerusalem, Sophronius. Caliph Omar Ibn el-Khattab offered Jerusalem a covenant—*dhimma*—of surrender that promised religious tolerance to Christians in return for payment of the "Jizya tax of submission." Sophronius also presented Omar with the keys of Jerusalem, the Holy City.

In AD 1073 Turkomen horsemen led by Atsiz Ibn Awak al-Khwarazmi conquered Jerusalem. They ravaged the city, set fire to heaped corn, chopped down trees, and destroyed the vineyards. They also despoiled the graves and threw out the skeletons. Christian pilgrims to the Holy City were not spared.

In AD 1099 the crusaders (Frankish knights) captured Jerusalem after a long–drawn-out siege and devastating battle against the Fatimid army and disintegrated Turkoman soldiers. The crusaders transformed the Muslim Dome of the Rock into a Christian church (Templum Domini), the Temple of the Lord, and the Al Aqsa mosque into the headquarters of the order of the Knights Templar. We have seen in the earlier chapter of this study that the Crusades were in response to the clarion and celebrated call of Pope Urban II on November 27, 1095, for the conquest of Jerusalem and the liberation of the Church of the Holy Sepulcher.

On October 2, 1187 (AD), Salah al–Din (Saladin) the Muslim warlord, led a multinational army of Arabs, Armeneans, Kurds, Turks, and Sudanese, and captured Jerusalem from the crusaders and converted Templum Domini and Al Aqsa to mosques. The Temple Mount, known to Muslims as Haram al-Sharif, was on Saladin's instructions to be cleansed of the infidel while the cross over the Dome of the Rock was thrown down. The paintings of Jesus Christ were torn into shreds while the cloisters north of the Dome of the Rock were demolished. Muslim dominion was effectively established over the Temple Mount.

Sometime in July 1244 (AD) Tartar horsemen from Manchuria and Mongola led by Barka-Khan overran Jerusalem, and in AD 1258 Mongol hordes from the East, conquerors of one of the world's largest empire, raided Jerusalem.

In AD 1264 Mamluks under Sultan Baibers (Baybers) captured Jerusalem and undertook the repairs of Dome of the Rock and the Temple

Mount. Under the Mamluk Turks unwalled and half-deserted Jerusalem was raided at will by Mongol horsemen. In October 1299 the Christian king of Armenia (Northeast Asia Minor) Hethoum II rode triumphantly into Jerusalem with about ten thousand Mongols sacking the city. The Hethoum-led Mongol occupation was short-lived. As they departed, the Mamluks negotiated their continued suzerainty over Jerusalem.

In AD 1480 bedouins, nomadic Arabs of Syria and Arabia, attacked Jerusalem almost capturing the Mamluk governor who escaped through the Temple Mount and out through the Jaffa Gate. According to some historical accounts, the bedouin attack left Jerusalem desolate.

On the August 24, 1516 (AD), the Ottoman sultan Suleiman (Selim the Grim) destroyed the Mamluk army near the town of Aleppo (Northwest Syria), and in March 20, 1517, Sultan Suleiman made his triumphant entry and took possession of Jerusalem. Jerusalem's Muslim cleric, the Ulema, handed Selim the keys of al-Aqsa and the Dome, at which he prostrated himself and exclaimed, "I am the possessor of the first qiblar."[11] Jerusalem and the Middle East remained under Ottoman rule for 400 years.

In AD 1590 a local Arab rebel invaded Jerusalem and seized the city, killing the Ottoman governor. The rebels were, however, defeated and expelled from the city. Indeed, the peace of Jerusalem was consistently breached by internecine wars and civil unrest against the Ottoman rulers and between contending forces among Ottoman rulers, such as the one that led to the bombardment of the Temple Mount on November 28, 1705, under the rulership of the Husseinis.

In AD 1799 the French emperor Napoleon Bonaparte invaded Palestine and announced to the world that he would restore Jerusalem to the Jewish people. But his defeat at Acre in the Eastern Mediterranean fore-stalled his ambition. As narrated by Simon Montefiore, Napoleon issued a pro-Zionist proclamation to the Jews on April 20, 1799, in the following words:

> Bonaparte, commander–in–chief of the Armies of the French Republic in Africa and Asia, to the rightful heirs of Palestine, the unique nation of the Jews who have been deprived of the land of your fathers by thousands of years of lust for conquest and tyranny. Arise then with gladness ye exiled and take unto yourselves Israel's Patrimony. The young army has made Jerusalem my headquarters and will within a few days transfer to Damascus so you can remain there (in Jerusalem) as ruler.[12]

Sometime around the first quarter of AD 1831, an Albanian warlord who ruled over Egypt, Mehmet Ali, conquered Jerusalem. By late 1831 Ali had vanquished all of the present-day Israel, Syria, and most of Turkey. His son Ibrahim (The Red) was given the charge of Jerusalem. When Ibrahim was at risk of losing the city in 1834, Mehmet Ali rallied round his son and repossessed Jerusalem from revolting fellahin.

In 1917 General Sir Edmund Allenby, a British army commander, invaded Jerusalem and by December 9, 1917, took possession of Jerusalem. British victory effectively ended the 400 years of Ottoman Turks' control of Jerusalem and the Middle East.

Eleven days after the declaration of an independent State of Israel, on May 14, 1948, and May 25, 1948, the Arabs, led by the Jordanians, conquered the Old City of Jerusalem. Jews were forbidden access to the Western Wall of the Temple Mount for the next eighteen years.

However, between the six days of June 1 and June 7, 1967, the Israelis, in what has become a famous in war history known as the Six-Day War, reconquered the Western Wall and the Old City of Jerusalem. A united Arab force of 500,000 men, 5,000 tanks, and 900 war planes were roundly defeated by an Israeli force of 275,000 men, 1,000 tanks, and 200 war planes. The goals of late President Gamal Abdul Nasser of Egypt and late President Aref of Iraq to, in their words respectively, "ensure the destruction of Israel" and to "wipe Israel off the face of the map," failed dismally.

Israel's Sinai Campaign of 1956, the War of Independence of 1948, the Six-Day War of 1967, the Yom Kippur War of 1973, and the invasion of Lebanon in 1982 are all wars fought for the very existence of Israel and for the soul of Jerusalem.

Jerusalem, coveted by nations and various powers—Egyptians, Assyrians, Babylonians, Medo-Persians, Greeks, Romans, Turks, Arabs, Mamluks, Byzantines, crusaders, Christians, Muslims, and adventurous soldiers, religious zealots, and fortune seekers—over which so much of human blood was ceaselessly spilled, became once again the city of the Jewish people. This return to Zion after the dispersal of the Jews to all corners of the world, as the Bible foretold, heralds the second coming of the Messiah, Jesus Christ. Jerusalem remains relevant in the apocalyptic vision.

Jerusalem, the city of war and peace, has a pivotal place in the *a-po-ka'ly-psis*, the unveiling of God's divine truth as set out in the Book of

Revelation, and as well in the Apocalypse, the battle of Armageddon, the war of the great day of God. Let's now examine Jerusalem in the unveiling of God's eternal plan for mankind and her place in the coming final battle between God's forces and Satan's army.

FINIS JENNINGS DAKE'S LISTING OF THE SIEGE AND CONQUESTS OF THE CITY OF JERUSALEM

By the tribe of Judah against the Jebusites about 700 years before the founding of Rome (Judg. 1:8)

By David against the Jebusites (2 Sam. 5:6–10; 1 Chron. 11:4–7)

By Shishak, king of Egypt, against Judah (1 Kings 14:25; 2 Chron. 12)

By the Philistines, Arabians, and Ethiopians against Judah (2 Chron. 21:16–17)

By Israel against Judah (2 Kings 18:13; 19:31)

By Syria and Israel against Judah (1 Chron. 28)

By Assyria against Judah (2 Kings 18:13; 19:37)

By Babylon against Judah (2 Chron. 36:6–7)

By Babylon against Judah (2 Chron. 36:10)

By Babylon against Judah (2 Chron. 36:17–20)

By Egypt against Judah after the captivities, 320 BC

By Scopus, a general of Alexander, about 299 BC

By Syria against Judah after the captivities, 203 BC

By Syria against Judah, 168 BC

By Syria against Judah, 162 BC

By Syria against Judah, 135 BC

By Hyrcanus the priest of Aristobulus, 63 BC

By Pompey against Aristobulus, 63 BC

By Herod with a Roman army who besieged the city in 39 BC

By Titus in AD 70 (Matt. 24:1–4; Luke 19:42–44; 21:20–24)

By the Romans again in AD 135 against the false messiah, 'Bar-Cochebas," who had acquired possession of the ruins. The city was obliterated and renamed Elia Capitolina and a temple of Jupiter was erected.

After 400 years of so-called Christian colonization, Chrosroes the Persian (about AD 559) swept through the country; thousands were massacred and the church of the Holy Sepulchre was destroyed. The Emperor Heraclius afterward defeated him and restored the city to the church.

The Caliph Omar, in AD 636–637, besieged the city against Heraclius. It passed into the hands of the Turks, in whose hands it remained until AD 1917.

Afdal, the Vizier of the Caliph of Egypt, defeated the Muslims in AD 1098 and pillaged the city.

In AD 1099 it was besieged by the army of the first Crusade.

In AD 1187 it was besieged by Saladin for seven weeks.

The wild Tartar hordes in AD 1244 captured and plundered the city, slaughtering the monks and the priests.

It was taken by General Allenby and the British in AD 1917.

Chapter 6

JERUSALEM: EPICENTER OF ARMAGEDDON

THE SECOND TO the final battle over the earth between Jehovah's forces led by the Messiah, Jesus, and His angelic hosts and Satan and his demonic forces followed by human foot soldiers, led by the political leaders of the earth who have turned their backs to the Lamb to make war against Him (Rev. 19:19) will take place in the vicinity of Jerusalem with global resonance. Yes, it is within the proximity of Jerusalem that the Bible Book of Revelation tells us the combined forces of the kings of the earth (presidents, prime ministers, premiers, military dictators, and their commanders) will be gathered for the war of the great day of God Almighty, Armageddon.

> And I saw three unclean spirits, . . . spirits of devils, working miracles, which go forth into the kings of the earth and of the whole world, to gather them to the battle of that great day of God Almighty. . . . And he gathered them together into a place called in the Hebrew tongue Armageddon.
>
> —REVELATION 16:13–14, 16

Armageddon or Megiddo is situated 90 kilometers (56 miles) north of the city of Jerusalem and 31 kilometers (19 miles) southeast of the modern city of Haifa. Megiddo is also a few miles southeast of Mount Carmel and overlooks the Jezreel Valley or the Plain of Esdraelon, also known as the valley or plain of Megiddo (2 Chron. 35:22; Zech. 12:11). Megiddo was strategic for the control of major north-south and east-west trade and military routes. Invading armies or caravans on their way through ancient Israel usually passed through this hill, mount, and valley with its extensive view stretching into tens of miles. Because of its commanding position, Megiddo was the center of many great battles.

One of the earliest battles at Megiddo was carried out under the Egyptian Empire, perhaps some few years before the Jewish Exodus. Pharaoh Thutmose II (circa 1490–1431 BC) launched a succession of campaigns into "Retenue," as the Egyptians called Palestine and Southern Syria. Seventeen campaigns in twenty years carried the Egyptian army as far as the Euphrates and reduced all the intervening city-states to vassals. Thutmose won his greatest victory when he defeated the coalition of forces under the prince of Kadesh at the great battle of Megiddo, referred to by historians as the first Armageddon.[1] Thutmose's records quote him explaining why he annexed Megiddo: "Capturing Megiddo is as good as capturing a thousand cities."[2]

When Napoleon Bonaparte the French general saw the valley of Megiddo, he declared it the world's most perfect battlefield. Kings warred and expired at Megiddo; wars were won and lost there. Indeed, more than thirty major battles have been fought at Megiddo. Jabin's army under the command of Sisera was defeated by Israel led by Barak and Deborah at Megiddo: "by the waters of Megiddo" (Judg. 5:19). King Ahaziah of Judah died at Megiddo as a result of injury sustained on the attacking orders of Jehu (2 Kings 9:27). King Josiah of Judah was killed at Megiddo after a military encounter with Pharaoh Neco (2 Kings 23:29, 30; 2 Chron. 35:22). Gideon overpowered the Midian raiders at Megiddo. In 1918 British general Edmund Allenby charged into the valley of Megiddo from the east with the rising sun to his back and liberated the region from the Turks of the Ottoman Empire. The most recent battle in the vicinity of Megiddo was during the Arab-Israeli war of 1948 when Israeli soldiers defended the land against Syrian and Iraqi forces. Indeed, the valley of Megiddo has been the center of battles involving Arabs, Druges, Egyptians, Persians, Saracens, Turks, and the British, among other nations.

The gathering of nations in Revelation 16:16 will be after the outpouring of the sixth of the seven bowls containing the last plague that will bring to an end God's anger on Satan-led nations whose way to Armageddon has been prepared with the drying up of the Euphrates River (Rev. 16:1, 12). The epicentral position of Jerusalem in the surely coming war of Armageddon is also foretold by the prophet Joel.

> In those days and at that time, when I restore the fortunes of Judah and Jerusalem, I will gather all nations and bring them down to the Valley of Jehoshaphat. There I will enter into judgment with them because of My inheritance, My people Israel. The nations have scattered the Israelites in foreign countries and divided up

my land.... Let the nations be roused and come to the Valley of
Jehoshaphat, for there I will sit down to judge all the surrounding
nations.

—JOEL 3:1–2, 12, HCSB

At the symbolic Valley of Jehoshaphat (Jehovah is judge or Jehovah
judges), the valley of God's judgment, the "valley of decision," Jehovah
judges the nations as deserving of His anger because of the rebellion
of nations against Him and the annihilatory plans against His chosen
ensign to nations—the State of Israel and the Israel of God.

Multitudes, multitudes in the valley of decision! For the Day of the
LORD is near in the valley of decision. The sun and the moon will
grow dark, and the stars will cease their shining. The LORD will roar
from Zion and raise His voice from Jerusalem; heaven and earth
will shake. But the Lord will be a refuge for His people, a stronghold
for the Israelites.

—JOEL 3:14–16, HCSB

Let us recall that during the reign of King Jehoshaphat (circa 873–849
BC or 936 BC as beginning of his reign by some scholars), Jehovah delivered Judah and Jerusalem from the military coalition of Ammon, Moab,
and the mountainous region of Seir, bringing confusion within the rank
and file of the invading forces, resulting in their slaughtering of one
another (2 Chron. 20:1–29).

In their coauthored book *Armageddon, Oil, and Terror*, John Walvoord
and Mark Hitchcock, assert that "it will be in the Middle East that the
future world government will have its center of political and economic
power."[3] According to them, the enigma of how the underdeveloped
Middle East could once again become the center of world history has
suddenly been solved by the world's economic dependence on oil and the
worldwide need to stop Islamic terrorism. In their words:

Already strategic geographically as the hub of three continents,
the Middle East is destined to be the center of a world struggle for
wealth and power so great that it will engulf the entire world in a
gigantic battle centered in the valley of Megiddo—also known as
Armageddon.[4]

The issue of the Temple Mount in Jerusalem also comes to the fore in
the march towards Armageddon. On June 7, 1967, Israeli forces captured

the Old City of East Jerusalem and thus established Israel's sovereign status, not only over Jerusalem but the Temple Mount, although Israel did not demolish the Muslim mosques nor did she rebuild the temple. It is apparent that Israel could not maintain sovereign right over the Temple Mount on Mount Moriah in view of the greater threat from the Arab world and the fact that it was yet to consolidate a sustainable hold on Jerusalem.

Indeed, it is generally agreed that no piece of land in the entire world is as volatile as the piece of land in Jerusalem where the Temple Mount sits. Today the Temple Mount faithful among the Jews are as determined to rebuild Solomon's Temple on the Mount of Moriah as the Muslims and the Palestinians are determined not to negotiate the mount as their holy place even at the risk of a third world war. The leadership of the Palestinian organization Hamas will never give up what they regard as their "exclusive right" to the Temple Mount and their commitment to war should the Islamic shrine on the mount be destroyed.

Also instructive is the fact that a stumbling block to the use of the Temple Mount by both Jews and Muslims is the exclusive nature of Judaism and Islam. For Judaism, the prophecy of Isaiah 2:2–3 gives the Temple Mount to Jews, for ultimately, nations of the world will troop down to the Jerusalem temple to worship the God of Israel.

> In the last days the mountain of the LORD's temple will be established as the highest of the mountains; it will be exalted above the hills, and all nations will stream to it. Many peoples will come and say, "Come, let us go up to the mountain of the LORD, to the temple of the God of Jacob. He will teach us his ways, so that we may walk in his path." The law will go out from Zion, the word of the LORD from Jerusalem.
>
> —ISAIAH 2:2–3, NIV

It is from this "mountain," the Temple Mount in Jerusalem, that Jehovah through His only and Spirit-begotten Son, the Messiah, Jesus, will

> Judge between nations and will settle disputes for many peoples. They will beat their swords into plowshares and their spears into pruning hooks. Nation will not take up sword against nation, nor will they train for war anymore.
>
> —ISAIAH 2:4, NIV

For Muslims, the great day of Allah's judgment will take place before the seat of justice on Jerusalem's Mount Moriah. To Islam, according to Randall Price, the balances, the al-Mizan, the arches and pillars on the Temple Mount, patiently wait for the scales that will measure the deeds of resurrected souls.[5] The Islamic doctrine of the subjugation of the nations of the world to Allah and the Koran as the final revelation of God does not provide any grounds for compromise on the Temple Mount. Herein lays the irreconcilable differences between Islam and Judaism and why the issue of the final control of the Temple Mount will be one of the issues that will lead to a devastating war with global impact. This of course is in addition to other propelling factors such as the economic and military interests of Russia, China, Germany, France, Great Britain, and the United States in the Middle East, and the plans by the enemies of Israel, one of which is Iran to wipe Israel out of the face of the earth.

For keen watchers of global history from secular and biblical perspectives, the physical and spiritual realms, how political leaders will inevitably march their nations to Armageddon is becoming increasingly clearer with each passing day. The bellicosity of Iraq and the nuclear threat to Israel remain clear and present dangers, not only to Israel but to the world. The Israeli-Palestinian daily war of attrition with Hamas continues and Hezbollah is not relenting on its attack on Israel. Iraq is at war with itself with daily terrorist attacks. Yemen is fighting terrorists. The Arab Spring has radically transformed the political landscape in the Middle East bestowing a not too certain future. Islamic fundamentalism and terrorism is spreading like wildfire. Uneasy peace prevails in the Korean Peninsula. North Korea boasts of intercontinental ballistic missiles that can strike mainland USA, a claim America describes as a bluff. South Korea wants to increase the range of her missiles. North Korea's detonation of a nuclear bomb in February of 2013 constitutes a very serious threat to global peace and peace in the Korean Peninsula. The USA, China, Russia, India, Pakistan, France, Germany, Israel, and other less-endowed military nations have stockpiles of nuclear, biological, chemical, and other light and heavy arsenals that are meant for present and future use and will one day be fully engaged. Civil war in Syria threatens the peace in the Middle East and global security.

Today various Islamic fundamentalist and terrorist groups across the world, such as Palestinian Islamic jihad, Egyptian Islamic jihad, Algeria's Armed Islamic Group, Islamic Change Movement of the Arabian Peninsula, Organization of Islamic Revolution, Hamas, Hezbollah,

Al-Qaeda, Taliban, and the world's leading exporter and sponsor of Islamic fundamentalism, the conservative Shiia State of Iran, are determined to sustain their terrorist struggle and war against their alleged dominance of the Judeo-Christian world order. This feeling has creeped into Africa with the spate of suicide bombings by Boko Haram in Nigeria. The peace of Mali is threatened by Islamic militants: Al–Shabaab is still out there in Somalia. Indeed, the future of Jerusalem and of the Temple Mount remains one of the most explosive issues of the Israeli-Palestinian conflict that has global implications. The fact that many world political leaders and the pope's Vatican believe that the internationalization of the city of Jerusalem could serve as the only way to engender a peaceful settlement between Israel and Palestine attests to the world's entanglement in the Israeli–Palestinian crisis. The nonmember observer status granted Palestinians in the United Nations in 2012 is a step towards greater internationalization of the Israeli-Palestinian debacle. It is also predicted that Jerusalem will be the epicenter of Armageddon because it will become the political capital of the king of the North described by scholars as the Antichrist who regards not the God of his fathers (Dan. 11:37). Daniel 11:45 relates that this king from the North who exalts himself "will pitch his royal tents between the seas at the beautiful holy mountain. Yet he will come to his end, and no one will help him" (NIV).

The "seas" referred to here by Daniel is believed to be the Mediterranean Sea and the holy mountain is Zion, Jerusalem, God's spiritual estate. It is from this invasion of Jerusalem in the war of Armageddon that the Lord's anger will "roar from Zion and thunder from Jerusalem" (Joel 3:16, NIV) and oversee the destruction of the kings of the North. Indeed, when the kings of the earth, including the king of the North (Antichrist) attack God's people, they will come all the way to their end.

Finally, it is important to emphasize that the land of Canaan on which sits Jerusalem is eternally holy unto Jehovah. In Deuteronomy 11:11–12, Moses, before his demise, told the children of Israel that Canaan the land they were to possess is "a land of mountains and valleys that drinks rain from heaven. It is a land the LORD your God cares for; the eyes of the LORD your God are continually on it from the beginning of the year to the end" (NIV). It is a land of everlasting possession to the children of Israel under God's watchful eyes (Gen. 17:8), the borders of which were established by Him from "the Red Sea, to the Mediterranean Sea, and from the desert to the Euphrates River" (Exod. 23:31, NIV).

We see in Ezekiel 43:7 that the glory of God which departed from

Israel from the Temple in Jerusalem and brought woes to Jerusalem and the nations, returns to the Temple on the Mount of Olives and Jehovah God, reestablishes Jerusalem as the seat of His earthly throne where He will live among the Israel of God forever.

> He said: "Son of man, this is the place of my throne and the place for the soles of my feet. This is where I will live among Israelites forever. The people of Israel will never again defile my holy name— neither they nor their kings—by their prostitution and the funeral offerings for their kings at their death.
>
> —EZEKIEL 43:7, NIV

Let us now direct our attention to other events that reestablish Jerusalem as God's dwelling place on earth resulting from the return of the glory of God to the temple in Jerusalem under Christ's kingdom rule. This is as a consequence of the invasion of Jerusalem by the kings of the North led by the Antichrist. Jerusalem becomes a heavy stone for the nations attacking it, cutting into pieces all those trying to heave it away. Jerusalem becomes an indestructible city, God's seat of judgment and redemption of the nations.

JERUSALEM: THE IMMOVABLE ROCK, GOD'S SEAT OF JUDGMENT AND REDEMPTION

It is very clear from Bible prophecy that the final attempt by an army of nations led by the Antichrist to annihilate the Jewish people and totally decimate Jerusalem will lead to Jehovah's intervention and the complete defeat of the invading forces. Through the instrument of Israel, Jehovah, to whom all "nations are as a drop of a bucket, and are counted as the small dust of balance... [and] are as nothing; and are counted to him less than nothing and vanity" (Isa. 40:15, 17), will demonstrate His victory over all nations as we read from chapters 12 to 14 of the prophetic Book of Zechariah. The unerring oracle reveals

> the word of the LORD concerning Israel. The LORD, who stretches out the heavens, who lays the foundation of the earth, and who forms the human spirit within a person declares: "I am going to make Jerusalem a cup that sends all the surrounding peoples reeling. Judah will be besieged as well as Jerusalem. On that day, when all the nations of the earth are gathered against her, I will

make Jerusalem an immovable rock for all the nations. All who try
to move it will injure themselves."

—ZECHARIAH 12:1–3, NIV

I will gather all nations to Jerusalem to fight against it.... Then
the LORD will go out and fight against these nations.... On that
day there will be neither sunlight nor cold, frosty darkness. It will
be a unique day—a day known to the LORD—with no distinction
between day and night.... On that day living water will flow out
from Jerusalem... The LORD will be king over the whole earth. On
that day there will be one LORD, and his name the only name.

—ZECHARIAH 14:2–3, 6–9, NIV

Zechariah 14:12–18 also contains the following yet to be fulfilled prophetic warnings to those nations that will ultimately attack Jerusalem for
the absolute destruction of the Jewish people:

This is the plague with which the LORD will strike all the nations
that fought against Jerusalem: Their flesh will rot while they are
still standing on their feet, their eyes will rot in their sockets,
and their tongues will rot in their mouths.... Then the survivors
from all nations that have attacked Jerusalem will go up year after
year to worship the King, the LORD Almighty and to celebrate the
Festival of Tabernacles.... The LORD will bring on them the plague
he inflicts on the nations that do not go up to celebrate the Festival
of Tabernacles.

—ZECHARIAH 14:12, 16, 18, NIV

Through Israel a worldwide faith will be built that will encompass all
nationalities, races, tongues, and tribes under Jehovah's appointed divine
kingship of the King of kings and Lord of lords, the Messiah, Jesus. But
before then, Jerusalem will become the center of a great battle with Christ
leading the hosts of heaven for her eternal restoration and the redemption of nations.

On that day his feet will stand on the Mount of Olives, east of
Jerusalem, and the Mount of Olives will be split in two from east
to west, forming a great valley, with half of the mountain moving
north and half moving south.

—ZECHARIAH 14:4, NIV

The same Jesus that was taken from the Mount of Olives in Jerusalem into heaven will come back in the same way He ascended into heaven as we read from Acts 1:11–12. Yes, the Messiah, Jesus, who was during His first advent oppressed and afflicted and yet opened not His mouth, and as a lamb to the slaughter, and as a sheep before her shearer opened not her mouth, will be back as a roaring and conquering Lion of Judah (Isa. 53:7).

Indeed, the earlier mentioned Feast of Tabernacles, known as the Festival of Booths, the Festival of Ingathering, and the Festival of Jehovah, as we read from Leviticus 23:39–43 is a festival of rejoicing and thanksgiving for all the blessings of God upon the children of Israel. According to Isaiah, "the redeemed of the LORD shall return, and come with singing unto Zion, and everlasting joy shall be upon their head: they shall obtain gladness and joy; and sorrow and mourning shall flee away" (Isa. 51:11).

It was expected that during this festival the Israelites could meditate in their hearts and joyfully reflect upon their God-given prosperity and abundance. As we read from Deuteronomy 16, Jehovah commanded the children of Israel to

> celebrate the Festival of Tabernacles for seven days after you have gathered the produce of your threshing floor and your winepress. Be joyful at your festival—you, your sons and daughters, your men servants and maidservants, and the Levites, the aliens, the fatherless and the widows who live in your towns.
>
> —DEUTERONOMY 16:13, NIV

As we have seen in the earlier quoted passages of Zechariah 14:12–18 and Isaiah 51:11, the nations, kindreds, and peoples that are saved from mankind's corrupt and wicked socioeconomic and political systems by Christ's Messianic kingdom will participate in the yearly Feast of Tabernacles. Zechariah also prophesied that the Feast of Tabernacles, which was a central feature of Jehovah's arrangement for approach to Him by the nation of Israel, will embrace all nations for true worship in His temple in Jerusalem—the tent of meeting for all nations.

The prophet Isaiah foretold that in the last days, when the mountain of the Lord's temple will be established on the top of the mountains and exalted above the hills,

> many people shall go and say, Come ye, and let us go up to the mountain of the LORD, to the house of the God of Jacob; and he will

teach us of his ways, and we will walk in his paths: for out of Zion shall go forth the law, and the word of the Lord from Jerusalem.

—Isaiah 2:3

The kingdom of God that Jesus spent days speaking to His disciples about was His future Messianic kingdom whose center will be the temple in Jerusalem, the Holy City of the future theocratic government of Jehovah's world new order. God will reveal Himself again at the end of days in Jerusalem. His sure promise is revealed by the prophet Zechariah, "I will return to Zion, and dwell in the midst of Jerusalem. Jerusalem shall be called the City of Truth, The Mountain of the Lord of Hosts, The Holy Mountain" (8:3, nkjv).

Jerusalem will indeed be the center of law and the worship of the one true God, Jehovah, during the Millennium and in the eternal ages when Jesus Christ will literally reign from Jerusalem. Then the law and the word shall go out from Jerusalem to the ends of the earth. Micah restates Isaiah's prophecy that in the latter days the law shall go forth out of Zion and the word of the Lord from Jerusalem (Mic. 4:1–2).

According to the prophet Joel from divine inspiration: "The Lord also shall roar out of Zion, and utter His voice from Jerusalem; and the heavens and earth shall shake: but the Lord will be the hope of His people" (Joel 3:16).

Isaiah equally pointed to a time when "Zion [Jerusalem] will be delivered with justice, her penitent ones with righteousness" and that God will restore her judges as in the days of old which will warrant that the city will be called "the City of Righteousness and Faithful City" (Isa. 1:26–27, niv).

As we have read earlier from Ezekiel, the glory of God departed from the temple in Jerusalem (Ezek. 9:3). This departed glory returns to the Temple and Jehovah reestablishes Jerusalem as the seat of His earthly throne where He will dwell among the Israelites and mankind forever (43:7). It is apparent from Ezekiel's vision that during the millennial Messianic reign of Jesus Christ, the altar of sacrifice will be reinstated in the restored temple. It is important to point out that the return of the temple does not replace Christ's once-and-for-all sacrificial atonement for human sins with His blood for universal redemption and salvation for all those who have received Him and exercise faith.

Israel, as Jehovah's "kingdom of priests [*cohanim*]" (Exod. 19:6) and the medium for His eternal blessings to all peoples and nations (Gen. 12:3), will fulfill their unfulfilled mission. They will in the millennial kingdom recognize Jesus as the Messiah and will reestablish the sacrificial ordinances of their everlasting covenant in recognition of God's benevolence, sovereign will, and Christ's salvific redemption.

In God's divine plan to ensure the national repentance, regeneration, and the impartation of spiritual life by His grace and benevolence to the Jewish people as to the Gentiles (the rest of nations), Israel and Gentiles will come to the full knowledge that Jehovah is the Sovereign Lord of the universe—the God above all other gods—and that Jesus is the Messiah. The Bible makes it abundantly clear that there will be a literal rebuilding of the temple in Jerusalem under a new inviolable covenant, which will provide a spiritual regeneration—a rebirth that will prevent the nation of Israel from again violating God's statutes and commandment—and this will extend to other nations.

Thus, once again, Jerusalem becomes the seat of the replica of Jehovah's heavenly sanctuary—the heavenly tabernacle of God. Let's remember that God chose Jerusalem to place the archetype of the heavenly temple where His ark (His earthly temple) was. First was the earthly tabernacle of Moses in the wilderness of Mount Sinai, then the tabernacle of David as well as the Temple of Solomon in Jerusalem approved and sanctified by God Himself (2 Chron. 7:16), then the second temple was rebuilt by Zerubbabel (520–515 BC) with the help of Persian King Darius; these were all material representations of the reality in the heavenly places. Jerusalem housed the shadow on earth of the substance in heaven until God's glory departed from it and now the glory returns with Christ's second coming.

Jesus Christ is "the man" whose name is "the Branch" who will build the temple.

> Tell him this is what the LORD Almighty says: "Here is the man whose name is the Branch, and he will…build the temple of the LORD. It is he who will build the temple of the LORD, and he will be clothed with majesty and will sit and rule on His throne. And he will be a priest on his throne.
>
> —ZECHARIAH 6:12–13, NIV

As Christ sits and rules on His throne, Jerusalem becomes the center of world worship of the one and only true God, Jehovah.

> And they will bring all your people, from all the nations, to my holy mountain in Jerusalem as an offering to the LORD —on horses, in

chariots and wagons, and on mules and camels," says the LORD. "They will bring them, as the Israelites bring their grain offerings, to the temple of the LORD in ceremonially clean vessels.

—ISAIAH 66:20, NIV

Isaiah 66:20 reveals that God, the Creator of the universe, intends to have and enjoy joyful feasts and sacrifices to Him from all nations during the millennial reign of His Spirit-begotten Son, Jesus Christ. We have also seen that the Feast of Tabernacles will be observed by all nations as revealed in Zechariah 14:16–18. The fact that there will be an earthly priesthood under Christ's kingdom rule as well as sacrifices and feasts is amply envisioned in Ezekiel 40:1–48; 43:19–27; 44:5, 30; 45:21–25; and a comparative analysis is given in Leviticus 23:1–44 with its fulfillment as an everlasting covenant in verse 21.

We can also firmly hold on to the conviction that these extrinsic, corporeal ceremonies are meant to satisfy the natural instincts in man for externalities, the outward observances in worship. These physical observances will not supersede the individual means of approach to God through Christ Jesus. Indeed, it should be emphasized that Christ, our Passover, has been sacrificed once and forever for us, for which we can willingly draw close to Jehovah anytime we desire.

Israel, under the millennial dispensation, will fulfill her proselytization mission as a priestly nation among the committee of nations (Exod. 19:5), under Christ's Messianic reign. Again, this is in fulfillment of Jehovah's eternal covenant with Abraham and promise to make his seed a blessing to all nations. Just as we today observe Christian and Muslim pilgrims making yearly pilgrimages to Jerusalem and Mecca, in Christ's millennial reign, Jerusalem and only Jerusalem will become the religious capital of the world—the center of world pilgrimage and worship of the one and only true God, Jehovah, and Jesus Christ, the Savior of the world.

Rebellion from Israel and other nations of the earth are ultimately brought down and Jehovah becomes all in all.

> Then the end will come, when he hands over the kingdom to God the Father after he has destroyed all dominion, authority and power. For he must reign until he has put all enemies under his feet. The last enemy to be destroyed is death. For he "has put everything under his feet." Now when it says that "everything" has been put under him, it is clear that this does not include God himself, who put everything under Christ. When he has done this, then the Son

himself will be made subject to him who put everything under him, so that God may be all in all.

—1 CORINTHIANS 15:24–28, NIV

All of these are for Jehovah to fulfill His purpose for Israel and for all His created obedient humans. The apostle Paul admonished,

I do not want you to be ignorant of this mystery, brothers and sisters, so that you may not be conceited: Israel has experienced a hardening in part until the full number of the Gentiles has come in, and in this way all Israel will be saved. As it is written: "The deliverer will come from Zion; he will turn godlessness away from Jacob. And this is my covenant with them when I take away their sins." As far as the gospel is concerned, they are enemies for your sake; but as far as election is concerned, they are loved on account of the patriarchs, for God's gifts and his call are irrevocable.

—ROMANS 11:25–29, NIV

Ultimately, Israel will fulfill Isaiah 49:6: "I will also make you a light for the Gentiles, that my salvation may reach to the ends of the earth" (NIV).

All believing Christians, outside the Jews, who worship Jehovah in spirit and in truth, have today received the light that Israel, by God's grace, has offered the world through the Jewish Jesus. All other non-believing Gentiles and Jews will ultimately come to the realization of Jehovah's supremacy when those Gentile nations hell-bent on totally destroying Israel and wiping it off the face of the earth will be annihilated in that great day of the Lord—the battle of Armageddon, which will herald Christ's Messianic kingdom and kinship. For Jehovah "has set a day when He will judge the world with justice by the man he has appointed [Jesus Christ]. He has given proof of this to everyone by raising Him from the dead" (Acts 17:31, NIV).

Babylon's imperial ruler Nebuchadnezzar came to the full realization that God's dominion is an everlasting dominion and that His kingdom is from generation to generation. Nebuchadnezzar also proclaimed, when his reason and understanding returned to him, that God "does according to His will in the army of heaven And among the inhabitants of the earth. No one can restrain His hand or say to Him, 'What have you done?'" (Dan. 4:34–35, NKJV).

Jehovah, the Elohim, the God of incomparable glory, asserts His sovereign authority over the kingdoms of the world. He puts an end to mankind's corrupt socioeconomic and political systems and sets up a new expression of His suzerainty over the earth. He gives His Spirit-begotten Son, Jesus Christ, auxiliary control in that kingdom (1 Cor. 15:27–28), so that it is referred to as the "kingdom of our Lord, and of his Christ" (Rev. 11:15). Jesus drew attention to earthly occurrences that would serve as signs of the imminence of this coming kingdom. Let us examine them.

Chapter 7

APPRECIATING CHRIST'S END-TIME WARNING

URING HIS EARTHLY ministry Jesus Christ told His disciples of signs that will gradually but surely lead to the end of the world's turbulent socioeconomic and political systems. This prophetic pronouncement should excite great interest in all students of Bible and secular history, as well as Christians and non-Christians alike.

> And you will hear of wars and rumors of wars. See that you are not troubled; for all these things must come to pass, but the end is not yet. For nation will rise against nation, and kingdom against kingdom. And there will be famines, pestilences, and earthquakes in various places....For there will be great tribulation, such as has not been since the beginning of the world until this time, no nor ever shall be.
>
> —MATTHEW 24:6–7, 21, NKJV

Jesus offered words of comfort to all those exercising faith in Him, pointing out that the predicted global violence and disasters should not come as a surprising or frightening phenomenon. Christ also promised comfortingly that He would be back on earth to intervene, not only to save and redeem Israel and the Israel of God (all those redeemed and exercising faith in Him), but to save mankind from self-annihilation: "If those days had not been cut short no one would survive, but for the sake of the elect, those days will be shortened" (Matt. 24:22, NIV).

Critics who rely too much or solely on their worldly intellect and the transient philosophy of men argue that natural and man-made disasters, wars, famines, and pestilences have always been integral to human experiences and world history. They also contend that the heightened frequency of natural disasters and wars are not signs of an impending end of the world as we know it but a natural "selective" evolutionary process and progression of mankind. These critics painfully miss the biblical truths of the spiritual essence of man's existence and his relationship with God. They appear to dwell either in the realm of the carnal or are misled by the plethora of false teachings associated with sects, cults, religious, and intellectual groups that are abound in the world today. While we must acknowledge that since the dawn of human history or the Adamic fall of man life on earth had always been lived on the edge of a precipice, this reality does not in any way condemn the human race to an eternity of tragic existence—endless circles of wars, disasters, diseases, sicknesses, and deaths.

The kingship of Christ should be understood from the visible and invisible perspectives of human existence. The visible world was created from an invisible heavenly one over which Jehovah, the Creator, presides as sovereign Lord and King. And just as earthly kings confer on their favored and chosen sons the status of heirs to their throne, God has bestowed on His Spirit and only-begotten Son, Jesus Christ, the kingship of His created earthly domain, having been offered out of love as a ransom sacrifice for forgiveness of sins and redemption of humanity. Christ's earthly kingship represents a physical and spiritual manifestation of Jehovah to man. It is the endorsement of a living and practical relationship with Him first through Christ and then a direct relationship with Him when Christ finally hands over the kingdom so that Jehovah will be all and all.

Let us recall that Jesus Christ called Cleopas and another disciple to whom He appeared after His resurrection on the road to Emmaus "fools" for not correlating Old Testament prophecies with events that had occurred to Him: "How foolish you are, and how slow to believe all that the prophets have spoken! Did not the Messiah have to suffer these things and then enter his glory?" (Luke 24:25–26, NIV).

The apostle Peter was led by the Holy Spirit to draw our attention to what men will become during the end times with a warning:

> Knowing this first: that scoffers will come in the last days, walking according to their own lusts, and saying, "Where is the promise of His coming? For since the Fathers fell asleep, all things continue as they were from the beginning of creation." For this they willfully forget: that by the word of God the heavens were of old, and the earth standing out of water and in the water, by which the world that then existed perished, being flooded with water. But

the heavens and earth which are now preserved by the same word, are reserved for fire until the day of judgment and perdition of ungodly men.

—2 Peter 3:3–7, nkjv

Christ, the Savior of the world, also warned that His coming will be sudden, unexpected, and all-pervasive: "For as lightning that comes from the east is visible even in the west, so will be the coming of the Son of Man. Wherever there is a carcass, there the vultures will gather" (Matt. 24:27–28, niv).

Peter teaches that we should understand the prediction of the imminence of Christ's second coming from the divine viewpoint according to thousand years as one day before God (2 Pet. 3:8).

For critics who lampoon and wave off the prophecy of Christ's second coming, this admonition from Jesus Himself calls for deep thought and sober reflection:

For in the days before the flood, people were eating and drinking, marrying and giving in marriage, up to the day Noah entered the ark; and they know nothing about what will happen until the flood came and took them all away. That is how it will be at the coming of the Son of Man.

—Matthew 24:38–39, niv

Indeed, the flood of Noah's day is not a myth. It is an historical fact. Its authenticity was confirmed by Christ Himself who was a witness of the deluge from heaven. The fact of the flood is also confirmed in flood legends from six continents and the islands of the sea. There are flood legends from Australia (Kurnai); Babylon (Gilgamesh epic); Bolivia (Chiriguano); Burma (Singpho); Canada (Montagnais and Crec); China (Lolo); East Africa (Masai); Egypt (Book of the Dead); French Polynesia (Raiatea); Greece (Lucian's account); Guyana (Macushi); Iceland (Eddas); India (Andaman Island, Bhil, and Kamar); Iran (Zend-Avesta); Italy (Ovid's Poetry); Malay Peninsula (Jakun); Mexico (Codex Chimalpopoca and Huichol); New Zealand (Maori); Peru (Indians of Huarochiri); Russia (Vogul); USA, Alaska, (Kolusches and Tlingit); USA, Arizona (Papago); USA, Hawaii (Legend of Nu-u); Vanuatu (Melanesians); Vietnam (Bahnar); and Wales (Dwyfan) legends.

All the aforementioned flood legends relate that at a certain period in human history, the world was destroyed by water. Most of these legends attribute the deluge to divine cause and more than half of them convey that there was a warning before the flood, while all agree that humans and animals were spared and were preserved in a vessel (Noah's ark of the Bible).

Some scholars of Bible and secular history have also made an interesting observation regarding the Chinese character for ship which is derived from the idea of eight persons in a vessel. This, they assert, bears a striking resemblance to the Bible account about Noah and his family; eight survivors of the deluge in an ark: "When once the longsuffering of God waited in the days of Noah, while the ark was a preparing, wherein few, that is, eight souls were saved by water" (1 Pet. 3:20). (See also 2 Peter 2:5, Genesis 7:13.)

Issues relating to signs of the end times, as prophesied by Jesus Christ who also foretold the complete destruction of Jerusalem and the temple, deserve a full study and are treated extensively in my upcoming book *Lucifer's War*. But suffice it to state that more than any other age or generation in human history, mankind lives today in an age of wars and rumors of wars, of nation rising against nation, and of kingdom against kingdom, including all kinds of natural and man-made disasters and human atrocities. Indeed, the capacity of man to self-destruct has attained the highest level of scientific and technological advancement and sophistication. The destructive effect of a twenty-first century global warfare with nuclear, chemical, and biological arsenals of mass destruction will make those of the First and Second World Wars and all other wars in ancient, medieval, and modern times combined pale into insignificance. An unabating culture of mutual fear and suspicion between nations, particularly between the nuclear superpowers, and between religious divides within and across nations, compounded by Islamic fundamentalism and global terrorism, propel the world to a nuclear Armageddon. Analysis of this mutual fear and suspicion has been treated earlier in the preface to this book.

In his letter to Timothy by divine inspiration, the apostle Paul paints a picture of the character of the ungodly man in the last days, which perfectly fits the general attitude of many men today. Man has increasingly become a predatory animal no better than a lion, a tiger, or a leopard; for these and other predators kill for food but man kills out of greed and hatred and for other self-preservatory economic, political, and religious philosophies and carnal reasoning.

But mark this: There will be terrible times in the last days. People will be lovers of themselves, lovers of money, boastful, proud, abusive, disobedient to their parents, ungrateful, unholy, without love, unforgiving, slanderous without self-control, brutal, not lovers of the good, treacherous, rash, conceited, lovers of pleasure rather than lovers of God—having a form of godliness but destroying its power. Have nothing to do with such people.

—2 TIMOTHY 3:1–5, NIV

Throughout the course of world history, nations, leaders, the rich and powerful, and economic and military interests have continued to engage in activities that lead to earth's decay and ruination. Religious, economic, and territorial warfare; rebellions; bad governance; greed; and corruption have continued to lead to expanding desertification and tremendous loss of arable land with its attendant famine and pestilences. Oil spills on land and in oceans, rivers, creeks, and rivulets have destroyed and continue to destroy productive areas of the earth, adversely affecting food sources. Gas flares, acid rains, and radioactive clouds cause collateral damages to vast expanses of human habitation. The contamination of air and water are the causes of various types of communicable and terminal diseases, premature births, and deformities. Industrial and municipal wastes increasingly constitute a health hazard and threat to life on land and in the seas and rivers. Ozone layer depletion, climate change, and the nuclear arms race constitute a clear and present danger to human civilization. But thankfully, Jehovah, the God of Creation, will ultimately destroy the wicked and all those destroying the earth.

The nations were angry and your wrath has come. The time has come for judging the dead, and for rewarding your servants the prophets and your people who revere your name, both great and small—and for destroying those who destroy the earth.

—REVELATION 11:18, NIV

For if God did not spare the angels who sinned, but cast them down to hell and delivered them into chains of darkness, to be reserved for judgment; and did not spare the ancient world, but saved Noah, one of eight people, a preacher of righteousness, bringing in the flood on the world of the ungodly; and turning the cities of Sodom and Gomorrah into ashes, condemned them to destruction, making them an example to those who afterward would live ungodly; and delivered righteous Lot... —if this is so, then the Lord knows how to

deliver the godly out of temptation and to reserve the unjust under
punishment for the day of judgment.

—2 PETER 2:4–9, NKJV

As the earth's political and military leaders prepare themselves for the
day of God's judgment, the great battle against God and His Anointed,
there are as well preparations in heaven to confront this Satan-led earthly
challenge. May we now turn our attention to this heavenly preparation for
the war of the great day of God and the defeat of "Gog" and his armies.

All flesh is as grass, And all the glory of man as the flower of the
grass. The grass withers, And its flower falls away, But the word of
the LORD endures forever.

—1 PETER 1:24–25, NKJV

WAR PREPARATIONS IN HEAVEN

All the earthly manifestations of the end-time foretold by Christ, beginning with the pangs of distress (tribulation) and the spread of the good
news of Christ's kingdom to all nations before the conclusion of the
present socioeconomic and political system as well as the gathering of
the armies of God opposing nations, come with heavenly preparations
as well.

The worthy Lamb who holds the seven stars in His right hand and who
has the seven spirits of God; who walks in the midst of the seven golden
lamp stands; the first and the last; who was dead and came to life; who
has eyes like a flame of fire and feet like fine brass; He who has the key
of David, who opens and no one shuts and shuts and no one opens; the
Amen, the Faithful and True Witness; the beginning of the creation of
God; is the only one worthy to open the scroll sealed with seven seals for
the final judgment of planet Earth. (See Revelation chapters 1–3 and 5.)
He is the only one worthy to take the scroll and to open its seals because
He was slain and with His blood purchased men for God.

Jehovah sits on His heavenly rainbow-encircled and emerald-like
throne in all glory, power, and majesty, and presides over the heavenly
court of the archangels, the living creatures, seraphs, cherubs, the twenty-
four elders, and myriads of angelic princes and messengers of His heavenly realm. Before Him and these heavenly hosts, Jesus Christ is found
worthy to open the scrolls with seven seals through which judgment is
pronounced and brought upon a confused and turbulent world with her
sea of humanity heading towards self-annihilation.

From the opening of the first seal, Christ, the warrior King, the conquering Lion of the tribe of Judah crowned with many diadems, sits on a white horse in power and majesty and begins His conquest as "the blessed and only Potentate, the King of kings, and Lord of lords" (1 Tim. 6:15). He battles against world leaders and nations that have denied and refused His kingship and are bent on exterminating His faithful and chosen ones on earth. Let us quickly recall that in 2 Kings 2:11–12, Jehovah's invisible heavenly war equipment is represented by fiery horses and chariots. The apostle John also saw vision of armies of cavalry numbering two myriads of myriads (two hundred million) empowered to execute the destructive judgment of Jehovah. All these "horses," which were apparently under the command of the four angels that had been bound at the Euphrates River, had death-inflicting power in both their heads and their tails (Rev. 9:15–19). In the symbolic vision of John, the glorified Jesus Christ, the faithful and true, sits on a horse, followed by the armies of heaven in white horses and in righteousness judges and makes war (19:11, 14).

John also relates the calamities that are unleashed on the earth following the opening of more seals as represented by different horsemen and their mounts. The opening of the second seal takes away peace on earth, rains down conflicts and wars. The third seal brings scarcity, famine, and pestilences, death on earth through which a fourth of the earth's population will be exterminated. Cosmic disturbances, massive earthquakes, supernatural planetary disorders followed the opening of the sixth seal which brought the kings of the earth, the great men, the rich men, the commanders, the poor and the lowly to their knees (Rev. 5:6–9; 6:1–17).

As we can see, this is a battle for final control of the earth between God and the anointed Christ and the Satan-led Antichrist army of rebellious nations. John's vision in Revelation 19:19 shows the nature of the coming battle and the belligerents: "And I saw the beast, and the kings of the earth and their armies, gathered together to make war against him that sat on the horse, and against his army."

Let us remember the divinely inspired words of the apostle Paul in his Epistle to the Ephesians:

> We do not wrestle against flesh and blood, but against principalities, against powers, against the rulers of the darkness of this age, against spiritual hosts of wickedness in the heavenly places.
> —Ephesians 6:12, NKJV

Before John's eyes, the vision of heaven opens and Jesus Christ, the one called "faithful and true," is revealed (Rev. 19:11–12). He is accompanied by the armies of heaven to fight against the beast and the kings of the earth (19:14). We should at this point quickly call back to memory that when an armed mob came to arrest Jesus at the garden of Gethsemane on Passover night of AD 33, He told His faithful disciples, who wanted to defend Him, to sheath their swords and asked if they did not know that if He wanted He could pray to Jehovah and His Father would provide Him with more than twelve legions of angels (Matt. 26:53). (See Matthew 26:36–56; Mark 14:32–52; Luke 22:39–53; John 18:1–12.)

Just like the multitude that came with swords and clubs to arrest Jesus at Gethsemane, the world's political, economic, military, religious, and intellectual leaders refuse to acknowledge the Messiah, Jesus, and His kingship and gather to battle Him. They are led by Satan, the prince of the power of the air, the spirit who works in the sons of disobedience and leads the world astray (Rev. 12:9; 1 John 5:19).

The psalmist had pointed to this coming war between Jehovah and Jesus Christ and earth's political leaders and military commanders when in divine inspiration he spoke of God sitting on His heavenly throne and laughing scornfully at the earthly "gods" conspiring to make Him irrelevant in the affairs of His created world and humans. This analogy may not be too apt, but their challenge could be likened to those of rebellious robots conspiring to control their manufacturer and assert total independence.

> Why do the nations conspire and people plot in vain? The kings of the earth rise up and the rulers gather together against the LORD and against His anointed, saying, "Let us break their chains and throw off their shackles." The One enthroned in heaven laughs; and the Lord scoffs at them. He rebukes them in His anger and terrifies them in His wrath, saying, "I have installed my king on Zion, my holy mountain. . . . I will make nations your inheritance, the ends of the earth your possession. You will break them with a rod of iron; you will dash them to pieces like pottery. Therefore, you kings, be wise; be warned, you rulers of the earth. Serve the LORD with fear and celebrate his rule with trembling. Kiss the son, or he will be be angry and your way will lead to your destruction, for His wrath can flare up in a moment. Blessed are those who take refuge in him.
> —PSALM 2:1–6, 8–12, NIV

Paul's prophetic words in His letter to the Thessalonians draw our attention to God's judicial punishments to disobedient humans,

> when the Lord Jesus is revealed from heaven with His mighty angels, in flaming fire taking vengeance on those who do not know God, and those who do not obey the gospel of our Lord Jesus Christ. These shall be punished with everlasting destruction from the presence of the Lord and from the glory of His power, when He comes in that Day, to be glorified in His saints, and to be admired among all those who believe.
>
> —2 THESSALONIANS 1:7–10, NKJV

It is of course apparent that a preponderance of the world's political and military leaders are out of tune with the divine prophetic messages of God in His manual for life—the Holy Bible. Most leaders of the nations of the earth behave like "gods," largely because they don't truly worship and fear Jehovah and Christ, His anointed One; and also because they trust more in their transient and limited powers over the lives of men. They are blinded by the allure and lust for power and human adulation and to the fact that they are just ordinary mortals in a vainglorious world.

Yes, most leaders have broken free from God and have made themselves "gods." This deification of man is also propelled by his transient material wealth and great scientific and technological advancements as well as the dangerous new age beliefs and networking gaining global acceptance. This development is further compounded by self-idolatry, sorcery, mental alchemy, and teachings like psychological salvation and scientism, including naked occultism, Satanism, and spiritism in governance and in businesses. The great apostasy prevalent in Christendom today is also winning its adherents. All these are signs of the end times, as Jesus foretold—a worldwide spiritual deception: "For false Christs and false prophets will rise and show great signs and wonders to deceive, if possible, even the elect. See, I have told you beforehand" (Matt. 24:24–25, NKJV).

There are, of course, dire consequences for the world's political leaders who turn themselves into "gods" and religious leaders who misdirect and miseducate their congregations and followers with false doctrines. These are men and women who are spiritually and physically led by demons, the angels that sinned, and the angels that did not keep their original positions but forsook their assigned place in heaven (Jude 6). The prophet Jeremiah reminds Israel and, by extension, nations of the world that the only true God is Jehovah, the Creator of the universe, and that He has pronounced that all those who aspire to the status of being "gods" will be destroyed because they are nothing more than the subjects of Satan who largely dominates the present world socioeconomic and political order, having been given a temporal power over all kindred, tongues and nations (Rev. 13:5, 7).

> But the LORD is the true God; he is the living God, the eternal King. When He is angry, the earth trembles; the nations cannot endure his wrath. Tell them this: "These gods who did not make the heavens and the earth will perish from the heavens."
> —JEREMIAH 10:10–11, NIV

Zephaniah prophesied Jehovah's rising up to the booty against nations.

> "Therefore wait for Me," says the LORD, "until the day I rise up for plunder; My determination is to gather the nations To My assembly of kingdoms, To pour on them My indignation, All My fierce anger; All the earth shall be devoured with the fire of My jealousy.
> —ZEPHANIAH 3:8, NKJV

Revelation 19:1–27 assures of the defeat of the beast, the kings of the earth, their armies, and the false prophets by the King of kings and Lord of lords, Jesus Christ, and His heavenly army of angels.

The prophet Ezekiel confirms the prophetic pronouncement of Jehovah's lasting judgment against nations refusing to acknowledge Him as the Creator and sovereign Lord of the universe and Israel as His "Ensign," His "Banner," to the world through which He has promised to show His universal magnificence and splendor.

> I will display my glory among the nations, and all the nations will see the punishment I inflict and the hand I lay upon them. From that day forward the people of Israel will know that I am the LORD their God. And the nations will know that the people of Israel went into exile for their sin, because they were unfaithful to me. So I hid my face from them and handed them over to their enemies.
> —EZEKIEL 39:21–23, NIV

The end-time invasion of Israel is a recurring theme in our expose of God's dismantling and destruction of Satan and man-led socioeconomic and political world order. We have in the preceding section seen how Jerusalem will serve as God's seat of judgment and redemption and how He will make Jerusalem an immovable rock to those attacking to destroy it. Jehovah's defense of Jerusalem, which is theologically both center of the land of Israel and center of the world, is nothing new (Ezek. 38:12). Indeed, ancient Israel and Jerusalem not only were located at a central point in respect of Eurasian and African continents, but were also the center of the pure, undiluted worship of the one and only true God, Jehovah, and were regarded by Him as "the pupil or apple of His eye" (Deut. 32:9–10). "For thus says the LORD of hosts: 'He sent Me after glory, to the nations which plunder you; for he who touches you touches the apple of His eye" (Zech. 2:8, NKJV).

In ancient times God used Israel as His execution force against God-dishonoring pagan nations and also fought the wars for them (Deut. 7:16; 20:16–17; 2 Chron. 20:29; Josh. 10:14). "Joshua captured all these kings and their land in one campaign, because the LORD, the God of Israel, fought for Israel" (Josh. 10:42, HCSB).

We should call back to memory the fact that a single angel killed 185,000 of the invading Assyrian army under Sennacherib (circa 704–681 BC) in defense of Judah under the kingship of Hezekiah (circa 716–687 BC) This was done not for the glory of Israel but for God's own glory and testimony to the world of pagan worshipers and unbelievers (2 Kings 19:35; 32–34).

Jehovah will again show His righteous indignation, His awesome and unmatchable power, in defense of Israel and Jerusalem in the "latter days" when a mighty army led by the Antichrist marches from the "North" supported by the military of anti-Semitic (anti-Israel) nations. This will be an army all riding on horses, a great horde, a mighty army advancing against "my people Israel like a cloud that covers the land" (Ezek. 38:14–16, NIV) (infantry, artillery, air strikes, and sea power). This is the coming of the man of sin, the son of perdition, the lawless one spoken, of by the apostle Paul in his second epistle to the Thessalonians.

> Let no one deceive you by any means; for that Day will not come unless the falling away comes first, and the man of sin is revealed, the son of perdition, who opposes and exalts himself above all that is called God or that is worshiped, so that he sits as God in the temple of God, showing himself that he is God.... And then the lawless one will be revealed, whom the Lord will consume with the breath of His mouth and destroy with the brightness of His coming. The coming of the lawless one is according to the working of Satan, with all power, signs, and lying wonders and with all unrighteous

deception among those who perish, because they did not receive the
love of the truth, that they might be saved.

—2 THESSALONIANS 2:3–4, 8–10, NKJV

An Italian proverb states: "to him who watches, everything is
revealed."[1] We can, if we open our eyes to world events and our hearts to
the living and sure words of God in the Bible, discern the end-time invasion of Israel from the ancient and modern day invasions and attacks on
that land. But let's once again recollect Israel's Six-Day War of June 1967
against hostile Arab and Islamic forces supported by the Soviets, who
provided arms, training, intelligence, and other logistics to their Arab
clientele. In spite of the formidable coalition, Israel won decisively in six
days. The Yom Kippur War of October 1973 saw Israel surrounded by an
enemy coalition led by Egypt, Syria, Jordan, and Iraq. Algeria, Kuwait,
Libya, Morocco, Pakistan, Saudi Arabia, Sudan, and Tunisia assisted
with financial aid, ground forces, combat pilots, and military equipment.
Cuba and Uganda also sent forces against Israel, while the then Soviet
Union assisted as a major sponsor of the anti-Israel coalition, though
they did not send ground forces. But Israel came out of this war as well as
an independent, respected, and also hated nation, particularly by many
Islamic nations.

Just as a cease-fire and a respite of uneasy peace followed the war of
attrition of rocket launches and air bombardment into Southern Israel
and Gaza between Hamas and Israel in eight days of November 2012, the
Israelis and the Palestinians will continue to witness a circle of intermit-
tent moments of peace and sudden conflicts until the Great day of God
Almighty at Armageddon. Indeed, "war will continue until the end" (Dan.
9:26, NIV). As Ezekiel, Joel, Daniel, and the apostle Paul envisioned, those
that will attack the land of Israel will be hell-bent on wiping Israel out of
the face of the earth, just as Ahmadinejad, the former Iranian president,
wants and pronounced on *Al Jazeera* cable news on October 26, 2005,
and as reported in the *New York Times* and UK *Guardian* of October 27,
2005. Khalid Meshal, Hamas leader, told Christiane Amanpour of CNN
that he does not believe in Israel's right to exist though he believes in the
two states solution.

UNDERSTANDING ARAB-ISRAELI CONFLICT

The passionate hatred of Israel by her Islamic Arab neighbors is of ancient
ancestry and can be traced to Bible prophecy. Let us go back in time to

the prophecy of Obadiah regarding the destiny of the nation of Israel in the consummation of God's redemption plan for mankind vis-à-vis Israel's relationship with the Palestinians, her Arab neighbors, and surrounding Islamic nations, as well as her status in the comity of nations and the rightful ownership of Jerusalem.

Obadiah states that in the day of God's judgment on all nations, there will be a holy remnant who will escape on Mount Zion (Jerusalem); that the house of Jacob will repossess their rightful inheritance; the house of Jacob will be a fire, the house of Joseph a flame, setting aflame and consuming the stubble which is the house of Esau, and that none of the house of Esau will remain because it is God's decree. Obadiah also foretold that those in the cities of the Negev will possess the mountain of Esau and those in the foothills or lowlands shall possess the land of the Philistines, the fields of Ephraim, and Samaria, while Benjamin will take possession of Gilead. The prophecy states further that those from the crowd of the people of Israel exiled among the Canaanites as far as Zarephath (Sidon area on the Mediterranean shore), as well as the exiled of Jerusalem as far as Sepharad (possibly a territory of Media), will repossess the cities in the Negev. Then, they victoriously will ascend Mount Zion to rule over Mount Esau and the kingdom and kinship will belong to Jehovah God (Obad. 1:15, 17–21).

The mountain or the house of Esau, as presented in Obadiah's prophecy, represents nations, kingdoms, or governments that were established by the descendants of Esau and exist today in the Middle East. They may also be traced to the Mediterranean, North Africa, and Asia Minor.

Of note in Daniel 2:35, 44–45 is the interpretation that mountains in biblical symbolism can represent kingdoms, ruling governments, or nations. In Daniel 2:35, the stone that struck the great image became a "great mountain" and filled the whole earth. In Daniel 2:44–45 we observe that the mountain that filled the whole earth is first described as a kingdom. Then as a divided kingdom; thirdly, as partly strong and partly fragile kingdom; and lastly, as the "mountain" or kingdom established by God Almighty which will stand forever, indestructible, and will consume all other human kingdoms. In Jeremiah 51:24–25 Babylon is described as a "destroying mountain" (a destructive kingdom).

Mountain can also represent a place of worship, since mountains and hills in ancient times served as sites of idolatrous worship and sanctuaries of false gods (Deut. 12:2; Jer. 3:6; Ezek. 18:6). Deuteronomy 12:2

states, "You shall utterly destroy all the places where the nations which you shall dispossess served their gods, on high mountains and on hills and under every green tree" (NKJV).

The prophecies of Isaiah 2:2–3 and of Micah 4:1–2 state, "In the latter days That the mountain of the LORD's house Shall be established on top of the mountains, And shall be exalted above the hills; And all nations shall flow to it" (NKJV).

The aforementioned prophecy paints a picture of mountain as a place of worship and as representing a kingdom. The worship of the one and only true God, Jehovah, will be magnified above all other fetish worship in heaven and on earth, and His kingdom will be established above all other human kingdoms to which all nations will pay obeisance.

It should therefore be apparent that the mountain of Esau depicts nations that emerged from Esau's descendants. We read from Genesis 25:22–23 that when Rebecca was pregnant, the twins within her struggled as if in contest. Worried about the uneasiness in her womb, she went before the Lord in supplication, to inquire if all was well. And the Lord replied, "Two nations are in your womb, Two peoples shall be separated from your body; One people shall be stronger than the other, And the older shall serve the younger" (NKJV).

We recollect that Esau sold his birthright to his junior twin brother, Jacob, for a meal of lentil stew and bread. As a consequence he lost his blessing as the firstborn of Isaac. Jacob, with the help of his mother, rightfully supplants Esau, having taken his firstborn right to receive the blessing of their father, Isaac. Isaac's blessing to Jacob, apparently sealed by Jehovah, is that he will become first among nations and curses will be upon those who curse him and blessing upon those who bless him. Isaac's reluctant blessing on Esau was that he will prosper, will live by his sword, and will finally, out of restlessness, assert his independence from his younger brother, Jacob (Israel).

As a free moral agent, Esau made personal choices, took singular decisions that alienated him from Jehovah, the God of his father; while Jacob took moral decisions that endeared him to the Lord. While Jacob, as directed by Isaac, went to Paddan-aram to Rebecca's relatives to choose a wife from a family that shared the same faith and worshiped the same God; Esau, on the other hand, took two pagan Hittite women, Judith and Basemoth, as wives without the consent of his parents. Esau also took a third wife named Mahalath, the daughter of Abraham's son Ishmael by the Egyptian handmaid Hagar. Esau's marital choices brought sorrow to

Isaac and Rebecca (Gen. 26:34–35; 36:2–3). Esau also became a skilled and adventurous hunter, "a wild man," unlike his meek, gentle, and pious brother, Jacob (Gen. 25:27). It should, therefore, not be surprising that God, through the prophet Malachi, pronounced, "I have loved Jacob, but Esau I have hated" (Mal. 1:2–3, NIV).

Jacob, whose name was changed to Israel after an encounter with God (Gen. 32:22–28), became one of the three great patriarchs of the Hebrew race, whose twelve sons became the progenitors of the tribes of Israel. The promised Seed, the Messiah, Jesus, through whom all the families of the earth will be blessed, is also from Jacob's (Israel's) lineage—the extension and outpouring of God's covenantal blessings on the other two patriarchs, Abraham and Isaac. On the other hand, Esau became the progenitor of the Edomites who became mortal enemies of the children of Israel. The psalmist called on Jehovah to "remember, O Lord, against the sons of Edom, The day of Jerusalem, Who said, 'Raze it, raze it, To its very foundation'" (Ps. 137:7, NKJV).

Indeed, the Edomites joined other enemies of Judah and Israel to plunder their land. They also derided the God of Abraham, Isaac, and Jacob, the Holy One of Israel, the God of all flesh and the universe, for which reason God directed three of His prophets—Jeremiah, Ezekiel, and Obadiah—to prophesy the destruction of the ancient Edomites and the final destruction of their anti-Israel descendant nations in the latter days (Jer. 49:7–22; Ezek. 25:12–14; 35:1–15; Obad. 1–16).

The agelong hatred of Israel by the Edomites appears to have been strengthened with Esau's marriage to the daughter of Ishmael, who was the progenitor of Israel's enemy nation, the Ishmaelites or Medianites. It would appear that the animosity Ishmael had towards Isaac was passed on to his descendants as we can discern from Psalm 83:4–6: "They have said, 'Come and let us cut them off from being a nation That the name of Israel may be remembered no more.' For they have consulted together with one consent; They form a confederacy against You; The tents of Edom and the Ishmaelites" (NKJV).

Like Esau, Ishmael had to fulfill the prophecy associated with his birth: "And the Angel of the LORD said to her [Hagar],... "And you shall bear a son. You shall call his name Ishmael.... He shall be a wild man. His hand shall be against every man, And every man's hand against him. And he shall dwell in the presence of all his brethren" (Gen. 16:11–12, NKJV).

While promising the centenarian Abraham that his nonagenarian wife, Sarah, would bear a son (Isaac, the son of promise), God also told

Abraham that Ishmael, his first son by Hagar, would become the father of twelve princes and the progenitor of a great nation. In fulfillment of Jehovah's promise, the twelve sons of Ishmael established territories from Havilah as far as Shur, East of Egypt towards Assyria (Gen. 25:12–18). It does appear that the nomadic Ishmaelites are closely related to the bedouins who traversed the Sinai Peninsula across northern Arabia into Mesopotamia, extending far into Southwest Arabia to the north of modern day Yemen.

The restless and wild Esau, who lost his inheritance to Jacob, married the daughter of Ishmael, who also lost his firstborn status to Isaac, thus unifying and consolidating the animosity of two disinherited sons— Ishmael and Esau (Ishmaelites or Medianites and the Edomites) against Isaac and Jacob (Israel). It is important to point out the Islamic prophet Mohammed claimed descent from Ishmael. It is scholarly acknowledged that the sons of Ishmael (except Kademah) are mentioned in Assyrian texts. The Qur'an (Koran) plainly expresses a correlation between the terms "Ishmaelite" and "Muslim Arab" which provides a link to the issue of land ownership.

When we link two nations' prophecy associated with Esau and Jacob to the prophecy of Ishmael's birth and that of Isaac and God's stated preferential decision, we will better understand the intractable enmity passed on through generations between the Arabs and the Jews and why the same problem persists in our twenty-first century era. We will also better appreciate that only God's divine intervention will bring lasting, permanent, and sustainable peace in the Middle East and on earth.

God's choice of Isaac and Jacob was not an arbitrary or irrational preference. His choice of Jacob over Esau is not only a reflection of good and bad choices made by the twins but is also an indication of His sovereign will and the fact that His decisions are never predicated on the dictates of men. He is the Potter and we are the clay (Isa. 45:9). Besides, "no one can restrain His hand Or say to Him, 'What have You done?'" (Dan. 4:35, NKJV).

The apostle Paul explains God's sovereign will regarding the dispensation of His covenant:

> For this is the word of promise: "At this time I will come and Sarah shall have a son." And not only this, but when Rebecca also had conceived by one man, even by our father Isaac (for the children not yet being born, nor having done any good or evil, that the purpose of God according to election might stand, not of works but of Him

who calls), it was said to her, "The older shall serve the younger." As it is written, "Jacob I have loved, but Esau I have hated.

—ROMANS 9:9–13, NKJV

It is also important to remind ourselves that Jehovah is the boundless and infinite God who knows the end from the beginning and had certainly foreseen that Esau's descendants, the Edomites, would attack the children of Israel on their way to the land of Canaan, the Promised Land, and ceaselessly pursue an agenda of war and extermination of His ensign to nations.

About fifteen hundred years before the coming of Christ, the Spirit of God came upon Balaam, who was employed by the Moabite/Medianite king, Balak, to use sorcery to pronounce a curse and the destruction of the children of Israel. Thrice he tried, and thrice he pronounced blessings instead of curses. Balaam's fourth prophecy by the Spirit of God pointing to the "latter days," refers to the Messianic rule that will destroy the children of chaos.

I see Him, but not now; I behold Him, but not near; A star shall come out of Jacob; A Scepter shall rise out of Israel, And batter the brow of Moab, And destroy all the sons of tumult. And Edom shall be a possession....Out of Jacob one shall have dominion, And destroy the remnants of the city.

—NUMBERS 24:17–19, NKJV

Ezekiel foretold what will happen to the invading forces of Gog on Jerusalem.

This is what will happen in that day: When Gog attacks the land of Israel, my hot anger will be aroused, declares the Sovereign LORD. In my zeal and fiery wrath I declare that at that time there shall be a great earthquake in the land of Israel. The fish of the sea, the birds of the air, the beasts of the field, every creature that moves along the ground and all people on the face of earth will tremble at my presence. The mountains will be overturned, the cliffs will crumble and every wall will fall to the ground. I will summon a sword against Gog on all my mountains, declares the Sovereign LORD. Every man's sword will be against his brother. I will execute judgment upon him with plague and bloodshed; I will pour down torrents of rain, hailstones, and burning sulphur on him and his troops and on the many nations with him. And so I will show my greatness and

my holiness and I will make myself known in the sight of many
nations. Then they will know that I am the LORD.

—EZEKIEL 38:18–23, NIV

Since mankind has opted to come to the full knowledge of God the
hard way, then He has no option but to deal ruthlessly with disobedient
humans as free moral agents for the choice they have made to challenge His sovereignty as Creator and God of all flesh and of the universe.
Mankind has been led by Satan into war with himself and his Creator,
and sure defeat and destruction await him.

Chapter 8

GOG'S DEFEAT AND DESTRUCTION OF THE WICKED

JEHOVAH OF ARMIES, the Lord of hosts, is a God of war (Ps. 80:7; 2 Sam. 22:35; Rev. 19:11). But, above all, He is love (1 John 4:8). And because He is love, He has decided to rescue and terminate the existence of the wicked ones of the earth.

> But the wicked will be cut from the earth, And the unfaithful will be uprooted from it.
> —PROVERBS 2:22, NKJV

> You should... destroy those who destroy the earth.
> —REVELATION 11:18

The destruction of Gog's invading army will be total, and there will be a burial place for them in the vicinity of Israel. The carcasses of this Gog-led congregation of a vast army from the North accompanied by many nations become food for birds and beasts and their skeletons are buried in the Valley of Hamon Gog.

The Prophet Ezekiel describes Gog as the head chieftain or the chief prince of Rosh, Meshech, and Tubal of the land of Magog, situated in the far corner of the earth, and that other members of the Gog-led northern military coalition include Persia, Ethiopia, Libya, Gomer, and Togarmah (Ezek. 38:2, 3–6, 15). Ezekiel also reveals that this Antichrist army will in the "latter years... come into the land of those brought back from the sword and is gathered out of many people, against the mountains of Israel... and brought forth out of nations" (Ezek. 38:8).

Meshech and Tubal, like Magog, are names given to sons of Japheth who is one of three sons of Noah, the other two being Ham and Shem, who repopulated the earth after the flood of Noah's day. The Book of

Genesis relates nations that descended from Noah through his sons: "The sons of Japheth were Gomer, Magog Madai, Javan, Tubal, Meshech and Tiras. The sons of Gomer were Ashkanezi, Riphath, and Togarmah" (Gen. 10:2, NKJV).

The Indo-European families of Aryan branch of speech emerged from Japheth, the Afro-Asiatic families of Hamitic branch of glotto— chronology from Ham, and the Asiatic families of the Semitic branch of speech descended from Shem.[1] Some Bible students and teachers have identified Magog, Rosh, Meshech, and Tubal as Russia and the former Soviet Republics; Gomer and Togarmah as Turkey, Armenia, and possibly all other Turkic speaking peoples of Asia Minor and Central Asia. Syria, Lebanon, and northern Jordan are also cited as members of the Gog-led coalition of Antichrist army.[2] John Hagee's sermon on the four blood moon, aired on Trinity Broadcasting Network (TBN) and Daystar Christian Network, identifies Russia, Germany, and Iran as major participants in this Antichrist coalition against Israel.

It is through the destruction of this Gog-led army and their burial in the Valley of Hamon Gog that God will entrench His holy name in the people of Israel and the nations of the earth who will come to Him as the sovereign Lord, the Holy One in Israel. He will, through the defeat and destruction of Gog and his army of nations, put an end to the profanity of His holy name (Ezek. 39:7–8).

> On that day I will give Gog a burial place in Israel, in the valley of those who travel east toward the Sea. It will block the way of travelers because Gog and all his hordes will be buried there. So it will be called the Valley of Hamon Gog. For seven months the house of Israel will be burying them in order to cleanse the land.
>
> —EZEKIEL 39:11–12, NIV

The Valley of Hamon Gog is also called the valley of Gog's crowd. Gog's crowd here represents the hostile attacking nations and world military powers that are led by Gog against Jehovah and Jesus Christ, Lord and Commander of the invisible heavenly armies, massed in defense of Israel and the Israel of God (Christian faithfuls). The burial of Gog and his entire crowd is in the valley of those passing through on the east of the sea. This is translated by Bible scholars as the Valley of Abarim east of the Dead Sea. The name Abarim is used in Numbers 33:47–48 with reference to the mountains east of the Dead Sea. The Israelites got to this territory almost at the end of their forty-year trek through the wilderness and encamped in the mountain of Abarim. The children of Israel descended from these mountains to the plains of Moab situated east of Jordan at the northern point of the Dead Sea.

The Israelites made their final encampment at this point before crossing the Jordan River. It was also at this point that God told Moses to "go up this mountain of the Abarim, Mount Nebo, which is in the land of Moab, across Jericho; view the land of Canaan, which I give to the children of Israel as a possession" (Deut. 32:49, NKJV).

Two deep valleys or gorges exist in this region, the Arnon and the Zered. The Arnon is about 3 kilometers (2 miles) wide at the apex and is about 520 meters (1,700 feet) deep. The Zered is an even more frightening ravine, its precipitous cliffs drop some 1,190 meters (3,900 feet). Either of these two canyons may serve as a literal, true representation of Ezekiel's prophetic burial place of Gog's crowd, "For I have spoken it, saith the Lord GOD" (Ezek. 39:5). Jehovah's action on His created humans and His earth, which is His footstool, is meant to preserve His creation; for without His intervention, mankind, led by Satan and his demonic and wicked human agents, will destroy all human forms. For example, the hydrogen bomb is a thousand times more powerful than an atomic bomb. While there have not been any hydrogen bombs used yet in warfare, there have been tests of the bomb. A common hydrogen bomb has the power up to 10 megatons while all the explosions in World War II totaled "only" 2 megatons, 20 percent of the power of a common hydrogen bomb. Just imagine the use of hydrogen, atomic, barrel, and cluster bombs, combined with middle- and long-range intercontinental ballistic missiles with nuclear warheads, as well as chemical and biological weapons and other arsenals of war in a third world war. Such a war, if unchecked, will consume humanity; and Jehovah will intervene to save the earth and all those who remain faithful to Him and to His anointed One, the Messiah, Jesus.

The already quoted Ezekiel 39:12 relates that for seven months after the defeat of Gog and the Antichrist invading nations at Armageddon, Israel will be engaged in the mass burial of corpses. Indeed, the burial period will stretch beyond seven months for at the end of seven months they will still be searching for corpses, "and when any seeth a man's bone, then shall he set up a sign by it, till the buriers have buried it in the valley of Hamongog" (Ezek. 39:14–15). This prophecy of the burial of Gog should not create any doubt in the discerning mind since Armageddon is not just global warfare but the war of God's great day of ingathering and destruction. With a world population of over seven billion humans and with a great company and a mighty army like a cloud to cover the land of Israel, then we can be sure that the slain will run into tens and hundreds of millions within and beyond the land of Israel.

Let us recall that the First World War consumed over 7 million military personnel. Germany lost 1.8 million humans, Russia 1.7 million, France 1.380 million, Austria 1.290 million, Britain 743,000, Italy 615,000, Romania 335,000, Turkey 325,000, and other nations combined over 800,000.[3] In the Second World War, more than twenty million people died. A global estimate of sixty million deaths has been given for World War II deaths.[4] And wars fought within nations and between nations since the Second World War have consumed not less than one hundred million lives and the figure is rising. In 1950 a United Nations force along with South Koreans, in a war between North and South Korea, killed an estimated one million four hundred and twenty thousand North Koreans and Chinese. Just as there were mass burials of corpses during the First and Second World Wars and in many wars of the twentieth and twenty-first centuries, there will be mass burials during and after the great war of the great day of God Almighty—Armageddon. It should be apparent that with great multitudes slain and scattered over a vast expanse of battlefields, it should take Israel the prophesied seven months to clear the putrid mess and properly clean the environment for sustainable human habitation. Clearly, there will be other battlefields; but Israel and its environ will host the major one. The Bible tells us through the divinely inspired prophecy of Jeremiah:

> A noise will come to the ends of the earth—For the LORD has a controversy with the nations.... Behold, disaster shall go Forth from nation to nation.... And at that day, the slain of the LORD shall be from one end of the earth even to the other end of the earth. They shall not be lamented, or gathered, or buried; they shall become refuse on the ground.
>
> —JEREMIAH 25:31–33, NKJV

Prophesying on the great day of the Lord, Zephaniah warned that it is a day of wrath, trouble, distress, devastation, desolation, thick darkness, and gloominess against the fortified cities and high towers and that God "will bring distress upon men, And they shall walk like blind men, Because they have sinned against the LORD; Their blood shall be poured out like dust, and their flesh like refuse" (Zeph. 1:17, NKJV).

It will also take seven years for Israel to clean up and dispose of all the weapons of war—guns, tanks, fighter jets, vehicles, and other arsenal's of war (Ezek. 39:9). The destruction of Gog and his army is played out so that self-conceited, stubborn, and wicked humanity, as well as faithful followers of God, will see the glory of Jehovah and Christ and the helplessness of man in the face of God's righteous indignation (38:22–23).

The defeat and extermination of Gog and his army at Armageddon ushers in Christ's thousand years of Messianic kingship, commonly known as the Millennium. Let's examine the literalness and the reality of this coming thousand years of Christ's kingdom reign on earth and what it brings for redeemed mankind. Jehovah, through the King of kings and Lord of lords, Jesus Christ, enthrones a world united in bonds of godly love and destroys a satanic wicked world chaotically divided by pride of tribe, race, and nation. The love of God and humanity becomes the core determinant for social and economic existence under the Messianic kingship of our Lord Jesus Christ. This comes at great cost to humanity—the Great Tribulation.

THE GREAT TRIBULATION
AND THE MESSIANIC KINGSHIP

Embedded in the *a-po-ka'ly-psis*—the unveiling or uncovering of the divine vision Jesus Christ shown to John in Revelation—is the good news of God's incoming kingdom in which mankind's chaotic and turbulent history comes to a cataclysmic and happy climax as Jehovah God and the Messiah, Jesus, carry out judgment on the earth and its Satan-dominated socioeconomic and political systems. The defeat of Gog and his forces heralds Christ's thousand years of kingship on earth. This is Jehovah's new world order and not the much talked about man's new world order or one world government. "The faithful witness, the firstborn from the dead and the ruler of the kings of the earth" takes over the governance of the earth (Rev. 1:5). Christ is the One who has redeemed mankind to God out of every tribe and tongue and people and nation.

> Blessing, and honour, and glory, and power, be unto him that sitteth upon the throne, and unto the Lamb for ever and ever.
> —REVELATION 5:13

The fact of the universal salvation for a crowd of mankind from all nations is captured in Revelation 7:9:

> After these things I looked, and behold, a great multitude which no one could number, of all nations, tribes, peoples, and tongues, standing before the throne and before the Lamb, clothed with white robes, with palm branches in their hands, and crying out with a loud voice, saying, "Salvation belongs to our God who sits on the throne, and to the Lamb."
>
> —REVELATION 7:9–10, NKJV

This is the great crowd that survived the Great Tribulation:

> So he said to me, "These are the ones who come out of the great tribulation, and washed their robes and made them white in the blood of the Lamb. Therefore they are before the throne of God, and serve Him day and night in His temple. And He who sits on the throne will dwell among them. They shall neither hunger anymore nor thirst anymore; the sun shall not strike them, nor any heat; for the Lamb who is in the midst of the throne will shepherd them and lead them to living fountains of waters. And God will wipe away every tear from their eyes."
>
> —REVELATION 7:14–17

The Great Tribulation has to take place before the Messianic kingship of Jesus Christ in the Millennium. What does the Bible say about tribulations and the Great Tribulation? Let us begin by stating that tribulation—a condition of affliction, distress, great suffering, misery, or severe trial—has been the lot of millions around the world in past ages and in our twentieth and twenty-first century eras. Mankind across continents and nations has continued to experience various forms of tribulation caused by wars, pestilences, famines, plagues, and natural and man-made disasters.

The early Christians suffered many tribulations, just as Jesus Christ told His apostles they would: "In the world you will have tribulation; but be of good cheer, I have overcome the world" (John 16:33, NKJV).

Christ also forewarned:

> They will put you out of the synagogues; yes, the time is coming that whoever kills you will think that he offers God service. And these things they will do to you because they have not known the Father nor Me. But these things I have told you, that when the time comes, you may remember that I told you them.
>
> —JOHN 16:2–4

Since the persecution and sacrificial crucifixion of Jesus Christ, the stoning to death of Stephen, and the persecutions and killings of all the apostles of Jesus Christ, except John the revelator, persecutions and tribulations of Christians have continued to this day and will continue until Christ's second coming. Christ's tribulation prophecy was fulfilled in the persecutions under Emperor Nero (circa AD 54–68) and all other persecutions under the Roman Empire. They were also fulfilled in the papal persecutions and inquisition of Christians (circa AD 1208–1834), the persecutions in England (circa AD 1401–1541), and in Scotland (circa AD 1527–1558). Christ's tribulation prophecy is equally fulfilled in the twentieth and twenty-first century persecutions of Christians in the former Soviet Union, Romania, China, Albania, Cuba, Czechoslovakia, Afghanistan, Iraq, Egypt, Lebanon, Nicaragua, Nigeria, Sudan, Vietnam, Pakistan, and many more countries.[5]

We can also relate the prophecy of Jesus Christ in Matthew 24:15–22 and Luke 21:20–24 to the tribulation which came upon Jerusalem in AD 70. In Matthew 24 Jesus warned the Judeans that when they see the "abomination of desolation" spoken of by Daniel the prophet, "standing in the holy place," they should flee to the mountains. In Luke 21, He prophetically warned, "But when you see Jerusalem surrounded by armies, then know that its desolation is near. Then let those who are in Judea flee to the mountains, let those who are in the midst of her depart, and let not those who are in the country enter her" (NKJV).

When in AD 70 Jerusalem was besieged by the Roman armies under General Titus, it resulted in severe famine conditions and colossal loss of life. We should recall that the Jewish historian Flavius Josephus narrates that 1,100,000 Jews died or were killed during the siege and war, while 97,000 survived. We have also seen from our references in this book, that the tribulation of the Jews continued with their persecution and ostracization in medieval Europe down to Hitler's holocaust in Nazi Germany. The black African continent also experienced many centuries of persecution and tribulation in the African slave expeditions and trade.

But there is a tribulation that the world is yet to experience. This is the Great Tribulation that Jesus Christ foretold in Matthew 24:21: "For then shall be great tribulation, such as was not since the beginning of the world to this time, no, nor ever shall be."

The prophet Daniel also gave an end-time prophecy of the Great Tribulation:

At that time Michael shall stand up, The great prince who stands watch over the sons of your people; And there shall be a time of trouble, Such as never was since there was a nation, Even to that time. And at that time your people shall be delivered, Every one who is found written in the book. And many of those who sleep in the dust of the earth shall awake, Some to everlasting life, Some to shame and everlasting contempt.

—DANIEL 12:1–2, NKJV

The prophet Jeremiah equally foretold this period of great tribulation to Israel and the world and described it as the time of Jacob's trouble: "Alas! For that day is great, So that none is like it, And it is the time of Jacob's trouble, But he shall be saved out of it" (Jer. 30:7, NKJV).

Revelation chapter 6 unveils the form and nature of the tribulation foretold by Jesus Christ, Daniel, and Jeremiah. First is the uncovering of the vision of Jehovah's chief opposer, Satan-led Antichrist, who counterfeits Jesus Christ, riding on a white horse with a crown on his head. He went on conquering and to conquer. He is the beast spoken of in Revelation chapter 13 who has been given authority for forty-two months (three and one-half years) and who blasphemes against God, God's name, His tabernacle, and those who dwell in heaven. He is the one that is worshiped by the unsealed kings and people of the earth; who has been given temporary authority over every tribe, tongue, and nation; and who has also been granted transient power to make war against the saints and overcome them.

He shall speak pompous words against the Most High, Shall persecute the saints of the Most High, And shall intend to change times and law. Then the saints shall be given into his hand For a time and times and half a time.

—DANIEL 7:25, NKJV

As Daniel also foretold the Antichrist will reign from Jerusalem and "plant the tents of his palace between the seas and the glorious holy mountain" (Dan. 11:45, NKJV). The Antichrist will also fulfill the prophecy in Revelation 13:

He causes all, both small and great, rich and poor, free and slave, to receive a mark on their right hand or on their foreheads, and that no one may buy or sell except one who has the mark or the name of the beast, or the number of his name. Here is wisdom, let him who has understanding calculate the number of the beast, for it is the number of a man: His number is 666.

—REVELATION 13:16–18, NKJV

We read from Revelation 19:11 that Jesus Christ also rides on a white horse. But unlike the Antichrist with just a crown, He has on His head many diadems or many crowns. And while the Antichrist wars in deceit and injustice for world dominance and the prevalence of evil, fear, and hatred on earth, Jesus Christ judges and makes war in righteousness for the victory of good over evil, love over fear and hatred.

Daniel reveals that the Antichrist will destroy many and will war against Jesus Christ but will eventually be destroyed by divine intervention.

> Through his cunning he shall cause deceit to proper under his rule; And he shall exalt himself in his heart. He shall destroy many in their prosperity. He shall even rise against the Prince of princes; But he shall be broken without human means.
>
> —DANIEL 8:25, NKJV

In Revelation chapter 6, the opening of the second seal brings down the symbolic red horse which takes peace away from the earth and entrenches conflicts and global warfare. The vision of the opening of the third seal shows a black horse on which sits someone with a pair of scales in his hands bringing worldwide famine and food shortages. The fourth seal unveils a pale horse on which sits one whose name is Death, accompanied by Hades through which a fourth of the earth's population is killed by means of warfare, hunger, and wild beasts. This signifies the fact that death and hell arise as consequences of war-induced disease epidemics and famine, as well as war itself. The opening of the sixth seal sends down Jehovah's wrath—cosmic disturbances, great earthquakes, supernatural occurrences on earth adversely affecting the sun, the moon, and the stars. The light of the sun fades out, the moon becomes red like blood, and the stars fall like asteroids on the earth. This is a foregleam of a worldwide environmental catastrophe. These are supernatural disorders in the heavens and on earth that show the helplessness and frailty of mighty and powerful men in the face of the righteous indignation and invincible power of almighty God. A fifth bowl, opened before the sixth one, reveals many that were martyred for their steadfastness to Jehovah, souls who were under the altar and "had been slain for the word of God and for the testimony which they held" (Rev. 6:9, NKJV). These were to rest for a while until the complete martyrdom of other servants of God during the tribulation.

The seven years of tribulation continues with the seventh seal, prelude to the sounding of the seven trumpets given to the seven angels who stand before God Almighty. The opening of the seventh seal ushers thirty minutes of portentous silence in heaven. This moment of ominous silence is followed by the sounding of the first trumpet by one of the angels. This brings hail and fire mingled with blood upon the earth through which a third of vegetation and all green grasses were incinerated. The blasting of the second trumpet sends down a huge mountain of fire into the sea, turning the sea into blood and destroying a third of living creatures and a third of ships therein. The third trumpet sends the great star from heaven into a third of the rivers and the springs of water turning them into bitter wormwood, killing many who drank from them.

Blowing of the fourth trumpet darkened a third of the sun, the moon, and the stars, causing pitch darkness to a third of day and night. The fifth trumpet sends up locusts from the bottomless pit that hurt men for five months, except those with God's seal on their foreheads. These are not ordinary locusts but diabolical spirits who have as king over them the angel of the bottomless pit whose name in Hebrew is *Abaddon* and translated in Greek as *Apollyon*, which means the Destroyer. These locust–like demons of torment are ordered not to harm the grass of the earth or any green thing or any tree but to torment unsealed men for five months, which is the normal life span of a locust. The blast of the sixth trumpet unveils the four angels who are bound at the great River Euphrates and were released to kill a third of mankind with three plagues of fire, smoke, and brimstone. This vision of the seventh seal and the plagues of the six trumpets are unveiled in Revelation chapters 8 and 9.

The sounding of the seventh trumpet by the seventh angel in Revelation 11:15 proclaims the kingdom of God Almighty with the opening of the temple of God in heaven and the revealing of the ark of His covenant in His temple. The opening of the tabernacle of the testimony in heaven releases the seven angels having the seven last plagues as we read in Revelation chapter 15. John sees a vision of something like a sea of glass mingled with fire, and the overcomers:

Those who have the victory over the beast, over his image, over his mark and over his name, standing on the sea of glass, having harps of God. They sing the song of Moses, the servant of God, and the song of the Lamb, saying: "Great and marvelous are Your works, Lord God Almighty! Just and true are Your ways, O King of the saints! Who shall not fear You, O Lord, and glorify Your name? For You alone are holy. For all nations shall come and worship before You. For Your judgment have been manifested."

—REVELATION 15:2–4

After this rendition, a loud voice from heaven gives the order for the outpouring of the seven bowls of the righteous indignation of God on the earth as revealed in Revelation chapter 16. These seven symbolic bowls brought the following literal plagues upon the earth: The first vial of wrath spread loathsome sores (boils) on the sea of mankind who had the mark of the beast and those who worshiped his image. The second bowl turns the sea into blood, killing every living creature within. The third vial turns the rivers and springs of water into blood. The fourth bowl is poured out on the sun, from which men are scorched with great heat and fire. The fifth vial of the wrath of God is poured out on the throne of the beast, the Antichrist, turning his kingdom into pitch darkness, bringing pain and suffering to him and his crumbling kingdom. The sixth bowl dries up the great river Euphrates, preparing the way of the kings of the East. This leads to the counterfeiting works of wonders by demonic spirits of Satan, which go out to the kings of the earth (world political and military leaders) and gathers them to the battle of the day of God Almighty at Armageddon. Let's quickly recall that the Euphrates is first mentioned in Genesis 2:14 as one of the four rivers once having their source in Eden, the other three being Pishon, Gihon, and Hiddekel. The Euphrates is the longest and most important river in Southwest Asia, some 2,700 kilometers (1,200 miles) in length rising from Northeast of modern day Turkey, extending some 100 kilometers (60 miles) in the Southeast corner of the Black Sea. At the time of the fall of Babylon (circa 539 BC), Cyrus, the Persian king, diverted the waters of Euphrates so that his troops could march through the riverbed into Babylon. The waters of Euphrates were thus dried up (Isa. 44:27–28). The drying up of the Euphrates is once again prophesied and envisioned as resulting from the outpouring of the symbolic sixth bowl by the sixth angel on the great river.

These pangs of distress lead to the fall of Babylon the Great, the world empire of false religion. This, in the interpretation of some Bible students, is represented by Christian Rome and all God dishonoring churches in Christendom that have imbibed the false doctrines of Babylonian worship and have injected her idolatrous religious practices into Christendom. They extend to all religions that have rejected the good news of eternal salvation and God's coming kingdom, through the millennial reign of Jesus Christ and the destruction of the present corrupt and wicked socio-economic, political, and religious systems, including the establishment of a new heavens and a new earth.

Jesus Christ Himself pointed to all these when He gave a foregleam of what is to come.

> And there will be signs in the sun, in the moon, and in the stars; and on the earth distress of nations, with perplexity, the sea and the waves roaring; men's hearts failing them from fear and the expectation of those things which are coming on the earth, for the powers of the heavens will be shaken. Then they will see the Son of Man coming in a cloud with power and great glory. Now when these things begin to happen, look up and lift up your heads, because your redemption draws near.
>
> —LUKE 21:25–28, NKJV

Some Bible scholars have interpreted the Revelation plagues as symbolic. But let us remember that Jehovah sent real plagues on Egypt to force the hand of Pharaoh to grant the children of Israel their freedom. Water was actually turned into blood, frogs covered the whole land of Egypt, lice invaded men and beasts, hail was rained down, locusts were sent down from the east wind, three days of pitch darkness descended on Egypt, and finally the death of all firstborn of Egypt including Pharaoh's son. (See Exodus chapters 7–11.) Let's also recall that the drying of the River Jordan and the Red Sea were literal miracles and supernatural occurrences from the hand of God.

Now if all of these took place literally and physically, what tangible evidence do we have for a symbolic interpretation of the Revelation plagues; and even more so when the Bible does not explain them as such? Why is it impossible to acknowledge the fact that with God everything is absolutely possible and nothing is impossible before Him? The God that created the heavens and the earth by His word can by the same word decree its judgment and destruction in whatever form, and pronounce its renewal.

> For by Him all things were created that are in heaven and that are
> on earth, visible and invisible, whether thrones or dominions or
> principalities or powers. All things were created through Him and
> for Him. And He is before all things, and in Him all things consist.
> —COLOSSIANS 1:16–17, NKJV

The defeat of the beast, the kings of the earth, and their armies by
Christ, the King of kings and Lord of lords; and the casting into lake of
fire of the beast and the false prophet who worked signs in the beast's
presence by which he deceived those who received the mark of the beast
and those who worshiped him; and the killing of all other human followers of the beast ends the seven years of tribulation and wars. It is this
destruction of the earth's socioeconomic and spiritual order that Christ's
millennial reign ushers in, which finally leads to the last war of Gog and
Magog, the final extermination of Satan and his demonic forces, and the
creation of a new heavens and earth after the Millennium.

Within the Millennium, a thousand years of Christ's earthly kingship, Satan is made ineffective, for he is imprisoned and fettered so as
not to negatively influence mankind until the conclusion of the thousand
years. Thereafter, he will for a very short duration be released before his
final extermination along with his demonic fallen angels and the mass
of nations he once again leads to war against God's Holy City and His
saints.

> Then I saw an angel coming down from heaven, having the key to
> the bottomless pit and a great chain in his hand. He laid hold of the
> dragon, that serpent of old, who is the Devil and Satan, and bound
> him for a thousand years; and he cast him into the bottomless pit,
> and shut him up, and set a seal on him, so that he should deceive
> the nations no more till the thousand years were finished. But after
> these things he must be released for a little while.
> —REVELATION 20:1–3

Now is the fulfillment of Matthew 25:31, 41. The Son of man comes in
His glory and all the holy angels with Him. He now sits on the throne of
His glory and gathers all nations before Him. He separates His sheep, the
blessed of His Father, from the goats. He sets the sheep on His right hand
and the goats on His left. He then invites the sheep into His kingdom
and their kingdom prepared from the foundation of the earth and the
goats He sends into everlasting fire prepared for the devil and his angels.

Jesus' illustration of the goats represents those persons who refuse to do well to the least of their brothers.

Within the Millennium is the first resurrection of all the just, the blessed and holy, the saints, those that were beheaded, those martyred for their witness to Jesus and for the word of God who had not worshiped the beast or his image and had not received his mark on their foreheads or on their hands. It is envisaged that the resurrection will cover from the Adamic period to the Millennium, from Christ's resurrection to the resurrection saints of the tribulation that will live and reign with Jesus Christ during the Millennium (Rev. 20:4–6).

The prophet Isaiah divinely envisioned life in the Millennium, which will surely be a glorious, peaceful, healthy, and orderly existence with longer life span for obedient mankind. We should call back to memory from the genealogy of Adam that Adam lived 930 years while Methuselah lived 969 years (Gen. 5:3, 25). Isaiah prophesied:

> No more shall an infant from there live just a few days, Nor an old man who has not fulfilled his days; For the child shall die one hundred years old, But the sinner being one hundred years old shall be accursed. They shall build houses and inhabit them; They shall plant vineyards and eat their fruit.... For as the days of a tree, so shall be the days of My people. And my elect shall long enjoy the work of their hands. They shall not labor in vain, Nor bring forth children for trouble.
>
> —ISAIAH 65:20–23, NKJV

A fascinating picture of planet Earth where there is friendship and harmony between animals and between animals and mankind is prophetically envisioned by the prophet Isaiah. This takes us back to the Garden of Eden where Adam and Eve communicated and lived peaceful with animals before the fall.

> The wolf also shall dwell with the lamb, and the leopard shall lie down with the kid; and the calf and the young lion and the fatling together; and a little child shall lead them. And the cow and the bear shall feed; their young ones shall lie down together: and the lion shall eat straw like the ox. And the sucking child shall play on the hole of the asp, and the weaned child shall put his hand on the cockatrice' [viper] den. They shall not hurt nor destroy in all my

holy mountain: for the earth shall be full of the knowledge of the LORD, as the waters cover the sea.

—ISAIAH 11:6–9

Isaiah 65:25 states that dust shall be the serpent's food. Isaiah also paints a joyful vision of Jehovah's restoration of planet Earth to one of environmental friendliness, unparalleled fertility, limitless provision of fresh and clean potable water, and abundant natural resources for the unpolluted use of the new man.

When the poor and needy seek water, and there is none, and their tongue faileth for thirst, I the LORD will hear them, I the God of Israel will not forsake them I will open rivers in high places, and fountains in the midst of the valleys: I will make the wilderness a pool of water, and the dry land springs of water. I will plant in the wilderness the cedar, the shittah [acacia] tree, and the myrtle, and the oil tree; I will set in the desert the fir tree, and the pine, and the box tree together: hat they may see, and know, and consider, and understand together, that the hand of the LORD hath done this, and the Holy One of Israel hath created it.

—ISAIAH 41:17–20

The cedar, the myrtle and the oil tree; three trees that normally grow in rich and fertile soils are prophesied to become companions of the desert-loving acacia as a result of God's divine provision—rivers in desolate heights, fountains in the midst of the valleys, and a pool of water in the wilderness, and springs of water in dry land.

The assured promise of God through the prophet Joel states:

Be not afraid, ye beasts of the field: for the pastures of the wilderness do spring, for the tree beareth her fruit, the fig tree and the vine do yield their strength.

—JOEL 2:22

And it shall come to pass in that day, that the mountains shall drop down new wine, and the hills shall flow with milk, and all the rivers of Judah shall flow with waters, and a fountain shall come forth out of the house of the LORD, and shall water the valley of Shittim [Acacias].

—JOEL 3:18

The word of Jehovah through the prophet Ezekiel also assures that "the tree of the field shall yield her fruit, and the earth shall yield her increase" (Ezek. 34:27). "And I will multiply the fruit of your trees and the increase of your fields, so that you need never again bear the reproach of famine among the nations (36:30, NKJV).

This restoration of all lands to full fruitfulness and enthralling beauty is equally confirmed by Zechariah: "For the seed shall be prosperous, the vine shall give her fruit, and the ground shall give her increase, and the heavens shall give their dew" (Zech. 8:12).

Christ's millennial reign will usher in universal peace, for, as Isaiah prophesied, "of the increase of his government and peace there shall be no end" (Isa. 9:7). The prophet Micah saw, as Isaiah did, that nations will no longer lift up weapons of war against themselves and that they shall convert their war arsenals into life-enhancing, productive uses (Mic. 4:3).

During the thousand years of the Messianic kingship of Jesus Christ, Jehovah, Creator of the heavens and earth, will assign to His obedient humans the perfect administration of His limitless stream of creation wealth, resources, and provisions throughout His inhabited earth. In God's new dispensation, new world order, the redeemed of the earth will witness the grace of His spiritual gifts in the full exploits of human talent, ability and creativity for peace and abundance on earth. Mankind will enjoy the endless stream of spiritual power and potentials the Lord Jesus innately has and dispenses according to His grace, wealth, and power, as exhibited in His earthly miracles during His first advent.

These are sure words, the blessed assurance of Jehovah, the Creator of the universe, whose words will never return to Him unfulfilled, for the word of God is not chained (Isa. 45:33; 2 Tim. 2:9, NIV). He calls on all the inhabitants of the earth and all nations to look unto Him and be saved for He is God and there is none else (Isa. 45:22). His counsel shall stand and He will surely do all His pleasure (46:10).

> In that day the deaf shall hear the words of the book, and the eyes of the blind shall see out of obscurity, and out of darkness.
>
> —ISAIAH 29:18

Yes, there shall be no more human deformities as Christ the King takes over theocratic governance of the earth. However, death isn't finally abolished until the end of the thousand years of Christ's reign.

> For he must reign, till he hath put all enemies under his feet. The last enemy that shall be destroyed is death.
>
> —1 CORINTHIANS 15:25–26

We also note that Death and Hades were cast into the lake of fire after the final battle of Gog and Magog at the expiration of the thousand years (Rev. 20:14).

Chapter 9

THE FINAL WAR: GOG AND MAGOG

W E HAVE EARLIER noted that after the thousand years of Christ's Messianic kingship, Satan will be released for a short time (Rev. 20:3). The instant annihilation of Gog and Magog—Satan and those nations in the four corners of the earth who are deceived and gathered by him to war against the camp of God's people and the city He loves—is also revealed in Revelation 20:

> Now when the thousand years have expired, Satan will be released from his prison and will go out to deceive the nations which are in the four corners of the earth, Gog and Magog, to gather them together to battle, whose number is as the sand of the sea. They went up on the breadth of the earth and surrounded the camp of the saints and the beloved city. And fire came down from God out of heaven and devoured them. The devil, who deceived them, was cast into the lake of fire and brimstone where the beast and the false prophet are. And they will be tormented day and night forever and ever.
>
> —REVELATION 20:7–10, NKJV

The battle of Gog and Magog brings to an end the waging of wars on planet Earth. The final defeat of Satan and the deceived nations in their last attempt to destroy the camp of the saints and Jerusalem, "the beloved city," fulfils several scriptures including Ezekiel 34:28 that tells us Israel "shall no more be a prey for the nations, nor shall beasts of the land devour them; but they shall dwell safely, and no one shall make them afraid" (NKJV).

A psalm of the sons of Korah, a song for Alamoth divinely envisions Jehovah the refuge of His people and conqueror of nations who puts an end to war tells us, "He makes war cease to the ends of the earth. He breaks the bow and cuts the spear in two. He burns the chariot in fire" (Ps. 46:9, NKJV).

Psalm 72:7 foretells that "in his days shall the righteous flourish; and abundance of peace so long as the moon endureth." That is until God's glory and the Lamb's glory serve as light to mankind (Rev. 21:23).

And as the source of perfect peace, He is the one who ultimately bestows it to nations, between nations, and for all peoples. The same Lord who destroys in His righteous and fiery anger wicked people and nations bestows peace to obedient mankind. "I form light and create darkness I make peace and create calamity; I, the LORD do all these things" (Isa. 45:7, NKJV).

Who is mortal man to question God's actions, or challenge His sovereign authority? For, indeed, "woe to him who strives with his maker. Let the potsherd strive with the potsherds of the earth! Shall the clay say to him who forms it, 'What are you making?' Or shall your handiwork say, 'He has no hands?'" (Isa. 45:9, NKJV).

Because earth is an extension of heaven made by the Creator King, Jehovah never gave up on His original plan for humans to dwell on earth forever. The psalmist wrote, "The meek shall inherit the earth; and shall delight themselves in the abundance of peace" (Ps. 37:11); it was affirmed by Jesus' statement in Matthew 5:5: "Blessed are the meek: for they shall inherit the earth."

It is as a result of His divine plan for mankind for all ages that Jehovah God directs the climax of world and human history to the creation of a new heavens and a new earth—a resurrected universe inhabited by resurrected people living with resurrected Jesus following the annihilation of Gog and Magog and Satan's destruction.

NEW HEAVENS, NEW EARTH

Jerusalem's pivotal position on which God's redemption plan for mankind and human history oscillates is once again played out in the last battle on earth—Jehovah's war against the armies of Gog and Magog. At the end of the one thousand years of the Messianic rule of Jesus Christ, Satan is unshackled and he goes out to deceive nations to fight against God's kingdom: "They went up on the breadth of the earth, and compassed the camp of the saints about, and the beloved city" (Rev. 20:9).

Through Satan's demonic deception a global army surrounds the "camp of the saints," and the "beloved city." The word *camp* was extensively used in most translations in Numbers 3:21–38 to describe the dwelling places of the priesthood families of the Israelites around the tabernacle under Moses' leadership. It is also used in Numbers 33:41–49 to describe the various destinations the children of Israel settled after their departure from Mount Hor up to their camping by the Jordan in the plains of Moab. "Camp" could mean a standing army and a military encampment, as in Joshua 10:5 (NKJV) where the five kings of the Amorites, Jerusalem, Hebron, Jarmuth, Lachish, and Eglon camped before the city of Gibeon to attack it for making peace with Joshua and the children of Israel.

The "camp of the saints" could very well stand for the peaceful and orderly city(ies) of the redeemed of the earth (the Israel of God) and also the "beloved city," representing the earthly Jerusalem from where Christ Jesus rules during the Millennium with a scepter of righteousness, having used an iron scepter to break the nations in pieces. We recall that Jerusalem is described severally and lovingly as the Holy City, the city of the great King, God's resting place, Jehovah's throne, and God's crown of glory, as we read from Psalms 48:1–3; 50:2; 78:68; 132:13–14; 135:21; Isaiah 62:1–3; and 1 Chronicles 29:23. At the end of the thousand years of Christ's Messianic kingship, Satan is released to deceive rebellious nations that have grown within the Millennium and to attack Christ's earthly theocratic government and the camp of the saints. Bible scholars have also interpreted the "camp of the saints" to mean the Lord and the church—the church being a wilderness community and God's beloved city cut off from the rest of the nations during the Millennium. While Christ will rule eternally, the first thousand years of His kingship is for the express purpose of ridding the earth of all rebellion, destroying all enemies of God, destroying sin and death, and ensuring the restoration of God's universal kingdom to its position above all other creations, as was in existence before Satan's rebellion and the Adamic sin and fall through Satan.

However, what should attract our greatest attention and interest is not the difference in our understanding and interpretation of the words *camp* and *beloved city*, but the ultimate destruction of Satan-led rebellious armies gathered from the four corners of the earth. The instant annihilation of this army with fire direct from God in heaven and the casting of Satan, the beast, and the false prophet into the lake of fire and brimstone where they will apparently be subjected to eternal torment along with the cowardly, unbelieving, abominable, murderers, sexually immoral, sorcerers, idolaters, and all liars into the lake which burns with fire and brimstone, which is the second death, heralds the new heaven, new earth and new Jerusalem (Rev. 20:13; 21:8).

We should note a salient distinction made between the final fate of Satan (including of course his demonic angels), the beast and the false prophet, and other sinful humans as we can discern from Revelation 20 and 21:

> The devil, who deceived them, was cast into the lake of fire and brimstone where the beast and the false prophet are. And they will be tormented day and night forever and ever.
> —REVELATION 20:10, NKJV

> But the cowardly, unbelieving, abominable, murderers, sexually immoral, sorcerers, idolaters, and all liars shall have their part in the lake which burns with fire and brimstone, which is the second death.
> —REVELATION 21:8, NKJV

> Then Death and Hades were cast into the lake of fire. This is the second death. And anyone not found written in the Book of life was cast into the lake of fire.
> —REVELATION 20:14–15, NKJV

The lake of fire is described and qualified as the second death. Those whose names were not found in the Lamb's Book of Life were cast into the lake of fire, which could be interpreted as condemnation to the second death, everlasting death, or a perpetual cutting off from the presence of Jehovah God and Christ Jesus. Let's quickly recall that in the last war and rebellion against God, the rebellious armies of Gog and Magog who gathered to destroy Christ's kingdom, the camp of the saints, the beloved city, were instantly devoured with fire from God. They were in a twinkle annihilated, incinerated, and were not condemned to any further punishment in a lake of fire for everlasting torment.

While it would not be totally out of place to conclude that Satan, his demonic angels, the beast, and the false prophet will be tormented forever and ever, and that other disobedient humans will be subjected to an everlasting state of lifelessness and nonexistence; from a literal interpretation of Revelation 20:10, 14–15; and 21:8, there are Bible scholars who hold the view of an everlasting torment for Satan and all other disobedient and rebellious spirit beings and humans. There is a second school of biblical scholarship who believe that what is implied in the lake of fire and brimstone and torment forever is symbolic and signifies an everlasting death for Satan his demons and all condemned rebellious humanity.

This latter school of eschatological interpretation quotes the example of Sodom and Gomorrah, and particularly the text in Jude 7 which speaks of eternal fire as it relates with the destruction of Sodom and Gomorrah:

> And the angels who did not keep their proper domain, but left their own abode, He has reserved in everlasting chains under darkness for the judgment of the great day; as Sodom and Gomorrah, and the cities around them in a similar manner to these, having given themselves over to sexual immorality and gone after strange flesh, are set forth as an example, suffering the vengeance of eternal fire.
> —JUDE 7–8, NKJV

The deduction from the aforementioned text in Jude 7 is that the "vengeance of eternal fire" is used as a symbol of everlasting annihilation with a rain of brimstone and fire from God on Sodom and Gomorrah (Gen. 19:24). John the Baptist referred to Christ's end-time judgment using the analogy of wheat, chaff, and unquenchable fire: "His winnowing fan is in His hand, and He will thoroughly clean out His threshing floor, and gather the wheat into His barn, but the chaff He will burn with unquenchable fire" (Luke 3:17, NKJV).

The eternal death school of thought also contends that the second death implies everlasting cutting off or death without any hope of ever living again, since "the wages of sin is death, but the gift of God is eternal life in Christ Jesus our Lord" (Rom. 6:23).

Besides, it is argued that symbolic Death and Hades are cast into the same lake of fire and brimstone as those delivered up from the dead by Death and Hades and are condemned. Death and Hades cannot suffer everlasting torment since they are not human. It follows therefore that since Death and Hades were cast into the lake of fire, which is the second death, and all those whose names were not found written in the Book of Life were also cast into the same lake of fire, it suggests total death for condemned humans. It is the extermination of death and all unsaved humans. Another argument advanced is the example of the prophecy regarding the destruction of Edom as recorded in Isaiah.

> And the streams thereof shall be turned into pitch, and the dust thereof into brimstone, and the land thereof shall become burning pitch. It shall not be quenched night nor day; the smoke thereof shall go up for ever: from generation to generation it shall lie waste.
> —ISAIAH 34:9–10

The deduction from the above text is that Edom was never hurled into some mythical hellfire to burn forever, but completely disappeared from the world scene as if she had been totally consumed with fire and sulfur. Edom's smoke will ascend forever in the sense that its final punishment was not everlasting torment but emptiness, wasteness, and nonexistence.

In Revelation 14:11 we read that the "smoke of their torment ascendeth up for ever and ever: and they have no rest day nor night, who worship the beast and his image, and whosoever receiveth the mark of his name."

Are we to correlate the above Revelation text with that of Edom's eternal fire and conclude that they are both symbolic and that the words concerning torment that ascends forever and ever and no rest for them day or night suggest everlasting cessation of life and nothing more? Is the statement "they have no rest day or night" really symbolic? Does it not mean just that?

For scholars, pastors, and teachers who believe in everlasting hellfire, it is the contention that when the unsaved die they go to Hades—the abode of punishment and torment. They interpret the parable or story of Jesus Christ concerning the rich man, Lazarus the poor man, and Abraham as a literal presentation of the fact that the wicked go at the moment of death to Hades—a place of afterlife torment (Luke 16:19–31), an intermediate state of afterlife.

> So it was that the beggar died, and was carried by the angels to Abraham's bosom. The rich man also died and was buried. And being in torments in Hades, he lifted up his eyes and saw Abraham afar off, and Lazarus in his bosom.
>
> —Luke 16:22–23, NKJV

Bible students and others who interpret the story of the rich man and Lazarus as a parable, readily cite Ecclesiastes 9:10. The text reads as thus: "Whatever your hand finds to do, do it with your might; for there is no work or device or knowledge or wisdom in the grave where you are going" (NKJV).

It is their contention that the aforementioned passage portrays an unconscious state of death until the resurrection—the first resurrection and Great White Throne Judgment resurrection. They also point out that if men are already judged in Hades suffering everlasting torment, what need will there be of a resurrection onto another judgment before the Great White Throne? The resurrection of the dead for judgment onto life everlasting or eternal damnation and not the resurrection of tormented humans in Hades (which in any case is the common grave of all mankind and not a place of torment) is a core doctrine of Christianity. The apostle Paul points to the centrality of the doctrine and faith in the resurrection of the dead: "But if there is no resurrection of the dead, then Christ is not risen. And if Christ is not risen then our preaching is empty and your faith is also empty" (1 Cor. 15:13–14, NKJV).

The point is that the dead, and not the consciously tormented, are resurrected for everlasting life or for everlasting separation from God. "The sea gave up the dead who were in it, and Death and Hades [graveyards, cemeteries] delivered up the dead who were in them. And they were judged, each according to their works" (Rev. 20:13, NKJV).

There are several passages of the Scripture from Matthew, Mark, and Luke quoting Jesus Christ on the issue of hellfire and everlasting fire, ostensibly buttressing the notion of everlasting torment:

> But whoever says, "You fool!" shall be in danger of hell fire.
> —MATTHEW 5:22, NKJV

> It is better for you to enter into life lame or maimed, rather than having two hands and two feet, to be cast into everlasting fire.
> —MATTHEW 18:8, NKJV

> Then He will also say to those on the left hand. "Depart from Me, you cursed, into everlasting fire prepared for the devil and his angels."
> —MATTHEW 25:41, NKJV

> And these will go away into everlasting punishment, but the righteous into eternal life.
> —MATTHEW 25:46, NKJV

> It is better for you to enter into life maimed, rather than having two hands, to go to hell, into the fire that shall never be quenched— where "Their worm does not die And the fire is not quenched."
> —MARK 9:43–44, NKJV

> And do not fear those who kill the body but cannot kill the soul. But rather fear Him who is able to destroy both body and soul in hell.
> —MATTHEW 10:28, NKJV

The above passage of Matthew 10:28 seems to suggest that there is total destruction, complete annihilation, in hell and that clearly the only one capable of doing so is Jehovah God. He only can kill or destroy both body and soul in hell. But another text conveying the message of Christ in this passage does so in a slightly different manner, which provides the ground for a different interpretation

> And I say to you, My friends, do not be afraid of those who kill the body, and after that have no more that they can do. But I will show you whom you should fear: Fear Him who, after He has killed, has power to cast into hell: yes, I say to you, fear Him!
>
> —LUKE 12:4–5, NKJV

Here we see a picture of casting into hell after death, which appears to be in harmony with the belief that the dead can be tormented in hell-fire. Perhaps Matthew 10:28 is meant to convey the same message or vice versa.

Christ's warning in Mark 9:43–47, describing hell as where the fire is not quenched and where worms don't die, echoes the same words of Isaiah used by the prophet to describe the latter-day reign and indignation of God:

> And they shall go forth, and look upon the carcases of the men that have transgressed against me: for their worm shall not die, neither shall their fire be quenched; and they shall be an abhorring unto all flesh.
>
> —ISAIAH 66:24

The above text is used by some Bible scholars to argue against the belief in everlasting hellfire, asserting that in Mark 9:43–47, Jesus alluded to Isaiah in describing Gehenna—the Valley of Hinnom. (In the days of Jesus Christ, Gehenna, also known as the Valley of Ben Hinnom, a deep narrow gorge Southwest of Jerusalem with Mount Zion to the north and the so-called "hill of evil counsel" to the south, was used as the garbage dump of Jerusalem. Into it were thrown all the filth and garbage of the city, including the dead bodies of animals and executed criminals. Fires constantly burned in the vale to consume the awful dumps while maggots worked in the fifth.) The contention, therefore, is that Christ's reference to Isaiah 66:24 was a symbolic one; not one of torture but rather of complete destruction, as is evident from the fact that the Isaiah text dealt not with persons who were alive but with the carcasses of men that were transgressing against God.

The *Dictionary of Biblical Imagery* explains hell in the following words:

> The best known biblical image for hell derives from a deep narrow gorge southeast of Jerusalem called gebenhinniom, "the valley of Ben Hinnom," in which idolatrous Israelites offered up child sacrifices to the gods Molech and Baal (2 Chron. 28:3, 33:6, Jer. 7:31–32; 19:2–6, NIV). Josiah defiled the valley to make it acceptable as a holy site (2 Kings 23:10) after which it was used as a garbage dump by the inhabitants of Jerusalem. As a result, the valley of Ben Hinnom became known as the dump heap, the place of destruction by fire in Jewish tradition. The Greek word gehenna, "hell" commonly used in NT for the place of final punishment, is derived from the Hebrew name for this valley.[1]

According to *Nelson's New Illustrated Bible Dictionary*, Jesus used the awful scene of the Valley of Hinnom as a symbol of hell. "In effect, He said, 'Do you want to know what hell is like? Look at Gehenna.' So hell may be described as God's 'cosmic garbage dump.' All that is unfit for heaven will be thrown into hell."[2]

Whatever interpretation or notion we hold on the controversial issue of hell and everlasting torment, let's be reminded that the most important message is the glory of the new heaven and earth, in which Satan, his demonic spirits, the beast, the false prophet, and wicked humans will have no place. Our concern and greatest challenge is to work in tandem with Jehovah's godly principles; His laws, statutes, and commandments; and to believe in the Messiah, Jesus, and to accept Him as our Lord and Savior.

If Satan and all the powers and principalities of darkness and all perpetrators and perpetuators of spiritual wickedness in high places, who have from succeeding generations contributed to human sufferings, tribulations, misery, deaths, wars, famine, pestilences, and to the destruction of the earth's natural order, are to be confined to everlasting hellfire, so be it. If they are to be cut off eternally, out of existence in perpetual state of nothingness and nonexistence, so be it; and better, so as to erase their memory totally from the universe. In either case, the earth and the heavens are rid of them and mankind is better off.

The most important proposition, therefore, is that as Bible-believing Christians, who have faithfully and with childlike spirits accepted the loving call of John 3:16, we must live daily in the hope of eternal life, which God, who cannot lie, promised before the world began, and acknowledge the gospel truth, which is after godliness (Titus 1:2).

Let us go back to our main discourse, the glory of new heavens and earth. The prophet Isaiah was divinely inspired to proclaim the coming new heavens and earth: "For as the new heavens and the new earth, which I will make, shall remain before me, saith the LORD, so shall your seed and your name remain" (Isa. 66:22).

The apostle Peter looked forward to a new heavens and earth: "Nevertheless we, according to His promise, look for new heavens and a new earth in which righteousness dwells (2 Pet. 3:13, NKJV).

Then, Christ showed John the vision of all things made new: "Now I saw a new heaven and a new earth, for the first heaven and the first earth had passed away. Also there was no more sea (Rev. 21:1, NKJV).

But just before John is shown the vision of the new heavens and earth, death and hell were cast into the lake of fire, which is described as the second death. The symbolic casting of death and hell into the lake of fire implies an end to death and the fulfillment of God's promise as revealed by the divine inspiration of His prophets: "He will swallow up death forever, and the Lord GOD will wipe away tears from all faces (Isa. 25:8, NKJV).

The prophet Hosea also gave a foregleam of the eventual end to human death and suffering: "I will ransom them from the power of the grave; I will redeem them from death: O death, I will be thy plagues; O grave, I will be thy destruction" (Hosea 13:14).

With the symbolic casting of death and hell into the lake of fire, God fulfils Revelation 21:4: "And God shall wipe away all tears from their eyes; and there shall be no more death, neither sorrow, nor crying, neither shall there be any more pain: for the former things are passed away."

This passing away of the former things, the destruction and regeneration of the present heaven and earth and earth's socioeconomic and political order, is laid bare in several Bible passages. The psalmist was inspired by the Holy Spirit to speak about the passing away of the present heaven and earth:

> Of old You laid the foundation of the earth, And the heavens are the work of your hands. They will perish but You will endure; Yes, they will all grow old like a garment; Like a cloak You will change them, And they will be changed.
>
> —PSALM 102:25–26, NKJV

In His Beatitudes, the Sermon on the Mount of Olives, Jesus spoke of the phasing out of heaven and earth: "Heaven and earth shall pass away, but my words shall not pass away" (Matt. 24:35).

In the Epistle of Paul to the Hebrews, he echoes Isaiah's prophetic words that the heavens and the earth will grow old like a garment and that like a cloak, God will fold them up (Heb. 1:10–12). The destruction of the old world order, the old and decayed heavens and earth, and their regeneration or renewal comes with awesome and frightening cosmic shakedown and meltdown, as we can read from several passages of the Scripture. Christ Jesus provides a foregleam of this end-time cataclysmic event, while pointing to the signs of His second coming: "Immediately after the tribulation of those days the sun will be darkened, and the moon will not give its light; the stars will fall from heaven, and the powers of the heavens will be shaken" (Matt. 24:29, NKJV). (See also Mark 13:24–27.)

In the Revelation of Jesus Christ given unto John, a vision of cosmic disturbances in the heavens and on earth was also shown to him:

> I looked when He opened the sixth seal, and behold, there was a great earthquake; and the sun became black as sackcloth of hair, and the moon became like blood. And the stars of heaven fell on earth, as a fig tree drops its late figs when it is shaken by a mighty wind. Then the sky receded as a scroll when it is rolled up, and every mountain and island was moved out of its place.
>
> —REVELATION 6:12–14, NKJV

The imagery of disorders in the sun, the moon, and the stars depict the inevitability of a fiery destruction of the old heavens and earth. The apostle Peter reminds us of the uninhibited power of the word of God in the fulfillment of the world's destruction by fire.

> For this they willfully forget: that by the word of God the heavens were of old, and the earth standing out of water and in water, by which the world that then existed perished, being flooded by water. But the heavens and earth which are now preserved by the same word, are reserved for fire until the day of judgment and perdition of ungodly men.
>
> —2 PETER 3:5–7, NKJV

Peter emphasized further that the heavens will pass away with a great noise, that the elements will melt with fervent heat and that both the earth and the works that are in it will be burned up (2 Pet. 3:10).

Malachi describes the day of the Lord's coming as a fiery encounter with the world: "But who can endure the day of His coming? And who can stand when He appears? For He is like a refiner's fire And like a launderers' soap. He will sit as a refiner and a purifier of silver" (Mal. 3:2–3, NKJV).

Yes! The earth and the heavens will be destroyed; and then they will be purified, refined, regenerated, and made new again. But there are differing views among Bible scholars, evangelists, and pastors regarding the extent of this end-time destruction. Will it involve the natural heavens, the vast expanse of the sky and everything in it (all the celestial bodies), or the universe? Will the entire earth, its natural habitats, all of God's created natural order, vegetation, rivers, seas, etc., be wiped out?

One school of thought believes that the physical universe, the earth, and the entire view of the heavens and its trillions of stars and heavenly bodies will apparently all be dissolved, reduced to emptiness as they were before creation. Are we to believe by this interpretation that planets like Mercury, Venus, Jupiter, Saturn, Uranus, Neptune, Pluto and other heavenly bodies will be dissolved? The other school contends that this is most unlikely and that the present heavens and earth will partially be destroyed and then renewed and rejuvenated. This latter school readily quotes Paul's words in the twelfth chapter of his Epistle to the Hebrews:

> But now he hath promised, saying, Yet once more I shake not the earth only, but also heaven. And this word, Yet once more, signifieth the removing of those things that are shaken, as of things that are made, that those things which cannot be shaken may remain.
> —HEBREWS 12:26–27

Accordingly, the things that cannot be shaken are the atmospheric heavens and earth, which are currently in place, and will never cease to exist but will merely be renovated by fire and exist in a renewed state. The removals of those things that can be shaken include the present corrupt world socioeconomic and political systems, man's sinful nature, disease germs, and spirits that induce men to corruption. Christ's millennial kingdom, with all its socioeconomic activities and worship, except the curse and its effects, will eternally continue and will not be dissolved by God's fire of refinement. God's original creation, the cosmos, the entire social order created at the time of Adam, is expected to remain forever, but it will be delivered from the present satanic bondage of corruption into the glorious liberty and manifestation of the sons of God (Rom. 8:18–25).

It is apparent from the seven trumpet plagues spoken of in Revelation chapters 8 and 9 that some parts of the earth will not be affected by God's righteous judgment. From the first trumpet, a third of the trees and green grasses were burned up (8:7). After the second trumpet, a third of the living creatures in the sea died and a third of the ships were destroyed (v. 9). When the third trumpet sounded, a third of waters became wormwood, and many men died from taking in the water (v. 11). After the fourth trumpet, a third of the sun, a third of the moon, and a third of the stars were darkened and a third of the day did not shine (v. 12). In Revelation chapter 9 we read that the fifth trumpet brought forth demonic locusts from the bottomless pit that were given authority to harm and torment only those who do not have the seal of God on their foreheads (vv. 3–5). The sixth trumpet released the four angels who were bound at the great River Euphrates to kill a third of mankind by the plagues of fire, smoke, and brimstone that came from the fiery mouths of the horses ridden by a two hundred million army of horsemen (9:13–21).

It is, therefore, logical to conclude that God's judgment will be selective, involving the process of sifting the wheat from the tares, gathering the wheat into God's barn and binding the tares and burning them (Matt. 13:30, 37–43). This selective process will involve His entire created universe.

In Matthew 24:29 and Mark 13:24–27, Jesus spoke of the darkening of the sun and the moon not giving off its light. Jesus also showed John this vision of the sun, the moon and the stars in Revelation 8:12. Modern science has revealed that the moon plays a vital role in earth's ecology and is the principal cause of ocean tides. The moon also contributes to the stability of the earth's spin axis. Without a perfectly fitted moon, the earth would vacillate like a spinning top, which would result in catastrophic climatic and tidal changes. In the marvelous designs of an omniscient God, He has given the earth two dynamic protective shields. These shields protect the earth from outer space, where lethal radiation is common and meteoroids are an ever present danger. All God needs to do to send fiery destruction to any part of the earth, is to remove, by His word, the earth's huge and powerful magnetic field that stretches far into space. Then it is exposed to the full intensity of cosmic radiation and the deadly forces emanating from the sun in form of solar flares, which in minutes release as much energy as billions of hydrogen bombs. It could be God's spoken word on the removal of the earth's magnetic field that would lead to the instant annihilation of the Satan-led army at the last battle of Gog and Magog. It could also be the cause of the great heat that scorched men in Revelation 16:8–9.

Those that will inherit this new heavens and earth refined by fire, are renewed, regenerated humans who have shed the old flesh of corrupted body and spirit. Indeed, the new heavens and earth herald God's perfect state as Jesus Christ delivers the kingdom to His Father and our Father, Jehovah God, so that God will become all in all. God's tabernacle comes down on earth to dwell with mankind, taking the place of the replica earthly tabernacle in Jerusalem, and all human trials, tribulations, daily worries, sicknesses, and deaths are put to an end.

> And I heard a loud voice from heaven saying, "Behold, the tabernacle of God is with men, and He will dwell with them, and they shall be His people. God Himself will be with them and be their God. And God will wipe away every tear from their eyes; there shall be no more death, nor sorrow, nor crying. There shall be no more pain, for the former things have passed away.
> —REVELATION 21:3–4, NKJV

In 1 Corinthians chapter 15, the apostle Paul explains that sinful human flesh cannot inherit this disease and death free new heavens and earth: "Now this I say, brethren, that flesh and blood cannot inherit the kingdom of God; neither doth corruption inherit incorruption" (v. 50).

This body that is not just made of flesh and blood is like the resurrected body that was sown in corruption and raised in incorruption, sown in dishonor and raised in glory, sown in weakness and raised in power, and sown in natural body but raised a spiritual body (1 Cor. 15:42–45). Let's recall that while replying to the Sadducees' question on the resurrection, Christ pointed out that in the resurrection there is no marrying nor giving in marriage but that humans will be like the angels of God in heaven (Matt. 22:29–32).

> The sons of this age marry and are given in marriage. But those who are counted worthy to attain that age, and the resurrected from the dead, neither marry nor are given to marriage; nor can they die anymore, for they are equal to the angels and are sons of God, being sons of the resurrection.
> —LUKE 20:34–36, NKJV

Paul also stated in Philippians 3:21 that Jesus Christ "will transform our lowly body that it may be conformed to His glorious body, according to the working by which He is able even to subdue all things to Himself" (NKJV).

It is important for us as Christians, believers, and faithful followers of Christ to have an unshakeable faith and a radiant hope on this coming glory and everlasting life of bliss under God's new world order, His eternal theocratic government of the final restitution of all things. It requires the spirit of an incurable optimist, a childlike faith, hope, and above all God's grace and divine revelation to accept the greatest miracle and supernatural occurrence that the world will ever get to know and experience. We should also exercise faith because Jehovah God created humans to live forever until the Satan-induced sin of disobedience to God's explicit commandment that brought the Adamic fall and death into the world. The longevity of mankind's early forbears from Adam down to Methuselah who lived 930 years and 969 years respectively (Gen. 5:1–32), points to the blessed assurance that once sin is removed from the earth, aging and death will cease. The prolongation of life beyond the limits of time and within the ceaseless movement of times and seasons, days and nights, summers and winters, is not an illusion but a coming reality.

Our God-given brains and ability to think, reason, and meditate on the meaning of life is not an accident of nature. And the source of eternal life has also provided everlasting life for all those who exercise faith and a healthy and genuine fear of Him in the new heavens and new earth free of chaos, conflicts, human wickedness, and satanic influences.

> Our God is a God of salvation, and escape from death belongs to the Lord GOD.
>
> —PSALM 68:20, HCSB

Indeed, as the apostle John was inspired to say, "The world is passing away, and the lust of it; but he who does the will of God abides forever" (1 John 2:17, NKJV).

The permanent seal of God's glory and His everlasting relationship with His created humans is established with the descent of the New Jerusalem.

Chapter 10

THE NEW JERUSALEM

AFTER THE MILLENNIUM and the extermination of the Satan-led final rebellion of the armies of Gog and Magog, the New Jerusalem is transplanted from heaven to the earth. The vision of the descent of this resplendent celestial city is shown to the apostle John by one of the seven angels who had the seven bowls filled with the last plagues of God.

> [The angel] came to me and talked with me, saying, "Come, I will show you the bride, the Lamb's wife." And he carried me away in the Spirit to a great and high mountain, and showed me the great city, the holy Jerusalem, descending out of heaven from God, having the glory of God. Her light was like a most precious stone, like a jasper stone, clear as crystal.
>
> —REVELATION 21:9–11, NKJV

The New Jerusalem is the city consecrated to the holiness, the highest spiritual purity, the absolute moral perfection of Jehovah God and Jesus, the Messiah. New Jerusalem is the Holy City of triumphant saints, the refined ones from among the redeemed of the earth in everlasting union of corulership and priesthood with God, Jesus Christ, the Holy Spirit, and a legion of angels—seraphim and cherubim—in the eternal governance of the new earth. It is clear from Revelation 20:4–6 that those who have been beheaded (killed by various means) for their witness to Jesus and for the word of God, and did not worship the beast, and are the beneficiaries of the first resurrection over whom the second death has no power, are citizens of the New Jerusalem. The citizenship extends to the 144,000 redeemed from the earth, who are the only ones that can sing the new song, who were not defiled with women, for they are virgins (possibly meaning purified of life and conduct) who followed the Lamb wherever He goes. These were redeemed from among men being first fruits of God and to the Lamb. And in their mouth was found no deceit, for they were without fault before the throne of God (14:1–4).

The apostle Paul gives us a picture of those that will inhabit the New Jerusalem in his Epistle to the Hebrews.

> You have come to Mount Zion, the city of the living God, the heavenly Jerusalem, the city of an innumerable company of angels, to the general assembly and church of the firstborn who are registered in heaven, to God the Judge of all, to the spirits of just men made perfect, to Jesus the Mediator of the new covenant, and to the blood of sprinkling that speaks better things than that of Abel.
> —HEBREWS 12:22–24, NKJV

Let us be reminded that before the descent of New Jerusalem, Jesus Christ had already spent His thousand years of Messianic kingship on earth and then superintending the annihilation of the Satan-led armies of Gog and Magog in the earth's last battle. Indeed, given the very short memory of men, a thousand years is actually a long period for rebellious men to forget God's judgment at Armageddon and to attempt another rebellion against Christ's kingdom rule and Jehovah's sovereignty. Now God descends on the earth with His tabernacle, His New Jerusalem, after the final annihilation of Satan and his rebellious followers.

> Behold, the tabernacle of God is with men, and he will dwell with them, and they shall be his people, and God himself shall be with them, and be their God.
> —REVELATION 21:3

The descent of God's tabernacle is in fulfillment of His promise, as revealed through divine inspiration by the prophet Ezekiel:

> My tabernacle also shall be with them: yea, I will be their God, and they shall be my people. And the heathen [nations] shall know that I the LORD do sanctify Israel, when my sanctuary shall be in the midst of them for evermore.
> —EZEKIEL 37:27–28

New Jerusalem is God's tabernacle dwelling among men, the theocratic capital of the entire universe from where God's presence is manifested everywhere in the new heavens and earth. In his *Commentary on*

Galatians, specifically Galatians 4:26 in which Paul described Jerusalem which is above as free and mother of us all, Martin Luther (1483–1546) commented thus:

> But the new and heavenly Jerusalem, which is the queen and a free-woman, is appointed of God in earth and not in heaven, to be the mother of us all, of whom we have been gendered, and yet daily are gendered. Therefore it is necessary that this our mother should be on earth among men. Notwithstanding she gendereth by the Holy Ghost, by the ministry of the word and sacraments, and not in the flesh....And this spiritual Jerusalem hath not any certain place, but is dispersed throughout the world, and may be in Babylon, in Turkey, in India or in the isles of the sea, wherever men receive the gospel of Jesus Christ.[1]

Here Martin Luther speaks of the spiritual essence of New Jerusalem. He speaks of the new and heavenly Jerusalem as the church. In other words, the faithful dispersed throughout the world who have one and the same gospel, one and the same faith in Christ, the same Holy Ghost, and the same sacraments.

Now, there are different interpretations regarding the New Jerusalem either as a literal city or as representing the church, the Israel of God. To some scholars, evangelists, pastors, prophets, and teachers, New Jerusalem symbolizes the whole Israel of God, redeemed by the Lion-Lamb of Judah from every tribe, and tongue, and peoples, and nations to become God's kingdom of priests. To others, New Jerusalem is a literal city and "city" means both the place and the people who dwell in it.

To this school of thought it is a bride because the inhabitants are the Lamb's Bride. It is God's dwelling place and seat of His theocratic governance. It is Christ's dwelling place as the King of kings and Lord of lords, Prince of Peace, great Counselor, and High Priest. It is the dwelling place of the angels and all those refined and cleansed as coheirs with Christ and corulers and priests over the earth.

It has been pointed out by Bible scholars that it is unscriptural to conclude that all those that will inherit the new heavens and new earth will be corulers with Christ and that all the redeemed of the earth will dwell in one city, the New Jerusalem. Apparently the Bible states that a mass of other redeemed humanity are not permanent dwellers of the New Jerusalem but will be granted entrance into the city as pilgrims.

And the nations of those who are saved shall walk in its light, and the kings of the earth bring their glory and honor into it. Its gates shall not be shut at all by day (there shall be no night there). And they shall bring the glory and honor of the nations into it. But there shall by no means enter it anything that defiles, or causes an abomination or a lie, but only those who are written in the Lamb's Book of Life.

—REVELATION 21:24–27, NKJV

The nations walking by means of the light of New Jerusalem are most certainly

the great multitude which no one could number, of all nations, tribes, peoples, and tongues, standing before the throne and before the Lamb, clothed with white robes, with palm branches in their hands, and crying out with a loud voice, saying, "Salvation belongs to our God who sits on the throne, and to the Lamb!"

—REVELATION 7:9–10, NKJV

Isaiah had a divinely inspired foregleam of this great worship of nations before God who sits on the throne and the Lamb: "'And it shall come to pass That from one New Moon to another, And from one Sabbath to another, All flesh shall come to worship before Me,' says the LORD'" (Isa. 66:23, NKJV).

The prophet Jeremiah also foretold "at that time Jerusalem shall be called The Throne of the LORD, and all the nations shall be gathered to it, to the name of the LORD, to Jerusalem. No more shall they follow the dictates of their evil hearts" (Jer. 3:17, NKJV).

Zechariah 14:16 seems to strengthen the position that there will be multitudes from the nations or peoples of the new earth who will not be inhabitants of the New Jerusalem, but will go on yearly pilgrimage to the Holy City and throne of the Lord, just as today Christian pilgrims go to Jerusalem and Moslem pilgrims to Mecca: "And it shall come to pass that everyone who is left of all the nations which came against Jerusalem shall go from year to year to worship the King, the LORD of hosts, and keep the Feast of Tabernacles."

There are also different views and interpretations as to the location and nature or characteristic of this Holy City of the eternal state of mankind. *Willmington's Guide to the Bible* describes the New Jerusalem as a "stationary city floating above the earth in space and the new earth becoming a satellite planet encircling the starry capital from which earth will receive its light."[2] But the argument against this position is that if the city is suspended in air, there will be no need for an elaborate foundation made with the finest and strongest precious stones. A counter argument in support of the "stationary floating city" position is that God, who is the architect, builder, and owner of the New Jerusalem (the tabernacle made with hands not of this creation [Heb. 9:11]), could easily have built the city with all its precious stone foundation completely in heaven, then float it with it's foundation in space by His pronouncement, His word. With God nothing is impossible (Luke 1:37).

Finis Jennings Dake presents an equally attractive picture of the positioning of the New Jerusalem, starting from the premise that the New Jerusalem site in heaven is called Mount Zion, as we can read from the books of Hebrews and Revelation.

> You have come to Mount Zion and to the city of the living God, the heavenly Jerusalem, to an innumerable company of angels.
> —HEBREWS 12:22, NKJV

> Then I looked, and there before me was the Lamb, standing on Mount Zion and with Him 144,000 who had his name and his Father's name written on their foreheads.
> —REVELATION 14:1, NIV

From the aforementioned position of New Jerusalem on Mount Zion, which Finis says refers to the highest mountain peak of the city on which God's capitol building is located, he concludes that "from all the statements in the scripture, it is clear that the city is a series of mountain peaks."[3] He explains that the city begins inside the walls as low foothills and increases in height until the highest peak is 1,500 miles high. And on that highest part is built the heavenly tabernacle, or capital building, where God sits as the supreme moral Governor of the universe. He concludes that on the mountains and in the valleys are built the many mansions of John 14:2: "In my Father's house are many mansions: if it were not so, I would have told you. I go to prepare a place for you."[4]

Perhaps this picture of Finis could best be appreciated if we consider God's everlasting covenant not only with the forbears of Israel but with the land of Israel as well, and His promise that through Israel He will show His glory to the rest of the nations. It is from Jerusalem that Christ will steer the nations for a thousand years and it is on Jerusalem that God's tabernacle or the New Jerusalem will rest from her descent from heaven, or be built. The land that Jehovah God allotted to ancient Israel includes the snowcapped mountains in the north and a mountain range that runs the length of the land like a huge backbone. If we are to expand on our vision of Finis Dake's interpretation, it is perhaps on this mountain range stretching from the mountains of Judah and Samaria to Mount Carmel, Mount Tabor, the mountains of Galilee, Mount Nebo, and to Mount Hermon, the tallest mountain in the Palestine area with its melting snows which supply water to Jordan River, that the New Jerusalem will be built. And perhaps it will extend far beyond, if these mountains are to stand in their positions after the great cosmic shake-down and meltdown that will be unleashed on the earth, particularly that of the seventh bowl of Revelation 16:17–20.

In analyzing the architectural measurements and dimensions of New Jerusalem, some Bible students, teachers, and ministers have offered a spiritual interpretation. For instance, this school of thought asserts that the 144 cubit high walls of the city (Rev. 21:17) symbolize 144,000 spiritually adopted sons of God. They posit further that the number 12 that appears in 12,000 furlong measurement of the city with the length, breadth and height being equal (v. 16), is used figuratively in organizational settings in Bible prophecy. They therefore conclude that the New Jerusalem is a superbly designed organizational arrangement for accomplishing God's eternal purpose and that New Jerusalem together with Christ the King represent God's kingdom organization. It is also their affirmation that the foundation of the city made of twelve precious stones of the highest and finest qualities (v. 19), emphasizes the priestly function of New Jerusalem of which Jesus, the great High Priest, is the lamp. This school of interpretation also provides a literal view of New Jerusalem as a city with priests, lighted with the brilliant luster of God's glory, and with permanently open majestic gates into which redeemed nations will walk and kings of the earth will bring their glory.

Far more important than all of these different interpretative views are the eternal qualities of New Jerusalem and its everlasting life provisions to redeemed humanity. Indeed, of immeasurable benefits and endless bliss to mankind and womankind is the water of the river of life that flows and the tree of life that grows from the eternal Holy City of God and the Lamb. Revelation 22:1–2 gives a vision of this river and tree:

> And he shewed me a pure river of water of life, clear as crystal, proceeding out of the throne of God and of the Lamb. In the midst of the street of it, and on either side of the river, was there the tree of

life, which bare twelve manner of fruits, and yielded her fruit every
month: and the leaves of the tree were for the healing of the nations.

This crystal clear river flowing out from God's throne reminds us of
the life-giving water that Christ spoke about during His earthly ministry
and dialogue with the Samaritan woman:

> Whoever drinks of this water will thirst again, but whoever drinks
> of the water that I shall give him will never thirst. But the water that
> I shall give him will become in him a fountain of water springing
> up into everlasting life.
>
> —JOHN 4:13–14, NKJV

Let us recall that over eight centuries before the revelation of John,
Ezekiel was also giving a vision of this river of water of life. In his vision
the river flowed out from the temple in Jerusalem and down into the
Dead Sea, and the heavily mineralized and chemically saturated water
was miraculously turned into clean fresh water teeming with fish. As in
John's vision, Ezekiel also saw on both sides of the torrent of river all
kinds of fruit-bearing trees (Ezek. 47:1–12). The tree of life that was in
the midst of the Garden of Eden and had since disappeared from man's
sight after the Adamic sin reappears in abundance in the New Jerusalem
(Gen. 2:9; 3:24).

These trees of life are God's bountiful and supernatural provisions for
giving eternal life to the redeemed of the earth. The leaves from them
will elevate all obedient sons and daughters of God to spiritual and
bodily perfection, erasing all corruption and building in incorruption.
Gloriously added to these overwhelmingly generous provisions of God
for eternal life are the permanent entrenchment of blessing and eradica-
tion of curse.

> And there shall be no more curse: but the throne of God and of the
> Lamb shall be in it; and his servants shall serve him: And they shall
> see his face; and his name shall be in their foreheads.
>
> —REVELATION 22:3–4

The Adamic curse of Genesis 3:10–19 is triumphantly abolished in
Revelation 22:3. With the tabernacle of God with men and His presence
among men, there is a certitude that the New Jerusalem and the entire
earth will be secured for all eternity. In the glorious radiant presence of

the Almighty God, eternal light shines on the New Jerusalem and the entire inhabited earth of the redeemed children of God.

Martin Luther, the great sixteenth century theologian, reflected on the blessed assurance of a new heaven and a new earth, wherein righteousness shall dwell in the following profound and lucid words:

> It will be no arid waste, but a beautiful new earth, where all the just will dwell together. There will be no carnivorous beasts or venomous creatures, for all those, like ourselves, will be relieved from the curse of sin and will be as friendly as they were to Adam in paradise. There will be little gods with golden hair, shining like precious stones. The foliage of the trees and the verdure of the grass will have the brilliancy of emeralds. We ourselves delivered from our mundane subjection to gross appetites and necessities shall have the same form as here, but infinitely more perfect. Our eyes will be radiant as the purest silver, and we shall exempt from all sickness and tribulation. We shall behold the glorious creator face to face. And then, what ineffable satisfaction will it be to find our relations and friends among the just! If we were all one here, we should have peace among ourselves, but God orders it otherwise, to the end we may yearn and sigh after the future paternal home, and become weary of this troublesome life. Now, if there be joy in the chosen, so must the highest sorrow and despair be in the damned.[5]

It is important to point out that the kingdom of God and of the Lamb on the new earth is not restricted merely to the ecclesiastical praise and worship or theocratic governance spheres, but it aims at absolute universality extending into every department of human life. Every loyal subject will endeavor to bring all human society, socioeconomic and ecclesiastical, into obedience to its law of righteousness. With the love and grace of God and the Messiah Christ and the assistance of angels, corulers with Christ, and the kingdom of priests in the New Jerusalem, a renewed, redeemed humanity is assisted to organize human society and all its institutions and organs upon a distinctively Christian (Christ-centered) basis. This coming kingdom of God is structured firmly on the foundation of the fatherhood of Jehovah God, the elder brotherhood and the redeeming blood of Christ Jesus, and the universal brotherhood of all redeemed citizens of the new world order—new heavens and new earth.

I strongly feel that I would have failed to give an apt or an appropriate conclusion to this book if I don't extract from the very deep spiritual insights of A. A. Hodge in his theological treatise on the kingdom of Christ, God's surely coming new heavens and earth. Hodge's words:

The baleful doctrine of human rights which is now turning all political societies into pandemoniums is never admitted in the kingdom of God. But the sublime doctrine of human duties in its stead binds all hearts and lives in beautiful harmony to the throne of the Prince, and to the happiness of all his subjects. This kingdom is to endure forever, gradually to embrace all the inhabitants of the earth; and finally the entire moral government of God in heaven and on earth…

The process by which this kingdom grows through its successive stages toward its ultimate completion can of course be very inadequately understood by us. It implies the ceaseless operation of the mighty power of God working through all the forces and laws of nature, and culminating in the supernatural manifestations of grace and miracle. The Holy Ghost is everywhere present and he works directly alike in the ways we distinguish as natural and supernatural, alike through appointed instruments and agencies, and immediately by his direct personal power. The special agency for the building up of this kingdom is the organized Christian church, with its regular ministry, providing for the preaching of the gospel and the administration of the sacraments. The special work of the Holy Ghost in building up this kingdom is performed in the regeneration and sanctification of individuals through the ministry of the church. But beyond this the omnipresent Holy Ghost works to the same end, directly and indirectly, in every sphere of nature and of human life, causing all the historic movements of peoples and nations, of civilization and of science, of political and ecclesiastical societies, to broaden and deepen the foundation and to advance the growth and perfection of his kingdom…

Its process is like that of the constructive power of the kingdom of nature, silent and invisible, yet Omnipresent and Omnipotent, like the rain and the dew, and the Zephyr and the sunlight. The kingdom comes intensively in each heart, like the leaven, which penetrates the whole mass silently yet irresistibly, like the growth of the mustard-seed, which from the least beginnings unfolds itself until it shoots out great branches and shelters the fowls of heaven. In this world the wheat and the tares, the good and the evil, grow together to the end. The net gathers in fish good and bad. One field brings forth thirty, another forty, and another an hundred-fold. In the end the tares shall be gathered and burned, and the pure wheat gathered without mixture in the eternal garner of the Lord. In the whole history of its coming the kingdom of God "cometh not with observation, neither shall they say, lo, here! Or Lo, there! For, behold, the kingdom of God is within you," But its consummation shall be ushered in suddenly and with overwhelming demonstrations of glory. "For as the lightning that lighteneth out of the one part under heaven shineth unto the other part under heaven; so shall also the son of man be in his day.[6]

Dietrich Bonhoeffer, the Lutheran martyr hung on April 5, 1943, for his outspoken opposition and resistance to Hitler's despotism, pointed out in one of his discourses that it is the grace of Jesus Christ that He still does not reveal Himself visibly to the world; for the very moment at which that happened would be the end, and thus judgment on the world.[7]

For now Christ lets His faithful bear witness to His hidden and manifest glory before the world through the spread of the good news of His coming kingdom until the last day when He returns visibly to judge everyone. So Jesus Christ, the risen One, avoids any visible reinstatement before the world, for that would be judgment on the world. Through His resurrection, ascension, and accession on God's right hand as King, we discern that God has not forsaken His created earth to Satan but has taken it back to Himself. Through Christ, God has bestowed on the earth a new future, a new promise, a new heaven and earth, and a new humanity. A radiant hope and an unshakeable faith in Christ's resurrection and Second Advent unshackle us from this transient carnal world and usher us into the new creation of God. This glowing hope and unflinching faith bestow upon us by grace the death of the righteous, as we go the way of all mortals here on earth, keeping us in the loving memory of God and Jesus Christ for the gift of everlasting life when the trump will sound and the dead in Christ will arise to eternal bliss: "For the Son of man shall come in the glory of his Father with his angels; and then he shall reward every man according to his works" (Matt. 16:27).

Finally, it is also imperative to emphasize that no matter the differences in our interpretation of the symbols or letters of Revelation or the Book of Daniel or our conception of the new heavens, the new earth, or the New Jerusalem, the most important message of salvation remains unchanged. And that is the unchangeable fact that "the Alpha and the Omega, the Beginning and the End...who is and who was and who is to come" (Rev. 1:8, NKJV), the Creator of all things, the consummation, the goal, the end and objective of all things has by His word willed a new heavens, a new earth, and a New Jerusalem wherein dwells eternal righteousness. He has by His word willed a perfect earth, a perfect body, and everlasting life for a renewed humanity who thirst for eternal life of bliss and who have freely taken from the water of the river of life and the tree of life. To these obedient servant kings belongs this timeless promise:

> And God shall wipe away all tears from their eyes; and there shall be no more death, neither sorrow, nor crying, neither shall there be any more pain: for the former things are passed away.
>
> —REVELATION 21:4

To them also belong Isaiah's inspired words of promise from Jehovah God:

> Thy sun shall no more go down; neither shall thy moon withdraw itself: for the LORD shall be thine everlasting light, and the days of thy mourning shall be ended.
>
> —ISAIAH 60:20

May God's kingdom be made manifest here on earth as He has established same in the highest heavens. May the undeserved kindness and the unmerited favor of the Lord Jesus Christ abide with you as you read this publication, and may you have a radiant hope and an unshakeable faith in the surely coming new heavens and new earth and the New Jerusalem. Amen.

NOTES

Preface
Israel: God's Ensign to Nations

1. Kenneth Barker and Donald Burdick, *Zondervan NIV Study Bible* (Grand Rapids: Zondervan, 2002).

2. Alfred M. Lilienthal, *What Price Israel?* (Beirut: Institute of Palestine Studies, 1969).

3. Abraham Lincoln, "Proclamation Appointing a National Fast Day," Abraham Lincoln Online, Speeches and Writings, found at http://www .abrahamlincolnonline.org/lincoln/speeches/fast.htm (accessed September 22, 2013).

Chapter 1
Israel in World History

1. *Insight on the Scriptures* (Brooklyn, NY: Watchtower Bible and Tract Society, 1988), 934.

2. John Hall and John Kirk, *The History of the World* (New York: Gallery Books, 1988).

3. James B. Pritchard, *Ancient Near Eastern Texts* (Jerusalem: The Hebrew University of Jerusalem, 1974), 285–286.

4. C. J. Gadd, *The Fall of Nineveh* (London: British Museum, 1923), #21,901.

5. *Insight on the Scriptures*, 580.

6. *Insight on the Scriptures*.

7. Flavius Josephus, *Jewish Antiquities* (bk. 11, chap. 5, sec. C-11, 337) in *The New Complete Works of Josephus*, trans. William Whiston (Grand Rapids: Kregel, 1999).

8. Flavius Josephus, *The Jewish War* (New York: Penguin Books, 1970), 899.

9. En.wikipedia.org/wiki/Pope Urban 11.

Chapter 2
Dispersal and Tribulation History

1. Lilienthal, 219–221.

2. Heinrich Graetz, *History of the Jews* (Philadelphia: Jewish Publication Society, 1919).

3. Lilienthal.

4. Friedrich Hertz, *Race and Civilization* (New York: Macmillan, 1928).

5. William Ripley, *Races of Europe* (New York: Appleton, 1898), 392.

6. Josephus, *The New Complete Works of Josephus*.

7. John Cornwell, *Hitler's Pope: The Secret History of Pius XII* (UK: Penguin Books, 2000), 24.

8. Ibid., 24–25.

9. Ibid., 25.

10. Georges Van Vrekhem, *Hitler and His God* (New Delhi: Rupa and Company, 2007), 307.

11. Ibid., 313.

12. Paul Johnson, *A History of the Jews* (New York: Harper & Row, 1987).

13. Van Vrekhem, 308–309.

14. Leon Poliakov, *History of Anti-Semitism* (New York: Vanguard Press, 1965).

15. Van Vrekhem.

16. R. Po-chia Hsia, *Myth of Ritual Murder, Jews and Magic in Reformation Germany* (New Haven, CT: Yale University Press, 1988).

17. John Whitney Hall and John G. Kirk, *History of the World* (North Dighton, MA: World Publication Group, 2005), 407.

CHAPTER 3
HITLER'S FINAL SOLUTION: THE JEWISH HOLOCAUST

1. Hyam Maccoby Oxford, quoted in Van Vrekhem, *Hitler and His God*, 306–307.

2. Leni Yahil, *The Holocaust: the Fate of European Jewry* (New York: Oxford University Press, 1990).

3. Joseph de Gobineau quoted in Van Vrekhem.

4. Robert Wistrich, *Hitler and the Holocaust* (New York: Modern Library, 2001).

5. Joachim Kohler, *Wagner's Hitler: The Prophet and His Disciple* (Malden, MA: Blackwell, 2000).

6. Lisa Pine, *Hitler's "National Community": Society and Culture in Nazi Germany* (London: Hodder Arnold, 2007), 101–110.

7. Kristallnacht information found at Touro Law, Touro College, Jacob D. Fuchsberg Law Center, http://www.tourolaw.edu/News/NewsDetails .aspx?id=39 (accessed September 30, 2013).

8. Adolf Hitler, *Mein Kampf*, trans. James Murphy (London: Hurst and Blackett, [1939?]), 409.

9. Ibid.

10. Eberhard Jackel, *Hitler in History* (Hanover, NH: University Press of New England, 1986).

11. Yahil Leni: *The Fate of European Jewry*. Oxford University Press, 1990.

12. Gerhard Weinberg, *A World at Arms: A Global History of World War II* (New York: Cambridge University Press, 2005), 473–474.

13. Leon Uris, *Exodus* (London: Corgi Books, [1958?]), 79–80.

14. Yahil, 365.

15. "Development and Execution: Origins" in "Holocaust," Master.com, Encyclopedia, http://www.nationmaster.com/encyclopedia/Holocaust (accessed September 30, 2013).

16. Page Smith, *The Historian and History* (New York: Knopf, 1964).

17. *Insight on Scriptures.*

18. Yahil, 270.

CHAPTER 4
ISRAEL AND NATIONS IN COVENANTAL REVELATION

1. Matthew Henry, *Matthew Henry's Commentary on the Whole Bible* (Peabody, MA: Hendrickson, 2005), 1453.

2. Adam Clarke and Ralph Earle, *Adam Clarke's Commentary on the Bible* (Grand Rapids: Baker Books, 1977), 701.

3. Henry, 1454.

4. Palmer O. Robertson, *The Israel of God: Yesterday, Today, and Tomorrow* (Phillipsburg, NJ: P & R, 2000), 35.

5. Walbert Bühlmann, *God's Chosen Peoples* (Maryknoll, NY: Orbis Books, 1982), 220.

6. Charles Spurgeon, *Spurgeon's Sermons on the Death and Resurrection of Christ* (Peabody, MA: Hendrickson, 2005), 153.

CHAPTER 5
ISRAEL IN THE FINAL REDEMPTIONS OF NATIONS

1. John Hagee, *Jerusalem Countdown* (Lake Mary, FL: Frontline, 2006), 54.

2. Josephus, *The Jewish War*, bk. 6, chap. 10, sec. 1, 438.

3. Josephus, *Jewish Antiquities*, bk. 7, chap. 3, sec. 2, 67.

4. Simon Sebag Montefiore, *Jerusalem: the Biography* (London: Weidenfeld and Nicolson, 2011).

5. Ibid.

6. Josephus, *Jewish Antiquities*, bk. 2, chap. 8, sec. 5, 337.

7. Ibid., bk. 12, chap. 5, sec. 3-V, 246–256.

8. Montefiore, 62–63.

9. Ibid., 134–135.

10. Ibid., 137.

11. Ibid.

12. Ibid., 316–317.

13. Finis Jennings Dake, *God's Plan for Man* (Lawrenceville, GA: Dake, 2001), 316–317.

CHAPTER 6
JERUSALEM: EPICENTER OF ARMAGEDDON

1. Hall and Kirk, 48–51.

2. Thutmose quote found at http://www.messengers-of-messiah.org/Tour/JezVal.html (accessed October 3, 2013).

3. John F. Walvoord and Mark Hitchcock, *Armageddon, Oil, and Terror* (Carol Stream, IL: Tyndale House, 2007).

4. Ibid., 34.

5. Randall Price, *The Temple and Bible Prophecy* (Eugene, OR: Harvest House, 2005), 448–449.

CHAPTER 7
APPRECIATING CHRIST'S END-TIME WARNING

1. Italian proverb found at http://www.maxioms.com/maxiom/44791
/to-him-that-watches-everything-is-revealed (accessed October 4, 2013).

CHAPTER 8
GOG'S DEFEAT AND DESTRUCTION OF THE WICKED

1. *Insight on the Scriptures*, 329.
2. Joel C. Rosenberg, *Epicenter* (Carol Stream, IL: Tyndale House, 2006),
132; Jack Van Impe *Revelation Revealed* (Troy, MI: Jack Van Impe Ministries,
1999), 204–205.
3. Belinda Gallagher, ed., *The World Wars* (UK: Miles Kelly, 2007), 211.
4. Weinberg, 894.
5. Harold J. Chadwick and John Foxe, *The New Foxe's Book of Martyrs*
(North Gainesville, FL: Bridge-Logos, 2001).

CHAPTER 9
THE FINAL WAR: GOG AND MAGOG

1. Leland Ryken, James C Wilhoit, and Tremper Longman, *Dictionary of
Biblical Imagery* (Downers Grove, IL: InterVarsity Press, 1998), 376.
2. Ronald Youngblood, F. F. Bruce, R. K. Harrison, and Thomas Nelson,
Nelson's New Illustrated Bible Dictionary (Nashville: Thomas Nelson, 1995),
556.

CHAPTER 10
THE NEW JERUSALEM

1. Martin Luther, *Commentary on Galatians* (Grand Rapids: Kregel, 1979),
284.
2. H. L. Willmington, *Willmington's Guide to the Bible* (Wheaton, IL:
Tyndale House, 1984).
3. Dake.
4. Ibid.
5. Martin Luther, *Table Talk* (Gainsville, FL: Bridge-Logos, 2004), 434.
6. A. A. Hodge, *Evangelical Theology* (Edinburgh, UK: Banner of Truth
Trust, 1976), 255–258.
7. Dietrich Bonhoeffer, *True Patriotism* (London: Collins, 1973).

BIBLIOGRAPHY

Alcorn, Randy. *Heaven*. Wheaton, IL: Tyndale House, 2004.

Armstrong, Karen. *A History of God*. New York: Knopf, 1993.

Bar-Zohar, Michael. *Beyond Hitler's Grasp*. Holbrook, MA: Adams Media, 1998.

Beitzel, Barry J. *Biblica: The Bible Atlas*. Lane Cove, NSW: Global Book, 2006.

Bonhoeffer, Dietrich. *True Patriotism*. London: Collins, 1973.

Bowker, John. *Beliefs That Changed the World*. London: Quercus, 2007.

Bhushan, K., and G. Katyal. *Nuclear, Biological, and Chemical Warfare*. New Delhi: APH, 2002.

Bühlmann, Walbert. *God's Chosen Peoples*. Maryknoll, NY: Orbis Books, 1982.

Cairns, Earle E. *Christianity Through the Centuries: A History of the Christian Church*. Grand Rapids: Zondervan, 1996.

Castleden, Rodney. *Natural Disasters That Changed the World*. Edison, NJ: Chartwell Books, 2007.

Chilton, Bruce. *Abraham's Curse: The Roots of Violence in Judaism, Christianity, and Islam*. New York: Doubleday, 2008.

Coll, Steve. *Ghost Wars*. London: Penguin Books, 2005.

Conner, Kevin J. *The Book of Daniel: An Exposition*. Vermont, VIC: KJC, 2004.

———. *Interpreting the Book of Revelation*. Portland OR: City Christian, 1996.

Conner, Kevin J., and Ken Malmin. *The Covenants*. Portland, OR: City Bible, 2003.

Cornwell, John. *Hitler's Pope*. UK: Penguin Books, 2000.

Dake, Finis Jennings. *God's Plan for Man*. Lawrenceville, GA: Dake, 2001.

Diprose, Ronald E. *Israel and the Church*. Waynesboro GA: Authentic Media, 2000.

Dowley, Tim, A. R. Millard, et al. *The Baker Atlas of Christian History*. Grand Rapids: Baker Books, 1997.

Easley, Kendell H. *Holman Illustrated Guide to Bible History*. Nashville: Holman, 2005.

Frame, John M. *No Other God*. Phillipsburg, NJ: P & R, 2001.

Gabriel, Mark A. *Islam and the Jews: The Unfinished Battle*. Lake Mary, FL: Frontline, 2003.

Gallagher, Belinda, ed. *The World Wars*. UK: Miles Kelly, 2007.

Gragg, Rod. *Forged In Faith*. New York: Howard Books, 2010.

Grudem, Wayne. *Bible Doctrine*. Nottingham, UK: InterVarsity Press, 1999.

Gurnall, William. *The Christian in Complete Armor*. Avon, UK: Bath Press, 1964.

Hagee, John. *Attack on America*. Nashville: Thomas Nelson, 2001.

———. *Beginning of the End: Final Dawn Over Jerusalem: Day of Deception*. Nashville: Thomas Nelson, 2000.

———. *Can America Survive?* New York: Simon and Schuster, 2010.

———. *Jerusalem Countdown*. Lake Mary, FL: Frontline, 2006.

Hall, John, and John Kirk. *The History of the World*. New York: Gallery Books, 1988.

———. *History of the World*. North Dighton, MA: World Publication Group, 2005.

Hamon, Bill. *Prophetic Scripture Yet to Be Fulfilled*. Shippensburg, PA: Destiny Image, 2010.

Hitchcock, Mark. *The Apocalypse of Ahmadinejad*. Colorado Springs: Multnomah Books, 2007.

Hitler, Adolf. *Hitler's Secret Book*. New York: Grove Press, 1961.

———. *Mein Kampf*. Translated by James Murphy. London: Hurst and Blackett, [1939?].

Hitti, Phillip K. *History of the Arabs*. London: Macmillan, 1981.

Hunt, David, and T. A. MacMahon. *The Seduction of Christianity*. Eugene, OR: Harvest House, 1985.

Hurnard, Hannah. *Watchman on the Walls*. Nashville: Broadman, 1997.

Johnson, Dennis E. *Triumph of the Lamb: A Commentary on Revelation*. Phillipsburg, NJ: P & R, 2001.

Josephus, Flavius. *The New Complete Works of Josephus*. Translated by William Whiston. Grand Rapids: Kregel, 1999.

Karsh, Efraim. *Islamic Imperialism: A History*. New Haven, CT: Yale University Press, 2006.

Keener, Craig S. *The IVP Bible Background Commentary: New Testament*. Downers Grove, IL: InterVarsity Press, 1993.

LaHaye, Tim. *The Merciful God of Prophecy*. New York: Warner Books, 2002.

LaHaye, Tim, and Edward Hindson. *The Popular Bible Prophecy Commentary*. Eugene, OR: Harvest House, 2006.

Lilienthal, Alfred M. *What Price Israel?* Beirut: Institute of Palestine Studies, 1969.

Lindemann, Albert S. *Esau's Tears*. New York: Cambridge University Press, 1997.

Lockyer, Herbert. *All the Messianic Prophecies*. Grand Rapids: Zondervan, 1973.

Luther, Martin. *Commentary on Galatians*. Grand Rapids: Kregel, 1979.

————. *Table Talk*. Gainsville, FL: Bridge-Logos, 2004.

MacCulloch, Diarmaid. *A History of Christianity*. London: Penguin Books, 2010.

MacGregor, Scott. *The Rise and Fall of the Antichrist*. Zug, CH: Aurora Production, 2006.

MacGregor, Scott, and Michael Roy. *The Future Foretold*. Zug, CH: Aurora Production, 2006.

Milne, Bruce. *Know The Truth*. Nottingham, UK: InterVarsity Press, 2009.

Moller, Lennart. *The Exodus Case*. Copenhagen: Scandinavian Publishing House, 2002.

Montefiore, Simon Sebag. *Jerusalem: the Biography*. London: Weidenfeld and Nicolson, 2011.

Munroe, Myles. *Rediscovering the Kingdom: Ancient Hope for Our 21st Century World*. Shippensburg, PA: Destiny Image, 2010.

Murray, Andrew. *Covenants and Blessings*. New Kensington, PA: Whitaker House, 1984.

Oren, Michael B. *Six Days of War*. New York: Penguin Books, 2003.

Owen, James. *Nuremberg: Evil on Trial*. London: Headline Review, 2006,

Pamphilus, Esebius. *Esebius' Ecclesiastical History*. Translated by C. F. Cruse. Peabody, MA: Hendrickson, 2009.

Pawson, J. David. *Come with Me Through Revelation*. UK: Terra Nova, 2008.

————. *Unlocking the Bible*. London: Collins, 2007.

Price, Randall. *The Temple and Bible Prophecy*. Eugene, OR: Harvest House, 2005.

Rees, Laurence. *Auschwitz: The Nazis & the Final Solution*. London: BBC Books, 2005.

Robertson, O. Palmer. *The Israel of God: Yesterday, Today, and Tomorrow*. Phillipsburg, NJ: P & R, 2000.

Rogers, Adrian. *Unveiling the End Times in Our Time: The Triumph of the Lamb in Revelation*. Nashville: Broadman and Holman, 2004.

Rogers, Paul. *A War Too Far*. London: Pluto Press, 2006.

Rosenberg, Joel. C. *Epicenter*. Carol Stream, IL: Tyndale House, 2006.

————. *Inside the Revolution*. Carol Stream, IL: Tyndale House, 2011.

Roy, Michael. *The Future Foretold: Ancient Prophecies Now Being Fulfilled*. Zug, CH: Aurora Production, 1999.

Schnittjer, Gary Edward. *The Torah Story*. Grand Rapids: Zondervan, 2006.

Schwab, George M. *Hope in the Midst of a Hostile World: The Gospel According to Daniel*. Phillipsburg, NJ: P & R, 2006.

Shawn, Eric. *The U.N. Exposed.* New York: Sentinel, 2006.

Sproul, R. C. *Truths We Confess.* Vol. 3. Phillipsburg, NJ: P & R, 2007.

Swindoll, Charles, and Roy Zuck. *Understanding Christian Theology.* Nashville: Thomas Nelson, 2003.

Timmerman, Kenneth R. *Countdown to Crisis: The Coming Nuclear Showdown with Iran.* New York: Crown Forum, 2005.

Torrey, R. A. *The Bible Answer Book.* New Kensington, PA: Whitaker House, 1999.

————. *What The Bible Teaches.* New Kensington, PA: Whitaker House, 1996.

Tyler, Patrick. *A World of Trouble: America in the Middle East.* London: Portobello Books, 2009.

Uris, Leon. *Exodus.* London: Corgi Books, [1958?].

Van Impe, Jack. *Revelation Revealed.* Troy, MI: Jack Van Impe Ministries, 1999.

Van Vrekhem, Georges. *Hitler and His God.* New Delhi: Rupa and Company, 2007.

Vine, R. D. *God's Answers to Your Questions.* England: Stanborough Press, [1952?].

Walvoord, John F., and Mark Hitchcock. *Armageddon, Oil, and Terror.* Carol Stream, IL: Tyndale House, 2007.

Water, Mark. *Encyclopedia of Bible Facts.* Chattanooga: AMG, 2004.

Weinberg, Gerhard. *A World at Arms: A Global History of World War II.* New York: Cambridge University Press, 2005.

Willmington, H. L. *Willmington's Guide to the Bible.* Wheaton, IL: Tyndale House, 1984.

Wright, Paul. *Bible Atlas with Charts and Biblical Reconstruction.* Nashville: Holman Bible Publishers, 2005.

Yahil, Leni. *The Holocaust: the Fate of European Jewry.* New York: Oxford University Press, 1990.

OTHER SOURCES

Alexander, David, and Pat Alexander. *The Lion Handbook to the Bible*. UK: Lion, 1983.

Cross, F. L., and Elizabeth A. Livingstone, eds. *Dictionary of the Christian Church*. Peabody, MA: Hendrickson, 1997.

Doniger, Wendy. *Britannica Encyclopedia of World Religions*. Chicago: Encyclopaedia Britannica, 2006

Gardner, Paul, ed. *New International Encyclopedia of Bible Characters*. Grand Rapids: Zondervan, 1995.

Henry, Matthew. *Matthew Henry's Commentary on the Whole Bible*. Peabody, MA: Hendrickson, 2005.

Insight on the Scriptures. Vols. 1 and 2. Brooklyn, NY: Watchtower Bible and Tract Society, 1988.

Isaiah's Prophecy. Vols. 1 and 2. Brooklyn, NY: Watchtower Bible and Tract Society, 2000.

The New International Webster Comprehensive Dictionary. Naples, FL: Trident Press International, 2003.

Pay Attention to Daniel's Prophecy. Brooklyn, NY: Watchtower Bible and Tract Society, 1999.

Renn, Stephen D. *Expository Dictionary of Bible Words*. Peabody, MA: Hendrickson, 2010.

Revelation—Its Grand Climax at Hand. Brooklyn, NY: Watchtower Bible and Tract Society, 1988

Ryken, Leland, James C Wilhoit, and Tremper Longman. *Dictionary of Biblical Imagery*. Downers Grove, IL: InterVarsity Press, 1998.

Survival into a New Earth. Booklyn, NY: Watchtower Bible and Tract Society, 1984.

You Can Live Forever in Paradise on Earth. Brooklyn, NY: Watchtower Bible and Tract Society, 1982.

Youngblood, Ronald, F. F. Bruce, R. K. Harrison, and Thomas Nelson. *Nelson's New Illustrated Bible Dictionary*. Nashville: Thomas Nelson, 1995.

INDEX

ABOUT THE AUTHOR

Dickson Agedah was born in Nigeria in 1957. He earned an honors degree in history from the University of Port Harcout, Nigeria, and worked in print media journalism as a reporter/researcher, sub-editor, bureau editor, and editor-in-chief. He is a Christian, Bible student, and author. His works include several books on socio-political and environmental issues in Nigeria: *The Military in Politics*; *Corruption and Stability of the Third Republic*; *Nigeria: Reinventing a Nation*; *Case for True Federalism*; and others. *ISRAEL* is his first Christian book. Dickson lives in Atlanta, Georgia with his wife Irene and their four children.

For information on some of Dickson Agedah's books, Google "Dickson Agedah."

CONTACT THE AUTHOR

Email: dicksonagedah@gmail.com